AFRICAN INTERVENTIONIST STATES

African Interventionist States

Edited by
OLIVER FURLEY and ROY MAY
African Studies Centre, Coventry University

Ashgate
Aldershot • Burlington USA • Singapore • Sydney

Published by
Ashgate Publishing Ltd
Gower House
Croft Road
Aldershot
Hants GU11 3HR
England

Ashgate Publishing Company
131 Main Street
Burlington, VT 05401-5600 USA

Ashgate website: http://www.ashgate.com

British Library Cataloguing in Publication Data
African interventionist states
1. Intervention (International law) 2. Peacekeeping forces - Africa 3. Africa - Politics and government - 1960-
I. Furley, Oliver II. May, Roy
327.1'72'096

Library of Congress Control Number: 2001095427

ISBN 1 84014 989 2

Printed in Great Britain by
Antony Rowe Ltd, Chippenham, Wiltshire

Contents

List of contributors

Christopher Clapham is Professor of Politics and International Relations at Lancaster University, and editor of The Journal of Modern African Studies. His main academic interests are in the politics of Ethiopia and the Horn of Africa, and of Liberia and Sierra Leone. Recent publications include *Africa and the International System* (1996), *African Guerrillas* (edited, 1998), and *Peacekeeping and Peace Enforcement in Africa: Methods of Conflict Prevention* (co-edited, 2000).

Tony Clayton was on the staff of the Royal Military Academy, Sandhurst, from 1965 to 1999. His publications include *The Zanzibar Revolution and its Aftermath*, C. Hurst, 1981; *France, Soldiers and Africa*, Brasseys, 1988; *The Wave of French Decolonization*, Longman, 1994; and *Frontiersmen, Warfare in Africa since 1950*, UCL, 1998. He is currently a Research Fellow at the Institute for the Study of War and Society, De Montfort University.

Gerry Cleaver is a lecturer in the School of International Studies and Law, Coventry University. He is also a member of the University's African Studies Centre where he is studying for his PhD on the practical problems associated with peacekeeping in Africa, a subject on which he has recently published articles. He teaches both African and Third World politics at undergraduate level as well as a course on African peacekeeping in the School's MA programme.

Oliver Furley is an Honorary Research Fellow and formerly Head of the Department of Politics and History at Coventry University. Previously he taught for many years at Makerere University, Uganda, and also in the universities of St Andrews, Edinburgh, the West Indies and Duke University, North Carolina. He is co-author with Tom Watson of *The History of Education in East Africa*, NOK Publishers, USA, 1978, and of *Uganda's Retreat from Turmoil*, Centre for Security and Conflict Studies, 1987. He has contributed chapters and articles on East African history, politics and conflict studies. He is editor of *Conflict in Africa*, Tauris Academic Studies, 1995.

Jeremy Levitt is Assistant Professor of Law at Depaul University College of Law. He is also Research Associate at the African Security Unit, Centre for Defence Studies, Kings College, London; and Research Fellow at the Center for International Development and Conflict Management, University of Maryland-College Park. He is a public international lawyer and political scientist with area expertise in public international law, conflict studies, state dynamics, and regional collective security in Africa. He has published several articles and chapters on causes of conflict, humanitarian intervention, peacekeeping, regional collective security, armed conflict, and democratisation in Africa.

Mel McNulty is a Senior Research Fellow at Nottingham Trent University. He worked previously at the University of Portsmouth where he completed a PhD on French military intervention in Africa. He has published on Rwanda and the Democratic Republic of Congo, and has worked recently on democratisation and the role of the military in Senegal and Cote D'Ivoire. He is currently editing *Conflict in Africa: An Encyclopaedia*, which is due for publication in 2002.

Norrie McQueen is head of the Politics department at the University of Dundee. He was previously Reader in International Relations at the University of Sunderland and his overseas experience includes posts in Australia and Papua New Guinea. He was a 'cooperante' in the education service in Mozambique in the years following independence. His publications include books on the decolonization of Portuguese Africa and on United Nations peacekeeping. He is currently working on the post-independence 'identity' of Portuguese-speaking Africa.

Simon Massey is a PhD student in the School of International Studies and Law at Coventry University where he completed his MA. His main research area is the theoretical and moral bases for peacekeeping operations in sub-Saharan Africa. He has published articles on this subject as well as on the politics of Chad and Guinea-Bissau.

Roy May is the Director of the African Studies Centre, Coventry University. He is also Head of International and Political Studies. He teaches undergraduate and postgraduate courses in African politics, development, aid and Third World politics. His original interest in the area came from service with the Royal West African Frontier Force in Sierra

Leone. He has published widely on Chad, the Franco-African relationship, the role of NGOs, militarism and peacekeeping in Africa.

Roger Southall is Professor of Political Studies at Rhodes University, South Africa. He has previously worked in universities in Uganda, Lesotho, Canada and the United Kingdom. He has published extensively on Africa and South Africa, and is editor of a forthcoming collection on Opposition and Democracy in South Africa which is to be published by Frank Cass. He is Managing Editor of *The Journal of Contemporary African Studies.*

Peter Woodward is Professor of Politics at the University of Reading, and was formerly at the University of Khartoum. His publications on north-east Africa include *Condominium and Sudanese Nationalism*, Rex Collings, 1979; *Sudan: The Unstable State*, Lynn Rienner, 1990; *Nasser*, Longman, 1992; and *Horn of Africa: State Politics and International Relations*, Tauris, 1996. He was Editor of *African Affairs*, the Journal of the Royal African Society, from 1986 to 1997, and Editor of *British Documents on Foreign Affairs: Africa*, University Press of America, from 1994 to 2000.

Acknowledgements

The editors wish to thank those who have helped in the production of this book: Professor Christopher Clapham for helpful advice about planning the structure of the book in its early stages; Arthur Owens, Social Sciences Librarian at Coventry University for his excellent biographical support; Marcie Edwards of the African Studies Centre for her unfailing work as editorial assistant, and Simon Massey for reading through the typescript. Thanks also to Coventry University Geography section for assistance with maps. The maps are published with the kind permission of the UN Cartographic Section.

List of abbreviations

ACRF	African Crisis Response Force
ACRI	African Crisis Response Initiative
ADF	Allied Democratic Forces (Uganda)
ADFL	Alliance of Democratic Forces for the Liberation of Congo
AFRC	Armed Forces Revolutionary Council (Sierra Leone)
ANC	African National Congress
APC	All People's Congress (Sierra Leone)
APC	Armoured Personnel Carrier
BCP	Basutoland Congress Party
BDF	Botswana Defence Force
BNP	Basotho National Party
CAR	Central African Republic
CEEAC	Communauté Economique des Etats d'Afrique Centrale
CIA	Central Intelligence Agency
CONCP	Conference of Nationalist Organisations of the Portuguese Colonies
CPLP	Communidade de Paises de Lingua Franca Portuguese
DRC	Democratic Republic of Congo
EAC	East African Community
ECOMOG	ECOWAS Monitoring Group
ECOWAS	Economic Community of West African States
ELF	Eritrean Liberation Front
EPLF	Eritrean People's Liberation Front
EPRDF	Ethiopian People's Revolutionary Democratic Front
FAA	Angolan Armed Forces
FAC	Forces Armées Congolaises
FAPLA	Angolan People's Liberation Army
FAR	Forces Armées Rwandaises
FARF	Forces Armées pour la République Fédérale
FAZ	Forces Armées Zairoises
FLEC	Cabindan Liberation Front

FNLA	National Front for the Liberation of Angola
HSM	Holy Spirit Movement (Uganda)
ICRC	International Committee of the Red Cross
IGAD	Inter-Governmental Authority for Development
ISDSC	Inter-State Defence and Security Committee
LCD	Lesotho Congress of Democrats
LRA	Lord's Resistance Army
MFDC	Mouvement des forces démocratiques de la Casamance
MFP	Marematlou Freedom Party (Lesotho)
MINURCA	United Nations Mission in the CAR
MISAB	Inter-African Mission to monitor the implementation of the Bangui Agreements (CAR)
MLC	Congolese Liberation Movement
MLSTP	Movement for the Liberation of Sao Tome and Principe
MPLA	Popular Movement for the Liberation of Angola
MPRI	Military Professional Resources Incorporated
MPS	Mouvement Patriotique du Salut (Chad)
NATO	North Atlantic Treaty Organisation
NDA	National Democratic Alliance (Sudan)
NIF	National Islamic Front (Sudan)
NIFAG	Nigerian Forces Assistant Group
NPFL	National Patriotic Front of Liberia
NRA	National Resistance Army (Uganda)
NRM	National Resistance Movement (Uganda)
OAU	Organisation of African Unity
OIC	Organisation of the Islamic Conference
OLF	Oromo Liberation Front
PAIGC	Partido Africano da Independencia de Guiné-Bissau e Cabo Verde
PALOP	African Portuguese Speaking Countries
PIAC	Popular Islamic and Arabic Conference
PLAN	People's Liberation Army of Namibia
RCD	Congolese Rally for Democracy
RECAMP	Renforcement des capacités africaines de maintien de la paix
RENAMO	National Resistance Movement (Mozambique)
RLDF	Royal Lesotho Defence Force
RPA	Rwandan Patriotic Army

RPF	Rwandan Patriotic Force
RUF	Revolutionary United Front (Sierra Leone)
SADC	Southern African Development Community
SADF	South African Defence Force
SANDF	South African National Defence Force
SEPAR	Southern Ethiopian Peoples' Administrative Region
SNM	Somali National Movement
SOFA	Status of Forces Agreement
SPLA	Sudan People's Liberation Army
SSDF	Somali Salvation Democratic Front
SWAPO	South West African People's Organisation
TPDF	Tanzanian People's Defence Force
TPLF	Tigray People's Liberation Front
UPDF	Uganda People's Defence Force
UNAMIR	United Nations Assistance Mission for Rwanda
UNAMSIL	United Nations Mission in Sierra Leone
UNHCR	United Nations High Commission for Refugees
UNITA	National Union for the Total Independence of Angola
UNITAF	United Nations Task Force (Somalia)
UNLA	Uganda National Liberation Army
UNLF	Uganda National Liberation Front
UNOMIL	United Nations Observer Mission in Liberia
UNOSOM	United Nations Operation in Somalia
UNSC	United Nations Security Council
UPG	Union pour le progrès en Guinée
WFP	World Food Programme
WNBF	West Nile Bank Front
ZANU-PF	Zimbabwe African National Union Patriotic Front

Map No. 4045 Rev. 2 UNITED NATIONS
March 2001

Department of Public Information
Cartographic Section

Map No. 4007 Rev. 6 UNITED NATIONS
April 2000

Department of Public Information
Cartographic Section

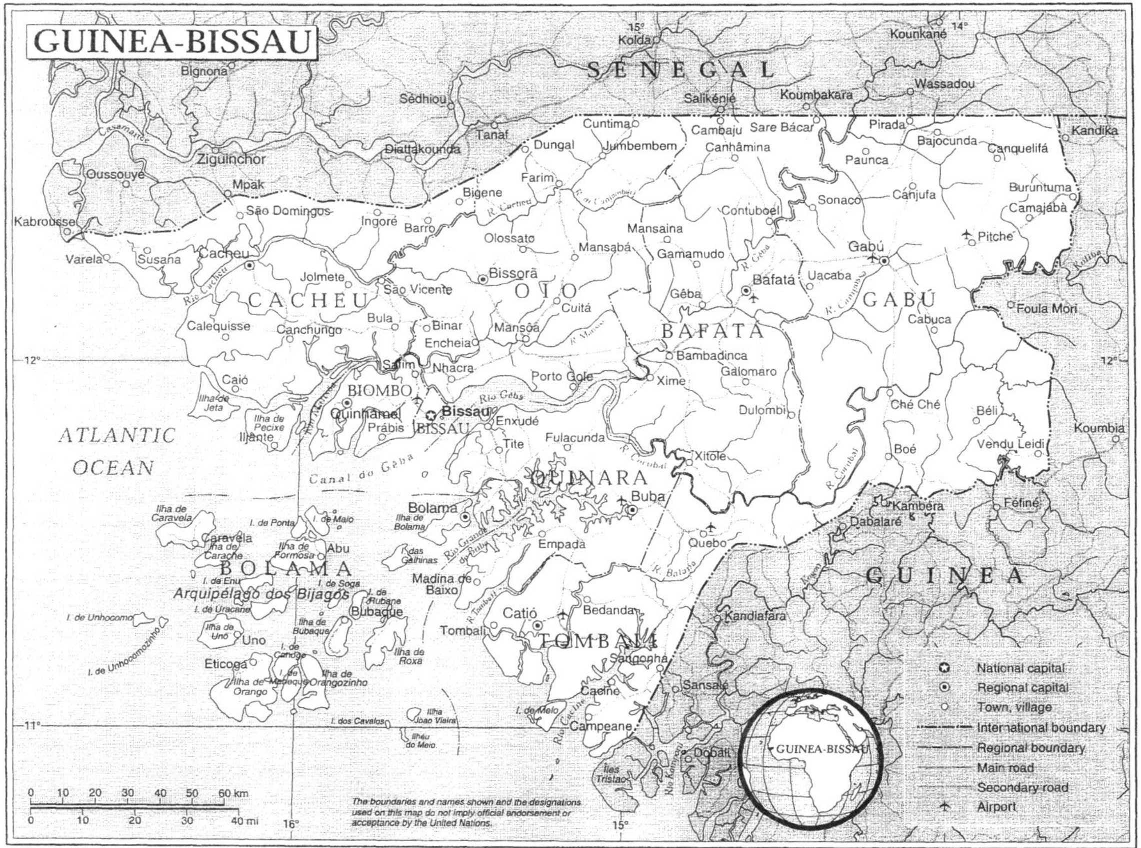

Map No. 4063 UNITED NATIONS
July 1998

Department of Public Information
Cartographic Section

Part One
Legal and Military Issues

1 Introduction

Oliver Furley and Roy May

The origins of this book arose from a desire to explore the role of African states as assertive actors, particularly in their role vis à vis other African states. For many years the dominant perception had been that of either ex-colonial or hegemonic powers intervening militarily (inter alia) in Africa to pursue their political, military or strategic goals. The focus we felt it important to analyse in more detail was that of the African states' use of military means to affect change in development in neighbouring states. As some of our case studies show, this is not as simple as it seems, as Massey shows very clearly in the case of Guinea Bissau, where external powers are still involved using local states as proxies.

Two specific pieces of earlier research had both demonstrated our interest in this field of study and contributed to the debate. The first of these being the Furley and May study of the Tanzanian invasion of Uganda and the second being the Armies on Loan article by Hughes and May.[1] Oliver Furley's long interest in the history and contemporary politics of Uganda has led him to an assessment of the role of the Tanzanian invasion of Uganda.[2] In retrospect, this may be considered as one of the key events in the long moves towards the escalation of interventions that this volume is concerned with.

Tanzania's invasion of Uganda in 1978 was one of the first really serious interventions into a neighbouring African state, constituting a large-scale invasion and the eventual deposition of the ruler, General Idi Amin. Tanzania was one of the poorest nations in Africa at the time, though, as Furley and May's chapter points out, it did possess a surprisingly large and well-equipped army. There were also compelling reasons for this intervention. Successive threats from General Amin, and claims to territory in Tanzania, heightened the already existing personal feud between the two leaders. Then came Uganda's incursions across the Kagera river into Tanzania, causing casualties and damage. Retaliation was obligatory and President Julius Nyerere's sense of outrage added to the political imperative. He counter-attacked, and as the war progressed, a succession of justifications was marshalled. It was to defend territorial sovereignty, to punish an aggressor, to rescue a people, on humanitarian grounds, from oppression by a tyrant; finally it emerged as a war to remove Amin and restore a democratically-elected government. But Nyerere's hopes of winning praise and approval from his fellow member-states of the OAU, and from the international community, were dashed. The final result of the war was approved but was viewed as a disturbing precedent. Nyerere was ahead of his time: the OAU never praised him for Tanzania's huge war effort, and he never got the compensation he kept demanding. The war bankrupted his country.

The Hughes and May research has identified as early as 1986 that there had been a significant contribution by African militaries to the political balance in Africa.[3] The research had classified interventions as *regime supportive*: to provide military assistance to a threatened regime or government, *regime opposing*: seeking the overthrow and destablisation of a regime or government, and *state supportive*: to ensure the survival of the state in the face of internal disruption and external aggression. The number and complexity of subsequent interventions have made it difficult to reapply these categories.[4]

For that research, the working definition used was that of James Rossenau's 'coercive military involvement in civil or regional conflict (or in anticipation of such conflict) which is intended to, or does, affect internal political outcomes'.[5] The exact nature of this intervention needs to be explored; clearly it can mean the direct military involvement of troops in another country in a variety of roles, either participation in a regional force (ECOMOG in Liberia and Sierra Leone) or participation in an African force, but intervention in a number of the cases dealt with in this book goes further than that, and could include:

- State sponsored guerrilla forces against the state (South Africa and RENAMO)
- Support rebels groups inside a state (Uganda)
- Support sides in a civil war (Guinea Bissau, DRC)
- Support for a peacekeeping force (ECOMOG, Liberia)
- Support for peace enforcement operations (ECOMOG, Sierra Leone)
- To prevent ethnicity-based cross-border interventions (Uganda, Rwanda)
- Bids for regional hegemony (Nigeria)

All of these are explored in this volume.

Since the Second World War, throughout the world it has been held as a norm of international behaviour that a nation's borders are inviolable and its internal affairs should not be subject to external interference. The UN Charter was founded on the very basis of the sovereignty of UN member states. In sub-Saharan Africa, even though the state borders are nearly all arbitrarily drawn, it was agreed by the colonial powers at the time of independence in the late 1950s and through the 1960s that the colonial boundaries be adhered to, if only to avoid chaos and conflict if attempts at alteration were made. The 1963 OAU Charter echoed the UN Charter in this, emphasising the inviolability of states and laying down the principle of non-intervention by one state in its neighbours or elsewhere on the continent. Members were pledged to respect the sovereignty and territorial integrity of each state and its inalienable right to a separate existence. To reinforce this, the OAU Cairo Conference of 1964 adopted the principle of *uti possidetis, ita possideatus* (as you possess, so you may possess).[6] It was not long before the doctrine of non-interference began to be eroded, and this intervention could be labelled 'intervention' as defined in the various ways set out above.

As some of our case studies show, it could be to 'punish' a state, or to defend its borders by pushing back an aggressive state to ward off further attacks, or indeed to gain access to and plunder its rich natural resources. But there have been many other types of intervention; where a government has actually invited a neighbour state to assist it in a civil war or revolt; where action is needed to enforce a peace agreement; where breaches of it would affect the whole region; or where a state or group of states intervene for humanitarian reasons, or indeed in defence of democracy, which has become the latest reason given for some interventions. As some of the case studies also show, economic motives at either individual or state level may also play a part. Many of these breach the UN and OAU charters and yet in the latter three categories, they have not been condemned as such: it seems, as Jeremy Levitt says in his chapter, especially in some of the interventions in states suffering civil war, that they derive a legal basis from customary international law, and that African continental law may be developing in relation to legitimate military intervention. Indeed, in a number of humanitarian interventions, the UN Security Council retroactively supported them, and so did the international community. In the cases of Sierra Leone and the Central African Republic, he claims that these show 'the international community will no longer permit the toppling of democratically elected governments'. He cites the treaty of ECOWAS, the West African group of states, which says that member states may introduce peacekeeping forces in internal conflicts in other states, when they 'threaten to trigger a humanitarian disaster', or pose a threat to peace and security in the sub-region, or 'erupt following the overthrow or attempted overthrow of a democratically elected government'. As Harbeson and Rothchild note in their excellent survey, the assistant secretary general of the OAU pointed out at the Kampala Forum that the 'principle of non-interference in the internal affairs of states is increasingly coming under scrutiny' and that by 1998, *Africa Confidential* could write that 'Africa's hallowed doctrine of non-interference in the affairs of sovereign states has been abandoned'.[7] John Kakande, a Ugandan journalist, was quite uninhibited when he wrote in 1997: 'It is now clear that the principles of non-interference by one country in the internal affairs of another no longer apply in Africa or anywhere else in the world. It is now the rule of "Might is Right"'. He therefore called on Uganda to send armed assistance to the Southern Sudanese rebel forces (SPLA) in the southern Sudan to create a buffer zone between Uganda and Sudan, whose government was said to be supplying bases for Ugandan rebels in the north, the Lord's Resistance Army. Rwanda, Angola, Zambia and Zimbabwe removed President Mobutu from Zaire and replaced him with Kabila 'and no one raised a finger', Kakande alleged. Angola overtly supported the civil war of the military dictator in Congo Brazzaville and again there was no condemnation by the OAU or any other body.[8] For him, the implication is clear: Uganda should not worry about incurring any blame for an armed intervention in Sudan.

In the space of two years from when Kakande wrote, the crumbling of the principle of non-intervention had gone much further. There is now 'a culture of intervention', as Norrie McQueen says in his chapter on Angola. Numerous and continuing interventions have meant that the sovereignty of states has been assailed and state borders in some cases have become almost meaningless. As the subtitle of Harbeson and Rothchild's study states, the African state system is in flux and that 'state weakness and state systems frailty have been mutually re-inforcing in Africa during post-Cold War times'.[9] 'Africa's frontiers in flux' was the headline for Achille Mbembe's long article in *Le Monde Diplomatique*, November 1999, in which he argued that new forms of territoriality have arisen, not matching official boundaries, norms or languages. Wars and anti-democratic movements have caused a flight from the state and the re-emergence of forms of sovereignty and political and social orders that bypass the state system. In what Mbembe calls the war belt from the Horn of Africa, through the Great Lakes and Congo, Congo Brazzaville and Angola to Sierra Leone and Liberia, the ties between state and subject are loosening while 'military princedoms have appeared in Rwanda, Uganda, Burundi, Ethiopia and Eritrea'. They join forces with their own diasporas which have been in place for years but whose citizenship has been disputed. In the DRC, armies of dissident adolescent mercenaries 'form groups that act like governments in the areas they control'. In West Africa, 'the new oil frontier' was causing the dissolution of the state, a de-territorialisation; clashes between native and non-native populations meant each locality answered to several jurisdictions – governmental, traditional and religious. In Angola, the borders of state sovereignty are hazy and the country is split; in Somalia the state has disappeared.[10]

Motives for intervention continue to proliferate: bids for political, economic and military hegemony in a region figure in a number of interventions, including those where a state contributes troops to a UN peacekeeping, or more literally a 'peace-enforcing' mission, as in Nigeria's dominant role in ECOMOG operations in Liberia and Sierra Leone. In the case of African armies contributing to UN missions, quite apart from political considerations, there are the motives of exercising the army in foreign terrain and thereby gaining valuable experience, as well as hopes of enhancing national prestige. The forces themselves are likely to be keen because it often means new uniforms, new equipment and extra pay. Troops who have worn the blue helmet of the UN gain an enviable panache thereby. Participation in a UN mission also keeps the troops occupied and lessens the dangers of a military coup at home. Also, as Simon Massey notes, Ugandan troops trained under the ACRI initiative were used against UDF in Uganda and also as part of the Ugandan force in the DRC and Senegalese troops trained under the RECAMP programme were used in the intervention into Guinea Bissau (though to no great effect!).

Tony Clayton in his chapter on African military capabilities emphasises the wide variety of military action in recent times, and the huge differences in both the size of African armies and their capabilities. He points out a major difficulty in recent and current African wars in that, in some cases, no side has the capacity for an all-out military victory, giving the examples of Sudan versus the SPLA, Ethiopia versus Eritrea, the Angolan army versus UNITA, etc. The possession of sophisticated weaponry is not often the key to success: the South African army was well equipped but its action in Lesotho in 1998 was 'a botched intervention'; on the other hand, the Tanzanian army was largely an army on foot when it intervened in Uganda in 1978-79, but was an organised and well-commanded force and it succeeded. Other campaigns are surveyed in this chapter which brings out great contrasts.

The civil war in Sierra Leone is a formless chaos, fought by youths on drugs, alcohol and reggae music; a faction in one state will support a faction in another, and inter- or intra-state conflicts merge. One of the themes of the chapter by Gerry Cleaver is how conflict in Africa increasingly resembles war in pre-colonial Africa: ‘bodies of men, usually ethnically bonded, fighting for economic assets in areas not demarcated by agreed borders’. The presence of vast numbers of refugees, often herded into camps, has also changed the character of conflicts: rebel groups such as the Interahamwe, the perpetrators of the Rwanda massacre, concealed themselves in these camps and were difficult to root out. The new economic warfare is to keep refugees in camps and use hunger as a weapon, often to obtain international humanitarian aid which is then misapplied.

A useful section of this chapter deals with the composition, training, capabilities and requirements of the peacekeeping forces in Africa. Sometimes these forces have a hidden agenda to support one faction or to develop a regional hegemony role, if they are organised by one of the continent’s regional organisations. They may be out to acquire assets, secure their own borders, acquire prestige and new equipment, etc. In the UN and in these regional groups, institutional memories are short, and experience and expertise may be quickly lost. In spite of this, Clayton points to some successes like MINURCA in the Central African Republic, an all-African endeavour. He concludes with a survey of the various response units and training programmes which are emerging, and makes a plea for an international military support staff college, training peacekeepers in agreed procedures.

In economic terms, several of Africa’s wars are now described as resource wars, where an interventionist state sees the opportunity to exploit turbulence in another country to purloin the avenues of export for some of the valuable products of that country. Thus the diamond trade which fuels the rebels in Sierra Leone is supported by Liberia, Burkina Faso and other states, and in the DRC’s civil war, the motives of the intervening states supporting President Kabila and also of those supporting the rebel groups, are clearly influenced by the prospects of enriching either the state or its principal actors by the diamond trade and the trade in other valuable resources.[11] Some of these economic links are explored in the chapter on the DRC.

The Legacy of Failures in Resolving African Conflicts

One of the reasons why intervention by African states in the continent's conflicts has recently become much more common is the fact that UN efforts at conflict resolution and peacekeeping have conspicuously failed. The Sudanese civil war, from 1955-1972, and again from 1983 to the present, has dragged on, seemingly impervious to pressures to find solutions, either by the major powers or by other initiatives. The result has been that Uganda, Zaire/DRC, Rwanda and other neighbours have been or still are actors in the conflict, but only in so far as it affected their own security interests. In Somalia, the descent into anarchy led to the sending of the UN Operation in Somalia (UNOSOM) to try to establish peace between the warlords. Its inadequacies led to its replacement by the Unified Task Force (UNITAF) with a mandate under Chapter VII of the UN Charter to make peace using force if necessary. It was dominated by American troops, and turned into a manhunt for Mohamed Aideed, regarded as the chief obstacle to peace. The attempt to capture him turned into a military disaster and a humiliation for the US government, which has had long-lasting repercussions not only for the policy of that government towards African conflicts but for member states of the UN as well. The big powers in general became loath to interfere with such conflicts, and preferred to confine themselves to a humanitarian role. America and France in particular disengaged themselves from active participation in peacekeeping attempts on the continent of Africa, and President Clinton's Decision Directive of May 1994, urging 'African solutions for African problems', was an attempt to signal both America's determination to steer clear of entanglements in African conflicts but also to promote new initiatives by African states to secure and maintain peace both in inter-state and intra-state crises. This was paralleled by the 1994 statement by Prime Minister Balladur that the French would support peacekeeping operations that would be 'proprement africaine ... capable d'intervenir rapidement en Afrique pour des operations de maintenir de la paix sur mandat des Nations Unies'.[12] From that time, the role of America, France, and indeed of the other major powers, was generally seen to be providing training facilities, and sometimes logistics, for African peacekeepers and peace enforcers.

The long civil war in the Sudan did not attract any wholehearted or prolonged intervention by either African states, beyond protecting their own borders, supplying the rebel SPLA with arms or resources, or in the case of Uganda, intervening to try to prevent its own rebels, the Lord's Resistance Army (LRA), from obtaining help from the Khartoum government. Peter Woodward's chapter on the Sudan shows how Sudan was itself an interventionist state, in the sense of lending support to rebel groups in Ethiopia and Eritrea, to the guerrillas of the LRA in northern Uganda, and to other groups in Chad and DRC. These were not direct interventions by military force, but Sudan employed surrogates to achieve certain ends. The raison d'être behind them was partly to protect borders, but more importantly for Sudan to become a 'beacon' as a fully-fledged Islamic state and a leader of Islamicism in that part of the world – a religious and ideological motive for intervention, which is largely absent from other interventions in Africa. Its support of terrorist groups finally caused a reaction and the US put Sudan on its list of states supporting terrorism. Woodward maintains that this contributed to a decline in Sudan's influence and a growing isolation. It did not receive significant help in quelling the civil war in the south which it seemed incapable of winning. In an effort to improve Sudan's relations with its neighbours it joined in the formation of the Inter-Governmental Authority for Development (IGAD) and the subsequent Sudan peace talks in the IGAD forum may possibly result in a new settlement in peace-making forged by one of Africa's regional organisations. If the civil war was brought to an end, this would indeed transform the climate of interventionism in the region, as so much of it has sprung from the struggle between the Khartoum government and the SPLA.

Rwanda provided the most conspicuous and the most tragic example of the UN's failure to intervene successfully in Africa. Before the genocide of April and May 1994, a force from one neighbouring state had of course already intervened. Uganda had harboured large numbers of Tutsi refugees from Rwanda, many of them dating back many years from when they first settled in Uganda, so much so that they were regarded as Ugandans and a significant number of President Museveni's National Resistance Army were Rwandans by origin. They formed themselves into the Rwandese Patriotic Front, and were determined to return to Rwanda and re-establish the former ascendancy of the Tutsis over the Hutus. In 1990 they invaded Rwanda, taking with them a good stock of weapons from the Ugandan army. Museveni denied that he knew about this proposed invasion, and this was not a case of intervention by the Ugandan state. However it is probable that he connived at it as he was probably not averse to an extension of Ugandan influence across the border, with people to whom he felt an affinity. Also, it might check the flow of refugees from that country into Uganda.

This was a time when France, a strong supporter of President Mobutu in what was then Zaire, was also supporting his neighbour, President Habyarimana in Rwanda, with arms, logistical support and military advice. France continued to support this predominantly Hutu regime right up to the time of the plane crash that killed Habyarimana and the genocide of the Tutsis and moderate Hutus that followed in 1994. Indeed, severe criticism has since been voiced regarding France's role which extended well beyond the time of the massacres. Her attempt to redeem the situation by initiating Operation Turquoise in which French troops set up a safety zone to safeguard lives in what was declared to be a humanitarian operation was also criticised because it appeared to save not only Tutsis but also many of the Interahamwe and ex-government troops who had perpetrated the massacres.[13] French public opinion and the press became extremely critical, so that Rwanda was almost as significant a turning point for French policies of military intervention in Africa, that Somalia had been for the US. The difference is that succeeding French governments continue to play an influential support role in Africa, though officially confining themselves to Francophone countries, as several chapters in this book describe.

Rwanda was also a turning point for UN policies of direct military intervention in Africa. Their peacekeeping force was far too small in Rwanda, in spite of warnings that a massacre was planned. The UN was not capable of quick action on the scale that was needed, and most of them were actually withdrawn, powerless to halt the killings. When a new, larger mission was sent, many months later, it had a new task of peace-building with the now-victorious Tutsi invading force, the Rwanda Patriotic Front. There were two major knock-on effects from this: the perpetrators of the massacre and the ex-government forces fled to Zaire, which sparked off the Congolese civil war, while the UN showed a great reluctance to send military missions to Africa thereafter, although a Canadian-led force, 'Operation Assurance', was all set to go in 1996 and was only prevented by the Rwandans clearing the refugee camps.[14] The stage was set for African regional organisations to take over, and for African states, not for the first time but now on an increasing scale, to intervene militarily for their own ends. Thus when the civil war in Rwanda's neighbour, Burundi, was continuing a partly similar ethnic struggle between Tutsi and Hutu, the UN did not send a force but confined itself to fact-finding missions. Instead when General Pierre Buyoya staged a military coup and set up a Tutsi military regime, it was the heads of the neighbouring East African states that took action, and they did not send an intervening force but imposed trade sanctions on Burundi. This new example of regional intervention albeit of a non-military nature was not to be lifted until Buyoya restored 'constitutional legality' to the country.[15] At the time of writing this appears to have met with partial success: constitutional institutions are being restored and the sanctions have been lifted, although the country remains in turmoil. The long-drawn out peace negotiations, led first by the late former President Julius Nyerere of Tanzania, and later by former President Nelson Mandela of South Africa, are an example of a different type of 'intervention' in Africa, where strong diplomatic pressure is applied by Africa's eminent statesmen and supported by the presidents of neighbouring states, the UN and the OAU. In gradual stages even the most reluctant of the warring parties are signing the proposed peace accord. If peace is achieved, this will be a significant success for diplomacy where no active intervention by military forces was involved.

Mel McNulty's chapter makes a case for Rwanda as taking the leading role among the interventionist states in the two Congo wars, first against President Mobutu and then against President Kabila. He points out that each of the nine states involved shared some similarities and overlaps in their motives in intervening: these were political, strategic and economic, which in Rwanda's case meant the search for external security, domestic stability, and latterly, for resources. It was in fact Rwanda that first suffered intervention, from Mobutu's Zaire and France in support, to defend President Habyarimana's shaky regime in Rwanda itself. This in turn meant that the Rwanda Patriotic Front, invading Rwanda from Uganda, held a lasting resentment against Mobutu's Zaire, which was seen as a source of regional instability perhaps more urgently by Rwanda than by the other intervening states. After the RPF took power in Rwanda, the defeated ex-FAR soldiers and the Interahamwe took refuge in Zaire and in 1994-96 used their bases in Zaire to attack Rwanda. Thus the counter-intervention by Rwanda into Zaire was inevitable, McNulty would argue.

Both Rwanda and Uganda helped the Congolese rebel Kabila to power as President of Zaire which became the Democratic Republic of Congo, but their presence was so overwhelming, becoming a 'quasi occupation' as McNulty observes, that Kabila turned against them and in 1998 he declared all foreign forces were to leave the country. The second war which consequently began is fought with a mixture of less convincing reasons, as Rwandan and Ugandan forces, occupying about half of the country, fight to retain their hold with the aid of several Congolese rebel groups who depend on them for support. The strategic reasons for intervention become less plausible when some of their forces are hundreds of kilometres deep in Congo away from their borders. Instead, it is likely that economic motives are much stronger. It has been called a resource war, and the nineteenth century European scramble for Africa has been replaced by 'Africa's scramble for Africa'. Indeed as McNulty points out, intervention is proving profitable, so that if for example, Rwanda's troops finally have to be pulled out, some financial or economic rewards may have to be found for them for fear they present a threat to their own government. It is partly for this reason that Rwanda's intervention, along with that of the other states, may not be a temporary affair but may lead to a permanent presence, perhaps fortifying ethnic unity in the eastern part of Congo. This opens up a question which has hardly been considered by the participants and peace negotiators in this war: how do the interventionist powers extricate themselves, and what effect is this likely to have on the sovereignty and territory of Congo? It is a war that may have a more profound effect on the borders and the concepts of sovereignty than any of the other conflicts in contemporary Africa.

This contemporary scramble for Africa is pursued in further detail in the chapter by Cleaver and Massey. Some of the intervening states' roles and actions have been considered in specific case studies such as those on Rwanda, Angola and Sudan. Thus this chapter aims both to reprise some of that material whilst expanding upon the motivation and the nature of some of the intervenees, notably Zimbabwe, Chad and Namibia.

Gerry Cleaver's chapter on international companies underlines the close connection between intervention by Africa's national armies on the one hand, and that by private security companies and mercenary forces on the other. A number of African governments facing civil war, invasion or serious security problems caused by guerrilla forces, in addition to accepting help from other African armies – 'armies on loan' – have resorted to the paid employment of these companies or have invited foreign mercenaries into their countries. Cleaver offers definitions of mercenaries and private security companies, making clear distinctions between the two. He cites several cases where they have played a significant part in eliminating violent opposition elements and in helping to bring about conditions to enable peace negotiations to be held.

The ending of the Cold War released experienced military manpower in many countries and at the same time, because of the withdrawal or diminution of involvement by most of the big powers, created a security vacuum in Africa which these companies and mercenaries could partially fill. The Angolan government came to rely on them quite strongly in their long civil war against the opposing forces of UNITA. They were used particularly to guard Angola's bases for oil and mineral extraction, as well as supplying expertise in the logistical and technological requirements of the war, and they took part also in actual combat with the enemy. Executive Outcomes was the most prominent of these companies, and they were employed in Angola and elsewhere, even though they suffered from an 'image problem' in that they were mainly formerly members of apartheid South Africa's special forces.

There was indeed a certain stigma attached to mercenaries or private security companies in that they joined wars for their own profit and were not particularly concerned with the cause for which they fought. In Sierra Leone, a desperate government employed both Executive Outcomes and later Sandline International to fight the Revolutionary United Front, and their assistance was vitally important, but their employment came in for international criticism and British officials in particular were criticised for their part in their procurement. The UN Special Rapporteur on mercenaries, Mr Enriques Ballesteros, summed up the doubts about the legitimacy of employing these companies when he said that they usurped the responsibilities that are the obligations of states themselves. Cleaver points to the dilemma, however, when African states feel there is no alternative to their use. It seems they are unlikely to go away and their use may well increase.

The book is organised into three main parts though the complex nature of the events and interventions make overlaps between these categories inevitable. The first part consists of an overview of contextual matters, specifically the changing legal framework in which the interventions occur and also an examination of the military capabilities of African states. The second part is about the states that one may class as intervenors and the third part looks at three case studies of states that are examples of those that have been intervened in. The final chapter in that section examines, within the context of state collapse, the concomitant growth of private security firms and mercenaries.

Notes

1 Hughes, A. and May, R., 'Armies on Loan', in Baynham, S. (ed) (1986), *Military Power and Politics in Black Africa*, Croom Helm, London.

2 Furley, O. W. and May, R. (1989), 'Tanzania's military intervention in Uganda', Conference on Uganda, May 1989, University of Copenhagen, Roskilde.

3 Hughes, A. and May, R., op.cit.

4 Hughes, A. and May, R., op.cit.: Out of the 29 interventions, 18 were classified as regime supportive, 6 as regime opposing and 5 as state supportive.

5 Rosenau, J. (1971) 'Intervention as a Scientific Concept', *Journal of Conflict Resolution*, 23, 2, June, cited by Hughes, A. and May, R., op.cit., p. 178.

6 Frynas, G. (2000) 'Foreign investment and international boundary disputes in Africa: evidence from the oil industry', Occasional Paper No 9, African Studies Centre, Coventry University.

7 Harbeson, J. W. and Rothchild, D. (eds) (2000) *Africa in World Politics: the African State System in Flux*, Westview Press, Colorado and Oxford, p. 12.

8 Kakande, J. (1997), 'Is the UPDF a Paper Tiger?', *New Vision* newspaper, 29 October 1997.

9 Harbeson, J. W. and Rothchild, D., op.cit, p. 4.

10 Mbembe, Achille (1999), 'African frontiers in flux', *Le Monde Diplomatique*, 14 November 1999.

11 See 'Diamonds in Sierra Leone' in *Africa Confidential*, 41, No 16, 4 August 2000, and 'The Glittering Prizes of War', *Africa Confidential*, 41, No 11, 26 May 2000.

12 Quoted by May, R., in 'France: down and out in Africa?', conference paper given at the ASAUK Biennial Conference 'Africa: past, present and future', Cambridge, September 2000.

13 Prunier, G. (1995), *The Rwanda Crisis 1959-1994: History of a Genocide*, Hurst and Co, London. See in particular, chapters 8 and 9.

14 Massey, S. (1997), 'Operation Assurance: the greatest intervention that never happened', *Journal of Humanitarian Affairs,* September.

15 Furley, O. W. (1998), 'Rwanda and Burundi: Peacekeeping amidst Massacres', in Furley, O. W. and May, R. A. (eds) *Peacekeeping in Africa*, Ashgate, Aldershot, pp. 239-261.

2 African Interventionist States and International Law

Jeremy Levitt

Introduction

Aims and Objectives

In the increasingly complex world of international law and the evolving nature of the state sovereignty and democratic governance regimes, a key question emerges: Is there a customary international law right of humanitarian intervention?[1] This chapter argues that the practices of African states and the United Nations in Africa since the end of the Cold War confirm that there is indeed a customary international law right of humanitarian intervention. African states have been the first to challenge holistically the classical notions of state sovereignty, territorial integrity, and non-interference in the internal affairs of states to alleviate grand human suffering and to preserve international peace and security. This chapter maintains that African states are largely responsible for spurring new norms of international law relating to the law of the use of force and the customary international law doctrine of humanitarian intervention.

The law *de lege lata* appears to recognise a right to unilateral humanitarian intervention by groups of states and regional actors in internal conflicts in three instances: 1) when there have been human rights abuses so egregious as to violate the *jus cogens* norms of international law; 2) when a government has collapsed and is spiralling into a state of anarchy; and 3) to safeguard democracy when a democratic regime has been violently and illegally overthrown against the will of its domestic populace.[2] These should be viewed as the normative criteria upon which humanitarian intervention may be based, as evidenced by the following cases: 1) the Economic Community of West African States (ECOWAS) Cease-Fire Monitoring Group (ECOMOG) interventions in Liberia (1990), Sierra Leone (1997), and Guinea-Bissau (1998), the Mission for the Implementation of the Bangui Agreement (MISAB) operation in the

Central African Republic (CAR) (1997), and the South African Development Community (SADC) mission in Lesotho (1998); 2) Chapter VII action by the United Nations in Iraq (1990), Somalia (1992), Yugoslavia (1992), Rwanda (1994) and Haiti (1993-1994); and 3) North Atlantic Treaty Organisation (NATO) action in Kosovo (1999).[3] This chapter, however, is only concerned with the African interventions that derive their legal basis from customary international law as opposed to the UN Charter.

Contemporary international law and international relations literature have failed to pay adequate attention to the impact of the aforementioned African case studies on the international system of peace and security, specifically regarding the development of new legal and policy norms. Therefore, this chapter purports to fill an alarming gap in international law, international relations, and Africanist literature. Given the numerous and arguably unsettled issues the topic engenders, the following analysis should by no means be considered a comprehensive treatment of the subject, but rather an attempt to shed light on the legal significance of African states' practice in these areas and to challenge the ethnocentric and linear bias in contemporary international law and security studies.

Legal Aspects of Humanitarian Intervention

Since the end of the Cold War it appears that customary international law has shifted from traditional prohibitions against forcible intervention in the internal affairs of states,[4] toward the recognition of a right to humanitarian intervention by groups of states and regional organisations in internal conflicts.[5] This shift appears to have been spurred by five internationally supported unilateral African interventions that occurred by regional actors between 1990 and 1998 (see Table 1),[6] and three popular African forcible military interventions by individual states that took place between 1997-1998 (see Table 1A). The legality of these interventions will be examined in an attempt to qualify in legal terms when it appears lawful for groups of states and regional organisations to employ the use of force in states for humanitarian purposes (i.e. invoke a right to humanitarian intervention) and to assess the current state of the law in this regard.

Table 2.1 Unilateral African Interventions, 1990-1998

Group	*Place of Intervention*	*Year of Intervention*	*Length of Mission*
1) ECOMOG	Liberia	1990	8 years
2) MISAB	CAR	1997	9 months
3) ECOMOG	Sierra Leone	1997	2 years
4) ECOMOG	Guinea-Bissau	1998	1 year
5) SADC	Lesotho	1998	1 month

Notes: Economic Community of West African States Cease-Fire Monitoring Group (ECOMOG); Mission for the Implementation of the Bangui Agreement (MISAB); Nigerian Forces Assistance Group (NFAG); Southern African Development Community (SADC).

Table 2.2 Lawful Forcible Military Interventions by Individual African States

Intervenor	*Place of Intervention*	*Year of Intervention*	*Length of Intervention*
1) Nigeria	Sierra Leone	1997	3 months
2) Senegal	Guinea-Bissau	1998	6 months
3) Guinea	Guinea-Bissau	1998	6 months

Under customary international law there are four recognised exceptions to the principle of non-interference in the internal affairs of states: 1) when a *de jure* government requests or consents to intervention; 2) when a group of states or a regional actor invokes a right to humanitarian intervention; 3) when a state acts in self-defence; and 4) as counter-intervention by a state to offset an illegal prior intervention by another state.[7] All of these interventions fall within the purview of the generally recognised exceptions to the principle of non-interference.

In consonance with the aforementioned exceptions, international law seems to recognise four types of intervention: 1) unilateral intervention by a *regional actor* acting on its own initiative (ECOWAS in Liberia, Sierra

Leone, and Guinea-Bissau; SADC in Lesotho; and NATO in Iraq and Yugoslavia); 2) unilateral intervention by a *state* or *group of states* acting on their own initiative (Nigeria in Sierra Leone, MISAB in the CAR, and Senegal and Guinea in Guinea-Bissau); 3) an intervention authorised by the United Nations but *not* taken by it (United States in Somalia and Haiti, France and Senegal in Rwanda, and, *retroactively*, the ECOWAS and MISAB interventions); and finally 4) an intervention taken by the United Nations (Yugoslavia and co-deployments in Liberia and the CAR). The legal basis for a *unilateral* intervention is different from an intervention taken under the authority of the United Nations. Any right of unilateral intervention must derive its legal basis from customary international law (items one and two above), whereas any intervention taken under the authority of the United Nations must derive its basis from Chapter VII of the UN Charter (items three and four above).[8] The analysis here is primarily concerned with unilateral intervention as described in number one above, since regional actors undertook five of the eight interventions under study. However, reference is also made to the types of interventions described in number two, because states and a group of states likewise carried out the remainder of the interventions under examination.

The following section will discuss the legality of the ECOWAS–ECOMOG interventions in Liberia, Sierra Leone, and Guinea-Bissau. It also examines the Nigerian intervention in Sierra Leone and the Senegalese and Guinean operations in Guinea-Bissau.

ECOWAS-ECOMOG Interventions in Liberia, Sierra Leone, and Guinea-Bissau

Liberia

1. Background

The Liberian Civil War began in 1989, when Charles Taylor, Liberia's current President, and a group of so-called 'dissidents' launched an attack against security personnel in Nimba County (located on the Liberian-Côte d'Ivoire border) and advanced toward the capital city of Monrovia. The group led by Taylor referred to themselves as the National Patriotic Front of Liberia (NPFL). The NPFL recruited soldiers from many groups foremost among them the Mano and Gio, and proceeded to crush then-

President, Sergeant Samuel Doe's (Doe) U.S.-backed Armed Forces of Liberia (AFL). By May 1990, the NPFL controlled significantly more territory than Doe's collapsing regime.

Liberian security forces suffered enormous losses on the battlefield, which led Doe, who was facing certain defeat, to make several unsuccessful appeals to the people of Liberia, the United Nations, and the U.S. government for military assistance. Finally, he appealed to ECOWAS to introduce a 'peace-keeping force into Liberia to forestall increasing terror and tension...' (i.e. restore his decrepit government to power).[9]

On 7 August 1990, the ECOWAS Standing Mediation Commission (hereinafter Commission) established the ECOMOG in Liberia to halt the 'wanton destruction of human life and property...[and]...massive damage...being caused by the armed conflict to the stability and survival of the entire Liberian nation'.[10] ECOMOG was mandated to '*restor[e]* law and order and *create* the necessary conditions for free and fair elections [emphasis added]'.[11] On 27 August 1990, ECOMOG entered Liberia to forestall the wanton destruction of human life and property and to prevent the state from descending into anarchy. The NPFL, which by then controlled approximately 90 per cent of the country, immediately attacked ECOMOG forces upon their arrival to Liberia. This caused ECOMOG to take on an offensive disposition toward the NPFL from the onset. Consequently, on 19 November 1992, the UN Security Council adopted Resolution 788, calling for a complete weapons embargo against Liberia - authorising ECOWAS to enforce its terms. Ten months later, on 22 September 1993, the Security Council adopted Resolution 866, which called for the creation of the UN Observer Mission in Liberia (UNOMIL), stating 'that this would be the first peace-keeping mission undertaken by the United Nations in co-operation with a peace-keeping mission already set up by another organisation, in this case the ECOWAS'.[12]

2. *ECOWAS Intervention*

The ECOWAS intervention in Liberia was lawful and derived its legal basis from customary international law and thereafter the UN Charter. In this sense, it was unique and the first of its type.

There is no concrete evidence that shows that ECOWAS established ECOMOG as a mechanism to support Doe's regime, nor that it relied on Doe's letter as a basis for the intervention. On the contrary, it did not intervene at a point when Doe's regime was salvageable, and might well have overrun Taylor's NPFL in August 1990 had it not been a genuine community enterprise.[13] In addition, not one decision or resolution of the ECOWAS Commission makes reference to Doe's letter, which suggests that it was not a factor in its decision to intervene. Conversely, several decisions of the Commission justify the intervention on humanitarian grounds.[14]

Had ECOWAS based its intervention on Doe's letter of request it would have been unlawful for two primary reasons. First, since the entire country was engulfed in the war, any intervention but an impartial one would have been a show of force against the political independence of the state. On this issue, Oscar Schacter aptly comments, 'no state today would deny the basic principle that the people of a nation have the right, under international law, to decide for themselves what kind of government they want...' including the '...right to revolt and to carry on armed conflict between competing groups.'[15] Therefore, had ECOWAS intervened to support or save Doe's regime, the NPFL or any other faction would have deprived the '...people in some measure of the right to decide the issue by themselves. It is, in terms of article 2(4), a use of force against the political independence of the state engaged in war'.[16] Second, since Doe was no longer considered the legitimate head of state by the Liberian masses, his government had collapsed, and the NPFL controlled the majority of the territory of the country, he did not possess the requisite legal authority to request foreign military assistance. Under international law, if a *de jure* government loses *de facto* control of the state, then it forfeits its right to speak for the state in totality until it regains control. On this point, Louise Doswald-Beck comments:

> ...That a regime may only be legally entitled to invite outside military help if it is a government within the meaning of the international law, and must therefore be in *de facto* control. If on the other hand, it needs to request assistance to quell an insurrection, i.e. a rebellion of some magnitude, it is by definition not in *de facto* control and thus cannot speak for the state.[17]

Hence, it is crucial for peace-making interventionist states to examine the state of affairs in a country *before* intervening. An intervention based on the request of a government is not necessarily lawful - as it depends on the character of affairs in a country at the time of the request. Since Doe was not in *de facto* control of Liberia when he requested assistance from ECOWAS, the latter could not rely on the request as a justification for the intervention. Consequently, no one had legal standing to represent the country as a whole and hence request external assistance, as the 'existence of *de facto* control is generally the most important criterion in dealing with a regime as representing the state.'[18] In addition, the ECOWAS-ECOMOG operation would not qualify as a valid *peacekeeping* operation because it did not obtain consent from Taylor, the country's *de facto* ruler and principal combatant, before intervening. It is a well-settled norm of international law and fundamental tenement of international peacekeeping policy that pre-intervention consent be obtained from all principal parties to a conflict before a *peacekeeping* mission is undertaken.[19] Since ECOWAS did not request or obtain Taylor's consent before intervening, the operation does not qualify as a lawful peacekeeping mission and thus renders Doe's request moot.

Under international law, regional actors are generally prohibited from taking action not prescribed in their organising instrument and subsequent protocols and treaties. At the time of the intervention, none of the ECOWAS instruments - including the 1975 ECOWAS Treaty, 1978 Protocol on Non-Aggression, and 1981 Protocol relating to Mutual Assistance on Defence -empowered it to intervene in purely internal conflicts (i.e. those that are not externally engineered). Therefore, given that the UN Security Council did not authorise the intervention, it must be shown that ECOWAS derived its basis from customary international law.

ECOWAS was entitled to invoke a right of humanitarian intervention because the Doe regime collapsed causing the state to slide into anarchy, resulting in death and suffering on a grand scale. It has been estimated that by August 1990 over 100,000 people had been killed and over 400,000 had been internally displaced, not including the thousands of refugees that fled into neighbouring Guinea, Sierra Leone, and Côte d'Ivoire. Few would dispute that the killing and maiming of tens of thousands of civilians (mostly women and children) by rebel and government forces was so egregious that it violated the *jus cogens* norms of international law (i.e. to persecute, oppress, exterminate, enslave, or deport civilian populations).[20] On this basis alone, the ECOWAS member states were obligated to fulfil their *erga omnes* obligations and intervene to stop the killing and safeguard the human rights of the people of Liberia.[21]

Although the UN Charter provided no legal basis for the ECOWAS intervention, it was supported by the United Nations and the whole of the international community. In fact, '[b]etween 22 January 1991 and 27 November 1996, the Council adopted fifteen resolutions directly relating to the situation in Liberia; in addition, the President of the Security Council issued nine statements in this connection.'[22] In virtually every resolution and statement, the United Nations commended ECOWAS for its efforts, not once making reference to ECOMOG's use of force offensively, which in effect tacitly legitimised such force. Moreover, Resolutions 788 and 866 placed a retroactive *de jure* seal on the ECOWAS intervention and empowered ECOMOG to enforce their terms.

Hence, detractors who question the legality of the ECOWAS intervention in specific and challenge the validity of the doctrine of humanitarian intervention in general must nonetheless deal with the daunting exercise of *theoretically* nullifying the *retroactive de jure seal* or *post de jure authentication* placed on it by the UN Security Council.

Sierra Leone

1. Background

In February and March of 1996, Sierra Leone held its first presidential and parliamentary elections in thirty years. The elections were held *during* the final stages of a five-year civil war. The Sierra Leone People's Party led by President Ahmed Tijan Kabbah was elected into power. Nevertheless, warring between the government and Revolutionary United Front (RUF), which contested the elections, continued unabated. On 30 November 1996, the government of Côte d'Ivoire, the ECOWAS, United Nations, Organisation of African Unity (OAU), and Commonwealth of States facilitated peace talks that culminated into the Abidjan Accord, ending the war.

On 25 May 1997, approximately six months after the war, several junior military officers led by Major Johnny Koromah and the RUF carried out a successful *coup d'état* against President Kabbah's democratically elected government, forcing him to flee to Guinea. Before leaving Liberia, however, Kabbah requested that Nigeria and ECOWAS intervene to forestall the conflict and restore constitutional order to the country.[23]

During the coup, Koromah's forces attacked ECOMOG and Nigerian Forces Assistant Group (NIFAG) contingents in order to avert a counter-offensive by them, and ECOMOG and NIFAG responded in kind. ECOMOG was stationed in Sierra Leone for peace-enforcement operations in Liberia, and NIFAG was providing security and training to the Sierra Leone Armed Forces pursuant to a Status of Forces Agreement (SOFA) between the two countries. Consequently, the coup was successful because

NIFAG officers allegedly leaked information to the coup plotters revealing when there would be a change of NIFAG guard units with others on the outskirts of Monrovia. The coup took place while NIFAG guard units were changing positions.

In response to Kabbah's request on 26 May 1997 and pursuant to its obligations under the SOFA, Nigeria (not ECOMOG) sent forces to Sierra Leone to restore law and order to the country and to protect Liberian citizens. However, Nigerian forces were met with strong resistance from the *junta* and were forced to retreat. Likewise, in early August 1997, pursuant to requests by the member states of ECOWAS, General Sani Abacha, former Nigerian head of state and ECOWAS Chairman, appears to have issued an 'executive directive' authorising an economic blockade against Sierra Leone to be enforced by the ECOMOG. On 30 August 1997, during the Twentieth Summit of ECOWAS in Abuja, the ECOWAS *officially* mandated the ECOMOG to enforce sanctions against the *junta* and restore law and order to the country. On 8 October 1997, the UN Security Council supported these various efforts by adopting Resolution 1132, which imposed an arms and petroleum embargo and travel restrictions against the junta. The resolution sanctioned ECOWAS to enforce its terms.

On 5 February 1998, 'responding to an attack by junta forces on its position at Lungi, ECOMOG launched a military attack on the junta', which led to its removal from power and expulsion from Free Town on 12 February 1998.[24] By early March 1998, 'ECOMOG [had] established itself successfully across most of the country.'[25] On 10 March 1998, President Kabbah returned to Free Town to resume his position as President of Sierra Leone. The leaders of Nigeria, Guinea, Mali, Niger, and the Vice-President of the Gambia accompanied him.

From a legal standpoint, it is important to note that there were *two* separate interventions in Sierra Leone: the first was taken under the authority of the Republic of Nigeria; the second by ECOWAS. The legality of each intervention will be discussed individually as they are justified on different grounds.

2. Nigerian Intervention

The Nigerian intervention in Sierra Leone was lawful for three reasons: 1) President Kabbah requested that Nigeria intervene; 2) the SOFA between the two countries permitted intervention in wake of an internal threat to the state; and 3) Nigeria was obligated and permitted to intervene according to the ECOWAS Revised Treaty of 1993.

From a legal standpoint, the Nigerian intervention should *not* be viewed as a humanitarian intervention, but rather as bilateral military assistance rendered to an allied nation. It is a well-settled norm of customary international law that *de jure* governments may request external military assistance to thwart internal rebellion.[26] Intervention is valid as long as the *de jure* government is in *de facto* control of the state at the time of the request, and such military assistance does not deprive the citizens of the state from choosing what kind of government they want.[27] If, however, the government has lost *de facto* control of the state and the civilian population either supports or is ambivalent about the rebellion (or new regime), then a state that militarily supports one side or the other in such a civil war is depriving the civilian population the right to decide the issue for themselves. As previously stated, such action is, according to article 2(4) of the UN Charter, 'a use of force against the political independence of the state engaged in civil war.'[28]

At the time of the intervention, Kabbah's regime, unlike Doe's in Liberia, controlled more territory than the *junta* and RUF and hence maintained *de facto* control of the state. Moreover, it was still recognised as the *de jure* government by the whole of the international community. More important, however, the civilian population of Sierra Leone continued to recognise the Kabbah government as its own and actively protested and took up arms against the *junta*. This is perhaps the first time in contemporary African history that well over 95 per cent of the civilian population of a state actively resisted the toppling of a democratically elected regime and refused to co-operate with and recognise its illegal incumbent, who under the constitution of the Republic was charged with protecting the political independence of the state, not violating it.

Further, the Nigerian intervention was also justified under the SOFA. The SOFA states that Nigeria 'shall have the right to apply force in the sustenance of the sovereignty and territorial integrity of the Republic of Sierra Leone' from internal or external threats,[29] and NIFAG shall have a right of self-defence against all attacks.[30] NIFAG was established to provide security for the government, train its troops, and avert future warring between the RUF and factions within the military against loyal government forces and militia. From this view, Nigeria was justified in sending reinforcements and using force to protect the rights of its citizens (i.e. NIFAG and ECOMOG troops and their families);[31] defend itself against armed aggression from the junta;[32] and fulfil its obligations under the SOFA by securing the integrity of the Kabbah government and people of Sierra Leone from the *junta*.

Finally, the ECOWAS Revised Treaty of 1993 (hereinafter Treaty) is perhaps the most persuasive evidence confirming the legality of the Nigerian intervention.[33] Article 58 of the Treaty obliges member *states* to 'undertake to work to safeguard and consolidate relations conducive to the maintenance of peace, stability and security within the region', and pledge to 'co-operate with the Community in establishing and strengthening appropriate mechanisms for the timely prevention and resolution of intra-State and inter-State conflict.'[34] Moreover, Article 58 calls on member states to 'establish a regional peace and security observation system and *peace-keeping* forces where appropriate.'[35] Consequently, under the terms of the Treaty, Nigeria was duty bound to send forces to Sierra Leone to restore law and order and to prevent the state from slipping into anarchy. For these reasons and taking into consideration that the United Nations did not reprimand Nigeria for taking unilateral action, the intervention must be considered lawful.

3. ECOWAS Intervention

The ECOWAS intervention in Sierra Leone can be justified on four grounds: 1) Kabbah requested that ECOWAS intervene; 2) ECOWAS was entitled to invoke a right to humanitarian intervention; 3) it was obligated to act under the ECOWAS Revised Treaty 1993; and 4) the UN Security Council retroactively authorised the intervention.

As previously stated, ECOWAS was entitled to act upon Kabbah's request and establish ECOMOG because Kabbah was the lawful head of state and because the coup was illegal under international law. Moreover, after the coup, Kabbah continued to be recognised as the *de jure* head of state by the international community. Since the civilian populace actively rejected the authority of the junta, and because the conflict did not escalate into a mass civil war, the *junta* leaders were *unable* to muster the requisite status (i.e. attain legal personality) to be considered *de facto* rulers. As a result, the ECOWAS was not required to obtain the consent of the *junta* before intervening, because Kabbah was legally entitled to speak for the state as a whole.

Shortly after the coup, the situation in the country became chaotic. Yet, it was not consumed by anarchy nor, arguably, at this juncture, had the *junta* and RUF committed human rights abuses that would have warranted humanitarian intervention. Nevertheless, ECOWAS could lawfully invoke a right of humanitarian intervention because the democratic government of Sierra Leone was illegally and violently dislodged against the will of its civilian populace,[36] who because of their opposition to the *junta* were threatened with death and suffering on a grand scale.[37] Moreover, civilian opposition by way of armed resistance and nationwide employment strikes against the *junta* intensified the situation and caused the state infrastructure to collapse. Had ECOMOG not intervened, fighting between the junta and the RUF on the one hand and the *Kamajors* and other civilians loyal to Kabbah on the other would have escalated, resulting in untold destruction and loss of life. Statements made by UN Secretary-General Kofi Annan are instructive here because they verify and perhaps validate the emergence of a *pro-democratic* right of intervention when democratically elected governments are overthrown; he comments that 'Africa can no longer tolerate, and accept as fait accompli, coups against elected governments, and the illegal seizure of power by military cliques.... For these reasons, ECOWAS was entitled to invoke a right to humanitarian intervention.'

As previously mentioned, the ECOWAS Revised Treaty of 1993 permits its member states to establish a regional peacekeeping force to resolve internal conflicts. That being the case and considering that Sierra Leone is a member of ECOWAS, the community was obligated, empowered, and legally entitled to mandate ECOMOG to restore law and order in Sierra Leone. Furthermore, similar to the case of Liberia, the UN Security Council placed a *retroactive de jure seal* on the ECOWAS operation by adopting resolution 1132, which sanctioned the ECOWAS to enforce an arms and petroleum embargo and travel restrictions against the junta.

One year after the ECOWAS intervention in Sierra Leone, its capacity to maintain law and order in West Africa was tested again in the conflict in Guinea-Bissau.

Guinea-Bissau

1. Background

Political turmoil in Guinea-Bissau dates back to the assassination of Bissau's revolutionary leader Amilcar Cabral by dissidents of the *Partido Africano da Independência da Guiné e Cabo Verde* (PAIGC) in 1973. The same year, Luis Cabral, Amilcar's brother, succeeded him but was subsequently overthrown by Vieira's faction in 1980. To the great dissatisfaction of Bissauans, Vieira ultimately pursued a capitalist path and buried Amilcar's popular socialist programme. In 1994, he won a bitter and controversial election where he was accused of election rigging and corruption. Vieira's 'popularity in the army slumped after he ordered the execution of several soldiers for an alleged coup attempt. For two years after the poll, such was the disarray in the army that he didn't appoint a chief of staff.'[38] 'Low pay and threats of mass dismissals' worsened the situation, which indefinitely damaged the morale of army personnel.[39] In the years that followed, the relationship between Vieira and key army official continued to deteriorate.

On 7 June 1998, the democratically elected government of President Bernardo Nino Vieira was threatened with a mutiny by high-ranking officers of the Armed Forces of Guinea-Bissau, led by Army Chief of Staff Ansoumane Mane. The mutiny was initiated after President Vieira fired Mane for not investigating claims that his officers were smuggling arms to the Casamance rebels in Southern Senegal. In addition, the mutineers opposed government plans to reduce the military by 50 per cent from its 1996 strength of 20,000.[40] By the end of June 1998, fighting between the mutineers and loyalist forces resulted in the deaths of several hundred civilians and caused over 250,000 persons to be displaced.

At the requests of President Vieira and pursuant to bilateral defence pacts, Senegal and Guinea intervened to quell the mutiny, evacuate their nationals and those of other countries, and restore constitutional legality and security to the country. Senegal and Guinea initially sent 1,300 and 400 troops, respectively, to the country. They did not intervene to enforce the peace, but rather to provide military assistance to Vieira. Although Senegal and Guinea were successful in preventing Vieira's regime from being toppled or collapsing, as partial combatants they were not in a position to serve as peace-enforcers.[41] Consequently, Vieira requested that ECOWAS deploy ECOMOG in the country.[42] During the eighteenth Foreign Ministers' Conference on Security in Abidjan, Côte d'Ivoire, on 30 June to 3 July 1998, ECOWAS Foreign Ministers made tentative plans to intervene *unilaterally* in Guinea-Bissau to restore law and order to the country.

However, a series of peace talks were brokered by the ECOWAS Committee on Guinea-Bissau and the Community of Portuguese Speaking Countries (CPLP) in Praia, Cape Verde, on 26 August 1998; Abuja, Nigeria, on 1 November 1998; and Lome, Togo, on 15 December 1998. In the talks, President Vieira and chief mutineer Mane *agreed* to the deployment of the ECOMOG to monitor the peace and imposition of a Government of National Unity. The Abuja Accord specifically provided for the deployment of the ECOMOG to replace the Senegalese and Guinean contingents.[43] On 26 December 1998, less than a week before ECOMOG was to be deployed in Guinea-Bissau, the UN Security Council adopted Resolution 1216, which 'welcomed' the role of ECOMOG in the implementation of the Abuja Accord, 'approved' the ECOMOG mandate, and 'affirmed' that 'ECOMOG may have to take action [i.e. force]...to discharge its mandate'.[44] Between December 1998 and March 1999, Benin, the Gambia, Mali, Niger, and Togo deployed approximately 800 ECOMOG troops in Guinea-Bissau to 'guarantee security along the Senegalese/Guinea-Bissau border, keep the warring parties apart and guarantee free access to humanitarian organisations'.[45]

2. *Senegalese and Guinean Interventions*

Under international law, the Senegalese and Guinean interventions were legal because both countries intervened pursuant to requests by President Vieira and in accordance with bilateral defence pacts, each of which provided for forcible military intervention in lieu of an internal or external challenge to the state. In this sense, the defence pacts are similar to the SOFA between Nigeria and Sierra Leone.

In the case of Guinea-Bissau, it is clear that Senegal and Guinea intervened specifically to quash the rebellion. Such action was permissible because under international law states are entitled to lend military assistance upon request from the head of state or other authorised agent of a *de jure* government, in this case Vieira. In addition, because the *junta* was not in *de facto* control of the state at the time the request was made and because the mutiny did not mature into mass civil war, Senegal and Guinea's timely actions did not violate the political independence of the state. Had the junta attained effective control of the state and the conflict matured into civil war, the intervention might still have been valid given that Vieira was democratically elected. As the cases of Haiti, Sierra Leone, and the CAR show, the international community is not likely to recognise and support regimes that attain power by toppling democratically elected governments. This is primarily because coups can interfere with a population's right to self-determination (i.e. to live under the form of government it chooses), and coups usually have devastating societal consequences. This lends further credence to the argument that, today, states have a pro-democratic right of intervention, which may fall outside the scope of humanitarian intervention, but nonetheless represents an independent norm closely linked to the human rights protective regime.

However, if it could be shown that the majority of the domestic population of Guinea-Bissau supported the coup, then a strong argument could be made that the Senegalese and Guinean interventions violated the international law principle of non-interference and interfered with the political independence of a state engaged in war. This argument, I believe, would be particularly compelling if there were ample evidence to show that the civilian population actively sought to overthrow the government for failing to govern in a democratic fashion (i.e. for suspending the constitution, postponing elections, dissolving parliament, banning political parties, and civic organisations and perpetuating corruption and cronyism). In this case, however, while Bissauan civil society and the army did not hold Vieira in high regard, it does not appear that they would have supported his violent ouster from power.

3. ECOWAS Intervention

The ECOWAS operation in Guinea-Bissau was legal for three reasons: 1) Vieira and Mane requested that ECOWAS intervene; 2) the ECOWAS Revised Treaty of 1993 (hereinafter Revised Treaty) and Framework for the Mechanism for Conflict Prevention, Management, Resolution, Peacekeeping and Security (1998) (hereinafter MCPMRPS Framework) obligated it to intervene; and 3) the UN Security Council approved of the mission.

President Vieira and former Army Chief of Staff and head mutineer Mane agreed to the deployment of ECOMOG in Guinea-Bissau. They determined that the ECOMOG interposition force would provide security along the Guinea-Bissau/Senegal border, keep the warring parties apart, and guarantee free access to humanitarian organisations attempting to provide humanitarian relief to the domestic population.[46] This fact is significant because unlike the cases of Liberia and Sierra Leone, *all* of the parties to the conflict formally consented to the deployment of ECOMOG, arguably making it the first of its kind in Africa. Hence, the intervention was legal as it took place at the request of the legitimate government, and although not necessary, of the mutineers as well.

Furthermore, similar to the case of Nigeria in Sierra Leone, the operation was justified under Article 58 of the ECOWAS Revised Treaty of 1993. However, unlike the cases of Liberia and Sierra Leone, ECOWAS *can* rely on the MCPMRPS Framework as a justification for the intervention. During the twenty-first Session of the Authority of Heads of State and Government in Abuja, Nigeria, 30-31 October 1998 - less than one month before ECOWAS intervened in Guinea-Bissau - the Authority of Heads of State and Government of the ECOWAS (AHSGECO) adopted and ratified the MCPMRPS Framework.[47] On 10 December 1999, just over one year later, the AHSGECO adopted the Protocol of the MCPMRPS (hereinafter Protocol) in Lome, Togo, which entered into force *provisionally* upon the *signature* by the AHSGECO and will *fully* or permanently enter into force when it receives nine ratifications.[48] At the time of this writing, it had yet to receive such ratifications. As previously stated, the MCPMRPS Framework provided the legal basis for the operation in Guinea-Bissau and is still in force pursuant to Article 3 of the Protocol, which recognises Paragraph 46 of the Framework as controlling on all conflict prevention, management, and resolution issues.

Under Paragraph 46 of the MCPMRPS Framework, ECOWAS may introduce peacekeeping forces in internal conflicts when they 'threaten to trigger a humanitarian disaster', 'pose a serious threat to peace and security in the sub-region', and 'erupt following the overthrow or *attempted* overthrow of a democratically-elected government'.[49] As evidenced by the actions of Senegal and Guinea, the geo-political and sub-regional implications of the conflict threatened to destabilise the region. When taken together with the fact that the *junta* attempted to overthrow Vieira's democratically elected government, ECOWAS could justify intervening under the Revised Treaty and the MCPMRPS Framework. Paragraph 46(iii) of the MCPMRPS Framework explicitly provides for a pro-democratic right of intervention, which comports with the law *de lege lata* in the West Africa region as highlighted in Article 25 of the Protocol and states' practice.

The ECOWAS was arguably entitled to invoke a right to humanitarian intervention because the coup posed a genuine threat of death and great suffering to the civilian population, and again, to safeguard Vieira's democratically elected regime because it was violently dislodged against the will of the people of Guinea-Bissau.[50] However, had the civilian population actively supported the coup, and there was no grand threat to their well-being (i.e. massive violations of human rights), then the intervention would need to be justified on other grounds.

The UN Security Council's reaction to the crisis in Guinea-Bissau was wholly unique. In July 1998, after ECOWAS foreign ministers made tentative plans to intervene *unilaterally* in Guinea-Bissau and approximately one week before ECOMOG was originally supposed to deploy in the country, the UN Security Council *approved* the ECOWAS intervention in the country. It endorsed ECOMOG's mandate to guarantee security along the Guinea-Bissau/Senegal border, keep apart parties at conflict, and guarantee free access of humanitarian workers - a mandate that clearly necessitated the use of force. As a result, the ECOWAS mission was a legal hybrid and can authentically be seen as both a unilateral intervention by ECOWAS and a multilateral one under the auspices of the United Nations, because both organisations took concurrent action. Once again, similar to the cases of Liberia and Sierra Leone, the UNSC placed a *retroactive de jure seal* on a *pre-authorised* unilateral intervention, albeit this time before troops had formally been deployed. Conversely, unlike the aforementioned cases, it did so by *endorsing* the ECOMOG operation as opposed to *authorising* it under Chapter VII or VIII of the UN Charter.

MISAB Intervention in the Central African Republic

1. Background

On 18 April 1996, the government of President Angel-Felix Patasse (of the Sara group) was destabilised by the first of a series of mutinies by segments of the Armed Forces of the CAR, due namely to 'widespread public discontent over social and economic problems exacerbated by prolonged non-payment of salary arrears'.[51] Many public servants, including members of the armed forces, had been demanding payment of salary arrears from 1992.[52] According to Premier Jean-Paul Ngoupande, the mutineers sought to overthrow Patasse's government.[53] However, the crisis was temporarily halted when Paris unblocked 700 million CFA francs, 'alongside CFA 300m from the CAR Treasury, to meet the arrears'.[54]

Thereafter, the state of affairs in the country worsened due to severe economic problems that were precipitated by the 1996 mutinies, and acute poverty that ran rampant throughout the country affecting 35.5 per cent of the population.[55] As a result, the country underwent successive army mutinies between November 1996 and January 1997, which were thwarted by robust military intervention by French Legionnaires (primarily of African origin). This intervention resulted in the deaths of two French soldiers and eventually led to a French withdrawal. The situation in the country, however, continued to deteriorate leading to two more military uprisings that further destabilised Patasse's government. On 18 May 1996, Sergeant Major Isidore Mathurin Dokodo, one of the leaders of the April mutiny, and Lieutenant Zao took over the capital for four days.[56] Both men are of Yakoma origin and along with 300 men from the Regiment *Mixte d'Intervention* managed to take over about two-fifths of Bangui and garnered a moderate amount of support from the civilian populace.[57]

The mutiny was in part a manifestation of deep-seated ethno-political tensions between followers of ex-President Andre Kolingba who was from the Yakoma group and his successor Patasse who was from the Sourmah-Kaba clan of the Sara (15 per cent of the population). The mutiny was triggered when the Presidential Guard (hereinafter Guard) attempted to arrest Captain Anicet Saulet Yavro for financial irregularities. Yavro was a senior representative of the Yakoma group and former head of the *Societe Centrafricaine de Telecommunications* under the Kolingba regime. Yavro attempted to evade arrest and shot and killed a member of the Presidential Guard. Thereafter, the same Yakoma troops who orchestrated mutinies earlier that year came to his aid and attacked the Guard and other loyalist forces. To make matters worse, the military did not trust that Patasse would implement a general amnesty in which they were entitled to under a separate agreement between the government and military in lieu of the April 1996 mutinies. They believed that Patasse would arrest their leaders and disband their regiment.[58]

France, said to have 2,500 legionnaires in the country, took the leading role in quashing the mutinies.[59] French troops used Puma helicopters to launch a retaliatory attack against the rebels for killing several French Legionnaires.[60] An estimated one hundred civilians and fifty mutineers were killed during the French assault.[61] As a result, French action was severely scrutinised in Paris, as Defence Minister Charles Millon's predecessor, Francois Leotard, and Socialist leader Lionel Jospin called for a parliamentary debate on the intervention. Consequently, amid growing pressure from the French parliament and President Patasse, who was known to harbour disdain for the country's former colonial master, French troops began to withdraw from the CAR in late September 1997.

Pursuant to requests by President Patasse during the Nineteenth Summit Meeting of Heads of State and Government of France and Africa held in Ouagadougou, Burkina Faso, in December 1996, the Presidents of Gabon, Burkina Faso, Chad, and Mali formed an International Mediation Committee (IMC) to help resolve the conflict. In accordance with the Conference on Consensus-Building and Dialogue, held in Bangui in late January 1997, and in response to requests by President Patasse, the member states of the IMC, chaired by President Omar Bongo of Gabon, established an Inter-African Force to Monitor the Implementation of the Bangui Agreements (MISAB) on 31 January 1997.[62] MISAB was mandated to restore peace and security to the country and monitor the implementation of the Bangui Agreements. In this regard, it was sanctioned to conduct operations to disarm the former rebels, the militia, and all other unlawfully armed persons, and maintain peace and security.[63] To support the MISAB's efforts, on 6 August 1997, the UN Security Council adopted Resolution 1125, which deemed the situation in the CAR a threat to international peace and security and authorised MISAB to take enforcement action to ensure the security and freedom of movement of its personnel.[64] The UN Security Council adopted additional resolutions in this connection. On 27 March 1998, the UN Security Council adopted Resolution 1159 creating the UN Mission in the CAR (MINURCA), to assist in the maintenance of peace, security, law and order; ensure security and freedom of movement of UN personnel and the safety and security of UN property; and provide police training for the national police and technical support to national electoral bodies.[65] The UNSC mandated Secretary-General Kofi Annan to 'secure a smooth transition between MISAB and MINURCA by 15 April 1998.'[66]

2. *MISAB Intervention*

The MISAB intervention in the CAR was lawful for three primary reasons: 1) similar to the ECOWAS missions in Sierra Leone, it acted upon the request of President Patasse; 2) MISAB was entitled to invoke a right of humanitarian intervention; and 3) the UN Security Council retroactively authorised the intervention.

Unlike the ECOWAS missions, the MISAB operation was not carried out under the auspices of a 'regional arrangement' (as implied in Chapter VIII of the UN Charter). Hence, the legality of the intervention may not be ascertained by referring to a treaty document, protocol, or other organising instrument. On the contrary, the MISAB was simply an *ad hoc* group of states that banded together to enforce the peace in the CAR. Under customary international law, as sovereign states, they were entitled to respond to Patasse's requests for assistance. Moreover, since MISAB was empowered to intervene under the terms of the Bangui Agreement, there was also a treaty basis for the intervention.

MISAB was entitled to intervene upon Patasse's request because, unlike the ECOWAS mission in Liberia, Patasse's regime did not collapse as did Doe's, nor was he forced to flee the country like Kabbah. Although the mutiny was for the most part successful, unlike the mutiny in Guinea-Bissau, the mutineers arguably appeared to be more concerned with receiving salary arrears than toppling the government. In fact, it may be argued that the May mutiny was apolitical and corporatist. As a result, the CAR conflict did not mature into a Liberian style civil war or evolve into one that had serious sub-regional implications like those in Liberia and Sierra Leone. For these reasons, then, the intervention did not violate the principle of non-interference, infringe upon the political independence of the state, nor interfere with the civilian population's right to self-determination. Therefore, the MISAB was lawful, impartial, and supported by all parties to the conflict. It was a genuine humanitarian peacekeeping mission designed to restore law and order to the CAR, not an operation designed to provide military support to Patasse's regime, as was the case with Nigeria's support of Kabbah and Senegal and Guinea's support of Vieira.

That being said, the mutiny nearly did result in the overthrow of Patasse's democratically elected regime. Akin to the ECOWAS operation in Sierra Leone in 1997 and the U.S.-led UN mission in Haiti in 1994, the MISAB was entitled to invoke a right of humanitarian intervention to safeguard Patasse's government and thwart a coup by the military apparatus of the state. The attempted coup violated international law, as 'the principle of democratic rule is today part of international law. While in a universal context the recognition of the principle has only had the effect of subtracting the question of democratic rule from the exclusive jurisdiction of states....'[67] The international community including African states has '...evaluated the principle of democracy to the category of a rule which is fully enforceable through appropriate regional collective mechanisms.'[68] In this sense, international law recognises a right to democratic governance and appears to place it on similar but not equal footing as the human rights protective regime. Hence, it appears that when undemocratic and violent means are used to unseat a democratic government against the will of the civilian population and when such an unseating threatens the stability of the state and the security of the said populace, states may invoke a pro-democratic right of intervention. While in theory, Western nations purport to have the strongest democratic traditions, in *practice*, this emerging norm is taking firmer root in Africa than in any other region. Time will tell whether such a right will fall within the rubric of humanitarian intervention or some other customary norm; either way, today, states' practice suggests that international law recognises a right to democratic governance as an exception to the principle of non-intervention.

Furthermore, similar to the cases of ECOWAS in Liberia and Sierra Leone, the legal validity of the operation was established when the UN Security Council, acting under Chapter VII of the UN Charter, adopted Resolution 1125. The resolution deemed the situation in the CAR a threat to international peace and security and authorised MISAB to ensure security and freedom of movement of personnel, and restore peace and security to the country in accordance with Bangui[69] - effectively placing a retroactive *de jure seal* on the intervention. Moreover, on 27 March 1998, when the UN Resolution 1159 established MINURCA to replace MISAB, for the second time in UN history, akin to the UN Observer Mission in Liberia (UNOMIL), the United Nations co-deployed forces with an operation already under way. By 15 June 1998, there were over 1,200 MINURCA personnel in the CAR including troops from Burkina Faso, Canada, Chad, Côte d'Ivoire, Egypt, France, Gabon, Mali, Senegal, and Togo. Ninety per cent of these troops were African, a significant number of whom were converted MISAB troops.[70]

SADC Intervention in Lesotho

1. Background

The root causes of the Lesotho crisis in 1998 can be traced to the Lesotho Congress for Democracy (LCD), which was elected into power in 1993, political rivalry associated with the Constitution of Lesotho entering into force on 2 April 1993, and the institutional struggles that followed, especially between elements of the security forces and the executive in 1994. From 1997 onwards, political tensions escalated as political rifts continued unabated between LCD on the one hand, and the Basotho

National Party (BNP), Basotholand Congress Party (BCP), and the Maramatlou Freedom Party (MFP) on the other. In early September 1998, such tensions found overt political expression when approximately 10,000 opposition protestors camped outside of the Palace of King Letsie III.[71] They were protesting amid allegations from opposition party leaders that the LCD rigged the May 1998 elections in which it won 79 of Lesotho's 80 voting districts. This situation was further exacerbated by the Troika Commission's (consisting of Botswana, South Africa, and Zimbabwe) untimely release of its findings with regard to the elections,[72] and by Prime Minister Phakalitha Mosisili's dismissal of a well-respected military officer for sympathising with election demonstrators.[73] Taken together, these factors exacerbated political discontent among segments of the civilian populace and numerous junior military officers, creating an extremely volatile environment.

On 11 September 1998, these officers began a mutiny, arguably orchestrated by Finance Minister Retselisistoe Sekonyana's BNP, against the government and arrested twenty-two senior military officials and forced their commander, Lieutenant General Makhula Mosakeng, to broadcast his resignation over Radio Lesotho.[74] Consequently, several violent clashes broke out between loyalist and opposition forces composed of divided segments of the army, police, and the civilian populace. Therefore, when Mosisili returned from a SADC meeting in Mauritius on 15 September 1998, he found the country in a state of disarray. Mutinous soldiers and other protesters forcefully stole and impounded eighty government vehicles from civil servants and stoned vehicles belonging to ministers, looted local homes and businesses, burned down government buildings, prevented government employees from going to work, and made death threats against Mosisili and other senior officials.[75] To make matters worse, on 18 September 1998 opposition parties demanded the 'government's resignation, the dissolution of parliament and the appointment by the King of an interim government including equal numbers from all major parties'.[76] At this juncture, the constitution of order in Maseru reached an intolerable state as elements in the Lesotho military and police force, which appeared to sympathise with the protestors, did not take action to quell the mutiny.

Fearing that a military *coup d'état* was imminent and uncertain about how long loyalist forces could maintain law and order, Prime Minister Mosisili requested that South Africa, Botswana, Zimbabwe, and Mozambique *militarily* intervene in Lesotho to restore law and order to the country in 'accordance with SADC agreements'.[77] The request could not have come at a worse time: President Mandela was touring the United States and Canada, Deputy President Thabo Mbeki was in Finland, Foreign Minister Alfred Nzo was visiting UN headquarters, and Deputy Foreign Minister Aziz Phadad was at the Commonwealth Games in Malaysia.[78] Hence, Safety and Security Minister Sydney Mufamadi (Mbeki's point person on the crisis) and Home Affairs Minister and Acting President Mangosuthu Buthelezi were left to deal with the crises. On 22 September 1998, after Zimbabwean President and former Chairman of the SADC Organ for Politics, Defence, and Security (hereinafter SADC Organ),[79] Robert Mugabe, refused to receive communications from Buthelezi about the Lesotho crisis, South Africa (600 troops) and Botswana (200 troops) sent 800 troops to Lesotho pursuant to Mosisili's request.[80] South African forces launched a robust intervention early that morning which resulted in the deaths of '49 soldiers on both sides and 170 mutinous Lesotho soldiers had been captured.'[81] Botswana soldiers arrived later in the day. After several days of chaos, the crisis was exacerbated with the arrival of reinforcements from South African and Botswana. Nevertheless, by the end of October 1998, Maseru began to return to normalcy, and the LCD and opposition parties signed a tentative peace agreement.

2. SADC Intervention

The SADC intervention in Lesotho was lawful for two primary reasons: 1) Prime Minister Mosisili requested that SADC militarily intervene to restore law and order to the country; and 2) the SADC Organ and the SADC Protocol on Politics, Defence, and Security (hereinafter SADC Protocol) obligated and empowered it to intervene.[82]

Similar to the cases of ECOWAS in Liberia, Sierra Leone, and Guinea-Bissau, and the MISAB intervention in the CAR, the SADC was entitled to rely on Mosisili's request as a basis for intervention. As previously mentioned, intervention by invitation of a legitimate government is a well-settled norm of international law.[83] Hence, since the LCD government was recognised by the international community and the Troika Commission as the legitimate government, Mosisili, as the foremost representative of the government, was entitled to request military assistance from SADC. In this regard, Mosisili's request for assistance was uniquely different from that of Kabbah, Vieira, and Patasse because he did not request the imposition of impartial 'peace-keepers' or partial 'peace-enforcers', but rather direct *military* aid. Regardless of the kind of intervention requested, however, his request was equally lawful.

It has been suggested that because Mosisili did not consult with King Letsie III before requesting military assistance from SADC states that the intervention was not 'constitutionally valid'.[84] Chapter VIII Article 92 of the Constitution of Lesotho states that,

> The King shall have the right to be consulted by the Prime Minister and other Ministers on all matters relating to the government of Lesotho and the Prime Minister shall keep him fully informed concerning the general conduct of the government of Lesotho and shall furnish him with such information as he may request in respect of any particular matter relating to the government of Lesotho.[85]

Whether or not Mosisili consulted with King Letsie is moot in considering the legality of the intervention. It was (and is) not the place of SADC or any of its member states to authenticate, interpret, or validate Lesotho's internal constitutional processes before responding to requests from the senior representative of its democratically elected *de jure* government arguably in effective control of the country. To argue otherwise would be to undermine and violate the international law principles of states' sovereignty, territorial integrity, and non-intervention in the internal affairs of *democratic* states, which form the structural fabric upon which the international system is based. SADC states had neither the authority nor the reason to question the efficacy of Mosisili's request for military assistance, and thus, under international law, could rely on the request as a valid basis for the intervention. Hence, akin to the cases of Sierra Leone, Guinea-Bissau, and the CAR, South Africa and Botswana were entitled to lend *military assistance* to the government of Lesotho.

Some analysts have perhaps rightly scrutinised the political and operational problems associated with the status and function of the SADC Organ and Lesotho crisis, respectively,[86] yet analyses that adequately consider the legal aspects of the intervention in Lesotho are lacking.[87] Hence, a distinction must be drawn between operational and *legal* concerns related to the mission, as the legal framework for the Organ had already been adopted at the time of the intervention and thus forms an important part of international/treaty law in the Southern African region.[88] In this regard, the Organ should be viewed as a *collective security appendage* of the SADC Treaty; the status of which is incontestable. Two relevant guiding *principles* of the Organ are to achieve solidarity, peace and security, and observe human rights, *democracy*, and the rule of law in the region.[89] Moreover, key *objectives* of the Organ are to 'protect the people...from instability arising from the *breakdown* of law and order'[90]; 'co-operate fully in regional security and defence through conflict prevention, *management*, and resolution';[91] 'promote and enhance the development of *democratic institutions* and practices within member states...';[92] 'promote peace-making and *peace-keeping* in order to achieve sustainable peace and security';[93] 'develop a *regional peace-keeping* capacity within national armies that could be called upon within the region, or elsewhere on the continent';[94] and 'co-ordinate the participation of member states in international and *regional peace-keeping* operations'.[95] More telling however, Objective (g) of the Organ states that when conflict can not be dealt with diplomatically, the Organ should recommend that the Summit consider punitive measures (i.e. the use of force).[96] Such measures are to be agreed upon in a Protocol on Peace, Security and Conflict Resolution.[97]

Although, at the time of writing this article, the SADC Protocol had not been fully ratified, it should be considered *soft law* as the Heads of State and Government of SADC have adopted it and the SADC Secretariat has taken steps towards its implementation.[98] Similar to the Organ, the Protocol clearly delineates its functions and the obligations of member states in this respect. Article 2 of the Protocol adopts all of the aforementioned key *objectives* of the Organ as core *functions*, and Article 5 lays down rigid guidelines as to when SADC member states may intervene in internal conflicts, namely, the following: large-scale conflict violence between sections of the population of a state, or between the state and/or its armed or para-military forces and sections of the population;[99] a threat to the *legitimate authority* of the government (such as a military coup by armed or para-military forces);[100] a condition of civil war or insurgency;[101] and any crisis that could threaten the peace and security of other member states.[102] The SADC Protocol also states that in internal conflict situations the 'Organ shall respond to an *invitation* by a member country to become involved in *mediating* a conflict within its borders'.[103] Hence, it is obvious that robust peacekeeping or peace enforcement is necessary to fulfil the functions outlined in Articles 2 and 5(2) of the Protocol. However, one key distinction between the ECOWAS and SADC Protocols is that in order for any of the sub-sections of Article 5 of the SADC Protocol to become operable, a government must *consent* to regional intervention.[104]

When taken together, the SADC Organ and Protocol lay a relatively unambiguous foundation for when SADC member states may *unilaterally* employ the use of force in states in internal conflict situations. Although both the Protocol and Organ state that 'military intervention'[105] and 'punitive measures'[106] should be taken 'in accordance'[107] with the UN Charter, the OAU, and international law,[108] the character of the Lesotho intervention would not support an interpretation that construes 'in accordance' to mean prior authorisation from the UN Security Council. From this background, the legal framework existed for South Africa (who at the time of the intervention was Chair of the SADC Summit of Heads of State and Government) and Botswana to intervene lawfully in Lesotho under the veil of SADC or individually. Mosisili's request for military assistance was also unambiguous, and according to Objectives (a)(d)(h)(o) of the SADC Organ and Article 2 sub-sections (a)(d)(h)(i)(m) of the Protocol, South Africa and Botswana were legally *obligated* and empowered to take enforcement action to forestall conflict in Lesotho. Furthermore, given the state of chaos in Maseru at the time of the request, and similar to the cases of Sierra Leone, the CAR, and Guinea-Bissau, it may be argued that SADC and/or South Africa and Botswana were entitled to intervene in Lesotho in consonance with Article 5(2) of the SADC Protocol and the emerging pro-democratic right of intervention under international law.[109]

It is doubtful, however, that SADC could validly invoke a right of humanitarian intervention. At the time of the intervention, there were no widespread violations of human rights that would shock the conscience of the international community; the government had neither collapsed nor was descending into anarchy; and although it is debatable whether the LCD government was in the process of being violently and illegally dislodged, the people of Lesotho were arguably ambivalent about the mutiny or attempted coup. If, however, it could be shown that the people of Lesotho had supported the mutiny and the crisis had evolved into mass civil war, it could be argued that Mosisili would not have been entitled to receive external military assistance to restore him to power. In such a case, under international law, partial military aid would interfere with the population's right of self-determination and under Article 2(4) of the UN Charter would amount to a show of force against a country immersed in civil war. Nevertheless, since this was not the case because Lesotho was not at civil war, SADC states were entitled to rely on Mosisili's request as the basis for intervening.

Conclusion

The case studies presented here demonstrate that African states are seeking African solutions to *humanities* problems. Over the past ten years, several key conflict and security mechanisms have emerged throughout Africa: the OAU's Mechanism for Conflict Prevention, Management, and Resolution; ECOWAS Framework and Protocol; SADC Organ and Protocol; and the Inter-Governmental Authority on Development (IGAD) evolving conflict mechanism. These mechanisms, taken together with African states' practice, demonstrate that the concept of regional collective security on the Continent has changed and continues to evolve.[110]

The eight cases under study - including the unilateral African interventions by regional actors and the lawful military interventions by individual African states - suggest that humanitarian intervention in purely internal conflicts is lawful when there have been human rights abuses that are so egregious as to violate the *jus cogens* norms of international law; a government has collapsed and is spiralling into a state of anarchy; or to safeguard democracy when a democratic regime has been violently and illegally dislodged against the will of its domestic populace. Nevertheless, these cases also suggest that it is often difficult to determine whether there is a valid basis for intervention. The above criteria for humanitarian intervention may not be adequate in situations where intervention could otherwise be justified. The cases of Sierra Leone, Guinea-Bissau, CAR, and Lesotho raise a vital question: Is there an international law basis for unilaterally intervening in a state when segments of the *military* threaten or attempt to overthrow a popular government that has attained power democratically? This question becomes increasingly difficult to answer when for example, it is *questionable* whether due to the crisis a government is: 1) legally entitled to request external assistance (i.e. arguably not in *de facto* control of the state); and 2) the state-of-affairs in the country would not justify a humanitarian intervention. Despite these difficulties, I believe the answer is yes.

The cases of Haiti, Sierra Leone, Guinea-Bissau, the CAR, and Lesotho illustrate that today the international community and the United Nations are willing to condone and support military interventions to safeguard democracy when militaries threaten or attempt to dislodge democratic and *popular* regimes. The above cases lend credence to the emergence of a *pro-democratic right* of intervention under customary international law, and thus an exception to the principle of non-intervention in the internal affairs of unpopular and *undemocratic* or *military* states. Yet, it is unclear whether such a norm would fit within the rubric of humanitarian intervention or form an independent norm of international law.

Basic human security is a prerequisite to enjoying fundamental human and development rights, but people cannot enjoy such rights in an insecure and unstable environment. Hence, democracy or governance by consensus is a prerequisite to establishing an enabling environment for peace, security, development, and the realisation of fundamental human rights. In this sense, any pro-democratic right of intervention would seem to fall within the rubric of humanitarian intervention due to the nexus of circular causation among undemocratic rule, gross violations of human rights, deadly conflict, and state collapse.

The UN Security Council's *post de jure authentication* of the Liberia, Sierra Leone, CAR, and Kosovo interventions; *pre-deployment authentication* of the Guinea-Bissau operational; *non-condemnation* of the Lesotho operation, and the United Nations' *co-deployment* of forces with ECOWAS in Liberia and with the MISAB in the CAR further illustrate that under certain circumstances the international community is willing to condone unilateral enforcement action for humanitarian purposes. Doctrine and states' practice in Africa and West Africa, in particular, seem to be spawning new norms of international law, but it would be a mistake for policy-makers and scholars to dismiss or compartmentalise these developments as Africa-specific. The international community has both legally and operationally supported these interventions, and as the U.S.-led NATO intervention in Kosovo and the Nigeria-led ECOWAS interventions reveal, the North-South ideological divide has closed on issues concerning the unilateral imposition of the use of force for humanitarian and democratic ends.

African states have been at the forefront of maintaining peace and security in Africa and throughout the world. However, as the cases of Somalia and Rwanda show, unless responsible and accountable political institutions emerge on the Continent, African states may paradoxically become the recipient of actions based on norms they are responsible for spawning (i.e. variegated Western solutions for African problems), or worse, no action at all.

Notes

1 In the past, humanitarian intervention has been defined as 'the justifiable use of force for the purpose of protecting the inhabitants of another state from treatment so arbitrarily and persistently abusive as to exceed the limits with which the sovereign is presumed to act with reason and justice'. Stonewell, Ellery, C. (1931) *International Law: A Restatement of Principles in Conformity with Actual Practice* 349. Today, humanitarian intervention has been defined as an intervention in a state involving the use of force (US action in Iraq and Somalia or ECOWAS action in Liberia, Sierra Leone, and Guinea-Bissau) or threat of force (UN action in Haiti), where the intervenor deploys armed forces and, at the least, makes clear that it is willing to use force if its operation is resisted—as it attempts to alleviate conditions in which a substantial part of the population of a state is threatened with death or suffering on a grand scale. See Greenwood, Christopher (1993) 'Is there a right to humanitarian intervention?', *The World Today*, 49, 24.

2 Significant portions of the Liberia, Sierra Leone, and the CAR analysis were extracted from prior work of the author. Levitt, Jeremy (1998), 'Humanitarian Intervention by Regional Actors in Internal Conflicts: The Cases of ECOWAS in Liberia and Sierra Leone', *Temple International and Comparative Law Journal*, Vol. 12, No. 2.

3 This, however, does not mean that all of these interventions qualify as a humanitarian intervention, but rather that precedent from each case study supports the conclusion that such a right exists. For example, the NATO intervention in Kosovo would not appear to fall within the rubric of humanitarian intervention given the robust military character and conduct of the operation. However, NATO did appear to have a valid legal basis for intervening (i.e. to forestall the genocide of Muslims in Kosovo). Although the operation was not authorised by the UN Security Council, it did receive support from the bulk of the international community. Hence, was it legal?

4 Customary international law can be defined as a 'general and consistent practice of states followed by them from a sense of legal obligation'. *Restatement (Third) of Foreign Relations Law,* 102 (2), (1987); To ascertain customary international law, judges resort to the 'customs and usages of civilized nations, and, as evidence of these, to the works of jurists and commentators…', The Paquete Habana, 175 US 677, 700, 20 S. Ct. 290, 299, 44 L. Ed. 320 (1900).

5 For a comprehensive delineation of the history of humanitarian intervention, *see generally* Fernando Teson, (1996) *Humanitarian Intervention: An Inquiry into Law and Morality.*

6 However, a unilateral intervention is one that derives its legal basis from customary international law rather than the UN Charter. A unilateral intervention may be one that is operationally multilateral.

7 Wippman, David (1995-96), 'Change Continuity in Legal Justification for Military Intervention in Internal Conflicts', *27 Columbia Human Rights Law Review,* 425, 446.

8 Greenwood, Christopher (1993), 'Is there a right to humanitarian intervention?', *The World Today*, Vol. 49, p. 34.

9 Letter addressed by President Samuel K. Doe to the Chairman and Members of the Ministerial Meeting of the ECOWAS Standing Mediation Committee, 14 July 1990, reprinted in Weller, M. (ed.) (1994) *Regional Peace-Keeping and International Enforcement: The Liberian Crisis*, p. 60 (hereinafter The Liberian Crisis).

10 See ECOWAS Standing Mediation Committee, Decision A/DEC.1/8/90, on the Cease-Fire and Establishment of ECOWAS Cease-Fire Monitoring Groups for Liberia, Banjul, Republic of Gambia, 7 August 1990, reprinted in *The Liberian Crisis*, supra note 9 at p. 61.

11 Idem. at p. 68.

12 *The United Nations and the Situation in Liberia*, U.N.Doc. [ST/] DPI/1668, 52nd sess., at p. 41 (1997).

13 Wippman, supra note 7 at p. 192.

14 ECOWAS Standing Mediation Committee Decision A/DEC.1/8/90, on the Cease-fire and Establishment of an ECOWAS Cease-fire Monitoring Groups for Liberia, Banjul, Republic of Gambia, reprinted in *The Liberian Crisis*, supra note 9 at p.67; see ECOWAS Standing Mediation Committee, Banjul, Republic of Gambia, Final Communiqué of the First Session, 7 August 1990, reprinted in *The Liberian Crisis*, supra note 12 at p. 73.

15 Schacter, O. (1984) 'International Law: The Right of States to Use Armed Force', 82 *Michigan Law Review*. 1620, 1641.

16 Idem.

17 Doswald-Beck, Louise (1985), 'The Legal Validity of Military Intervention by Invitation of the Government', *1985 British Yearbook of International Law,* 189, pp. 195-196.

18 Idem. at p. 194.

19 There are two exceptions to this rule: 1) when states have been authorised to act by the UNSC (Chapter VII enforcement action); 2) when states invoke a customary international law right of humanitarian intervention. In either case, the issue of consent is moot.

20 A *jus cogens* norm, also known as a peremptory norm of international law is a norm accepted and recognised by the international community of states as a whole from which no derogation is permitted and which can be modified only

by a subsequent norm of international law. These norms sit atop the hierarchy of international law and enjoy the greatest clout, pre-empting both conflicting treaties and customary international law. Vienna Convention of the Law of Treaties, 23 May 1969, Art. 53 1155 UNTS, 332, 344. Princz v. Federal Republic of Germany, 26 F. 3d 1166, 1179 (D.C. Cir. (1994) (quoting R. Jackson, 'Final Report to the President on the Nuremburgh Trials (Oct.7, 1946)', cited in R. Jackson, *The Nuremburgh Case XIV-XV* (1971); United States v. Alfried Krupp, reprinted in *10 Trials of War Criminals Before the Nuremburgh Military Tribunal Under Control Council Law*, 1395 (1950).

21 An *erga omnes* obligation is an obligation that rests with the whole of the international community to protect people from systematic and gross human rights violations including slavery, genocide and racial discrimination. *Barcelna Traction Case* (Belgium vs. Spain), 1970 I.C.J. Rep. 3 para. 33-34 (Second Phase).

22 *The United Nations and the Situation in Liberia*, UN Doc [ST/] DPI/1668, 52nd session, at p. 35 (1997).

23 *African Research Bulletin*, May 1997, at p. 12695; see also, 'Kabbah Urges ECOWAS Leaders to Restore Him to Power', *Panafrican News Agency*, 2 September 1997.

24 *Fourth Report of the Secretary-General on the Situation in Sierra Leone*, UN SCOR, 53d session, U.N. Doc. S/1998/249 (1998).

25 Idem.

26 *See generally*, Beck, supra note 13.

27 Schacter, supra note 15 at p. 1641.

28 Idem.

29 *Status of Forces Agreement Between the Government of the Federal Republic of Nigeria and The Government of the Republic of Sierra Leone Concerning the Provision of Military and Security Assistance to the Republic of Sierra Leone*, Article 21.1.1 (1997).

30 Ibid. Article 21.1.2.

31 Gardner, R. N. (1991), 'Commentary on the Law of Self-Defence', in Damrosh, Lori Fisler and Schaffer, David (eds), *Law and Force in the International Order*, pp. 49, 52; Lillich, R. B. (1991), 'Forcible Protection of National Abroad: The Liberian Incident of 1990', *German Year Book of International Law*, Vol. 35, p. 205; and Doswald-Beck, Louise (1984), 'The Legality of the U.S. Intervention in Grenada', *Netherlands International Law Review*, Vol. 31, pp. 355, 361.

32 Alexandrov, Stanimir A. (1996) *Self-Defence Against the Use of Force in International Law*; Schacter, supra note 15 at p. 1638.

33 Economic Community of West African States Revised Treaty, 24 July 1993.

34 Ibid. Article 58 – Regional Security.

35 Ibid. Article 58 – Regional Security.

36 For more on this issue see, Levitt supra note 7 at pp. 369-71; see also, Tuomala, Jeffrey C. (1994) 'Just Cause: The Thread that Runs so True', *Dickson Journal of International Law,* Vol. 15.

37 However, without a genuine threat of death or great suffering to the domestic populace of a state, it has yet to be resolved whether a right to pro-democratic intervention exists. Nevertheless, based on the diversity of justifiable circumstances that led to the U.S.-led UN mission in Haiti, the ECOMOG operation in Sierra Leone and Guinea-Bissau, MISAB intervention in the CAR, and SADC operation in Lesotho, it appears that a pro-democratic norm that falls outside of the purview of humanitarian intervention is fast developing.

38 'Guinea-Bissau: Manes' Men', *Africa Confidential*, Vol. 39, No. 13, 26 June 1998.

39 Idem.

40 Idem.

41 Soon after the mutiny, Senegal deployed 1,300 troops to Guinea-Bissau, and Guinea 400 troops.

42 *Panafrican News Agency*, 'ECOWAS Puts Out Plan to End Bissau Mutiny', 5 July 1998.

43 Report of the Secretary-General Pursuant to Security Council Resolution 1216 Relative to the Situation in Guinea-Bissau, S/1999/294, 17 March 1999.

44 UNSC Resolution 1216 (1998), Adopted by the UN Security Council at its 3958th meeting on 21 December 1998.

45 Ibid.

46 *Report of the Secretary-General Pursuant to Security Council Resolution 1216 Relative to the Situation in Guinea-Bissau*, S/1999/294, 17 March 1999.

47 *Framework Establishing the ECOWAS Mechanism for Conflict Prevention, Management, and Resolution, Peace-keeping, and Security*, A/DEC.11/31/98, Abuja, Nigeria, 31 October 1998.

48 *Protocol Establishing the ECOWAS Mechanism for Conflict Prevention, Management, and Resolution, Peace-keeping, and Security*, A/DEC.12/10/99, Lome, Togo, 10 December 1999.

49 *Framework Establishing the ECOWAS Mechanism,* supra note 48 at Section II Peace-keeping Paragraph 46. Paragraph 46 is repeated and expanded under Article 25 of the Protocol.

50 See generally, Fielding, Lois (1995) 'Taking the Next Step in the Development of the New Human Rights: The Emerging Right to Humanitarian Intervention Assistance to Restore Democracy', 5 *Duke Journal of Comparative and International Law,* p. 329.

51 *Report of the Secretary-General Pursuant to Resolution 1136 (1997) Concerning the Situation in the Central African Republic*, U.N. SCOR, 53rd sess., U.N. Doc. S/1998/61 (1998); 'Central African Republic: Angel on a Pinhead', *Africa Confidential,* 10 May 1996; and, 'CAR: Mutineers' Mistake', *Africa Confidential*, 7 June 1996.

52 'Central African Republic: Angel on a Pinhead', *Africa Confidential*, 10 May 1996.

53 'CAR: Echoes of Zaire', *Africa Confidential*, 29 November 1996.

54 'Central African Republic: Angel on a Pinhead', *Africa Confidential*, 10 May 1996, p. 3.

55 *Report of the Secretary-General on the United Nations Mission in the Central African Republic*, S/1998/540, 19 June 1998.

56 'CAR: Mutineer's Mistake', *Africa Confidential*, Vol. 37, No. 12, 7 June 1996.

57 'Echoes of Zaire', *Africa Confidential*, Vol. 37, No. 24, 29 November 1996.

58 'CAR: Mutineer's Mistake', *Africa Confidential*, Vol. 37, No.12, 7 June 1996. The participants of the May mutiny, led by Sergeant Major Isidore Mathurin Dokodo, were the same group that mutinied earlier that year.

59 'CAR: Mutineer's Mistake', *Africa Confidential*, 7 June 1996, This represented the fourth time that French troops have intervened to save Patasse's regime. 'CAR: French Leave', *Africa Confidential*, 10 October 1997.

60 'CAR: French Leave', *Africa Confidential*, Vol. 38 No. 20, 10 October 1997.

61 Idem.

62 *Report of the Secretary-General Pursuant to Resolution 1136*, supra note 50.

63 *Report of the Secretary-General Pursuant to Resolution 1136 (1997) Concerning the Situation in the Central African Republic*, S/1998/61, 23 January 1998.

64 Idem.

65 Approximately 1350 personnel partook in the mission. UNSC resolution 1159 U.N. SCOR, 3867th mtg., U.N. Doc. S/RES/1159 (1998).

66 Idem.

67 Teson, Fernando R. (1996), 'Collective Humanitarian Intervention', 17 *Michigan Journal of International Law,* 335.

68 Idem.

69 UNSC resolution 1125 U.N. SCOP, 3808th mtg, U.N. Doc. S/RES/1125 (1997).

70 *Report of the Secretary-General on the United Nations Mission in the Central African Republic*, S/1998/540, 19 June 1998.

71 'Lesotho/Swaziland: Militants and Monarchs', *Africa Confidential*, Vol. 39, No. 19, 25 September 1998.

72 The Troika Commission (or Langa Commission) was established by the parties at conflict to investigate allegations of foul play by Lesotho's Independent Electoral Commission. It was presided over by Deputy President of the South Africa's Constitutional Court, Pius Langa.

73 'Lesotho/Swaziland: Militants and Monarchs', *Africa Confidential*, Vol. 39, No. 19, 25 September 1998.

74 Idem.

75 'Mosisili's letter requesting military assistance', *Electronic Mail & Guardian,* 22 September 1998.

76 Idem.

77 Idem.

78 'South Africa-Lesotho: To a Little Kingdom', *Africa Confidential*, Vol. 39, No. 20, 9 October 1998.

79 *SADC Organ for Politics, Defence and Security*, supra note 81; see generally, Tsie, B. (1998) 'Regional security co-operation in Southern Africa', *Global Dialogue*; Brammer, H. (1999), 'In search of an effective regional security mechanism for Southern Africa', *Global Dialogue*, pp. 21–22; and Breytenbach, Willie (2000) 'Failure of Security Co-operation in SADC: The Suspension of the Organ for Politics, Defence and Security', *South African Journal of International Affairs*, Vol. 7, No. 1, Summer; and Aardt, Maxi van (1997), 'The SADC Organ for Politics, Defence and Security: Challenges for Regional Community Building', *South African Journal of International Affairs,* Vol. 4, No. 2, Winter.

80 South Africa and Botswana later increased these numbers to 1,000 and 460, respectively. 'South Africa - Lesotho: To a Little Kingdom', *Africa Confidential*, Vol. 39, No. 20, 9 October 1998.

81 'Flames devour a city without a fire brigade', *Electronic Mail & Guardian,* Johannesburg, South Africa, 24 September 1998.

82 *The Southern African Development Community (SADC) Organ for Politics, Defence and Security*, Gaborone, Botswana, June 28, 1996, compiled in *Africa: Selected Documents on Political, Security, Humanitarian and Economic Issues,* Institute for Strategic Studies, University of Pretoria, at 32-35, Ad hoc Publication No. 33 (Nov. 1996); and '*Protocol on Politics, Defence, and Security in Southern African Development Community (SADC) Region'*, compiled in African Legal Materials, *African Journal of International and Comparative Law*, March 1999, at 197.

83 Falk, Richard (1996), 'The Complexities of Humanitarian Intervention: A New World Order Challenge', 17 *Michigan Journal of International Law,* 491, 502; see also, Schacter, Oscar (1984), 'The Right of States to Used Armed Force', 82 *Michigan Law Review,* 1620, 1626.

84 'South Africa-Lesotho: To a Little Kingdom', *Africa Confidential*, Vol. 39, No. 20, 9 October 1998.

85 *The Constitution of Lesotho*, Chapter VIII Article 92 (2 April 1993).

86 *SADC Organ for Politics, Defence and Security*, supra note 81; *See generally*, Tsie, B. (1998) 'Regional security co-operation in Southern Africa', *Global Dialogue*; Brammer, H. (1999), 'In search of an effective regional security mechanism for Southern Africa', *Global Dialogue*, pp. 21–22; and Breytenbach, Willie (2000), 'Failure of Security Co-operation in SADC: The Suspension of the Organ for Politics, Defence and Security', *South African Journal of International Affairs*, Vol. 7, No. 1, Summer; and Aardt, Maxi van (1997), 'The SADC Organ for Politics, Defence and Security: Challenges for Regional Community Building', *South African Journal of International Affairs,* Vol. 4, No. 2, Winter. One key reason why the Organ is dysfunctional is because of geo-political tensions between Mandela and Mugabe. For example, Mandela would like the Organ to be under the political and jurisdictional control of the Summit of the Heads of State and Government of SADC whereas, President Mugabe insists that the Organ be autonomous.

87 Hough, M. (1998), 'Collective Security and its Variants: A Conceptual Analysis with Specific Reference to SADC and ECOWAS', *Strategic Review for Southern Africa*, Vol. 20, No. 2, pp. 38-39, November.

88 For purposes of this analysis, whether or not South Africa and Botswana followed internal SADC procedures before deploying forces does not appear to affect the legality of the operation in the broad sense because as the forgoing analysis will show, it appears to have been justified under the SADC Treaty, Organ, and Protocol.

89 *SADC Organ for Politics, Defence and Security*, supra note 82, at Principles (c)(d).

90 *SADC Organ for Politics, Defence and Security*, supra note 82, at Objective (a).

91 *SADC Organ for Politics, Defence and Security*, supra note 82, at Objective (d).

92 *SADC Organ for Politics, Defence and Security*, supra note 82, at Objective (h).

93 *SADC Organ for Politics, Defence and Security*, supra note 82 at Objective (i).

94 *SADC Organ for Politics, Defence and Security*, supra note 82 at Objective (l).

95 *SADC Organ for Politics, Defence and Security*, supra note 82 at Objective (o).

96 *SADC Organ for Politics, Defence and Security*, supra note 82 at Objective (g).

97 Idem.

98 Soft law should be considered as 'guidelines of conduct which are neither strictly binding norms of law nor completely irrelevant political maxims, and operate in a grey zone between law and politics.' Such guidelines 'may nevertheless in actual practice acquire considerable strength in structuring international conduct'. Soft law 'may also be relevant from a sociological perspective of international law with regard to the process of the formation of customary law or treaty law and the related issue of "legitimacy" in the international legal system'. Malanczuk, Peter (1997), *Akehurtst's: Modern Introduction to International Law*, Seventh Revised Edition, New York: NY Routledge, pp. 54-55.

99 SADC Protocol for Politics, Defence and Security, supra note 82, at Article 5(2)(1)(a).

100 Art. 5(2)(1)(b).

101 Art. 5(2)(1)(c).

102 Art. 5(2)(1)(d).

103 Art. 5(2)(2).

104 It should be noted that this type of policy would appear to be overly state-centric and counter-productive when the state is the referent object of oppression.

105 *SADC Organ*, supra note 82, Principle (g).

106 *SADC Protocol*, supra note 82, Article 5(4).

107 Idem.

108 The SADC Organ and Protocol both make reference to the United Nations and OAU; however, only the Protocol makes a specific reference to international law.

109 Article 5(2) states that internal conflicts that could be subjected to regional intervention include a threat to the legitimate authority of the government (such as a military coup by armed or para-military forces).

110 On these issues, see generally, Levitt, Jeremy (2001), 'Conflict Prevention, Management, and Resolution: Africa-Regional Strategies for the Prevention of Displacement and Protection of Displaced Persons: The Cases of the OAU, ECOWAS, SADC, and IGAD', *Duke Journal of Comparative and International Law*, Vol. 11, No. 1, Winter/Spring; and Olonisakin, Funmi and Levitt, Jeremy (1999) 'Regional Security and the Challenges of Democratisation in Africa: The Case of ECOWAS and SADC', *Cambridge Review of International Affairs,* Autumn/Winter.

3 African Military Capabilities in Insurrection, Intervention and Peace Support Operations

Tony Clayton

This chapter sets out to consider the capabilities of African armies to carry out their roles as national ground forces either for intervention or home defence. Such consideration must however extend to the types of conflict in which they may be committed; these can involve combat with insurrectionary groupings of men, warlord factions, militias not members of professional armies but well trained in the handling of weapons which they have acquired or seized. The main focus of the chapter will, however, be on the military requirements of successful peace support operations and how capable African armies may be for this, increasingly important and necessary, role.

The strengths of African armies appear moderately impressive on paper.[1] The major powers have ground force standing armies totalling 100,000 in the case of Ethiopia, 98,000 in Angola, 62,000 in Nigeria, 54,000 in South Africa (to reduce to 25,000), 35,000 in Zimbabwe, 30,000 in Tanzania and 20,000 in Kenya, with the smaller countries possessing armies of between one and fifteen thousand. Angola possesses a large tank force including Russian T72s, a 1970s generation vehicle. The Ethiopian and Nigerian armies include numbers of 1960s generation medium tanks, with in the case of Nigeria more modern light tanks; both possess armoured personnel carriers and reconnaissance vehicles, towed and self-propelled guns and multiple-barrelled rocket launchers together with light air defence missiles and guns. Other armies with small numbers of tanks include Zambia, Zimbabwe, Tanzania and Uganda. South Africa's 220 more modern tanks are probably the most powerful armoured force south of the Sahara. Kenya, with its 'air cavalry' strategy based around over thirty attack and a dozen transport helicopters, leads in effective air land warfare capabilities. Most nations have either light artillery or mortars, or both; armoured-cars in varying numbers, and light anti-aircraft guns or missiles, together with radar air defence warning systems.

The general field training standards of African armies vary very considerably. On paper the South African Army should be the best, but the reorganisation of the South African National Defence Force has incurred formidable problems. The African National Congress government wishes to 'punch above its weight' with strong armed forces but it reduced the percentage of GDP devoted to defence from 4.7% to 1.5%. Further the efforts to amalgamate the eight different regular, former insurgent and ethnic homeland forces, each with different training, ideology and experience has created a grave imbalance in spending between equipment and personnel. In consequence existing equipment is not being replaced and new equipment is not being developed. At personnel level friction and resentments from the past still remain, and there is a serious shortage of officers at unit command level with the necessary experience. Probably overall the best trained Black African armies are those of Kenya and Ghana. Much depends on the funding made available for training, usually far from adequate, and the abilities and enthusiasm of officers. Evidence suggests a decline in professionalism in several African armies; funds available for officer training are insufficient and in several armies, particularly in West Africa the career of an officer is seen as a path to a later lucrative civilian employment. Drug taking, at all ranks, is not uncommon, Nigeria being the worst example. Standards can vary greatly even within armies. Where political or 'dash' arrangements have favoured the career of an indifferent officer poor performances will follow all down the line. Two general points, common to most African armies can however be made. Most armies train essentially on a savannah war programme or on forest/savannah alternation programmes, the enemy being in both cases another army trained for the same form of warfare. Such training would of course include cordon and search evolutions. Very few African officers and units, however, have had proper training for fighting in built-up areas, with its complexities of four man brick block and street clearing and possible use of sewers – a training difficult to provide in African conditions. Also, while the leading African armies possess their paper strengths in terms of battle and logistic equipment their maintenance standards are often very poor, with vehicles unserviceable or soon becoming so, particularly in the field. One reason for this is that the non-commissioned officers sufficiently skilled for servicing can almost certainly earn more money elsewhere, a second is that spare parts may not be available, since they require foreign exchange. The quality of supplies, and food purchased locally may be sub-standard with perhaps a 'kickback' from the contractor to the logistic staff commander. Irregularities also occur with petroleum supply. Signals equipment and signallers though have in general a better reputation. Medical facilities for casualties and sick are almost invariably inadequate – if they exist at all.[2] In sum, the smaller African armies where infantry is lightly equipped and armour limited to light armoured-cars are little more than gendarmerie, and the larger armies require a number of weeks' intensive training and preparation for effective ground combat. It is because of these weaknesses that a number of African conflicts, Sudan versus the Sudan Peoples' Liberation Army, Ethiopia versus Eritrea, UNITA versus the Angolan Army, the civil warfare in Chad and Somalia, Uganda's war with the Lord's Resistance Army, all become protracted and stalemate, no side having the military capacity for all-out victory.

Nigeria, Angola and South Africa possess air forces with sizeable numbers of 1960s and 1970s fighter and air-to-ground strike aircraft. Ethiopia possesses small numbers of 1980s MIG-23 and 29 aircraft, a few up to date Sukhoi 27s, with avionic radar detection equipment and helicopter gun-ships. Zimbabwe, Zambia and Tanzania have smaller numbers of obsolescent and no doubt worn machines. Kenya has a small number of more modern machines. Smaller African countries' air forces are limited to transport, liaison and reconnaissance light aircraft or light helicopters. African air forces face the same or worse dilemmas over servicing and spare parts as armies, and the numbers of aircraft actually operational must be well below paper strengths.

A recent example of a botched intervention by a supposedly powerful African army, that of South Africa's intervention in Lesotho in 1998, highlights several of these problems as well as those particular to South Africa. A force of 600 of the newly restructured South African National Defence Force, not especially trained for intervention, was despatched to Maseru to suppress an armed mutiny against the pro-South African king and after a dubious election result. The force was inadequate in size – having to be reinforced by a unit from Botswana – and badly served in terms of prior intelligence, planning and logistic preparation. In consequence both it and the Lesotho Defence Force suffered unnecessary loss of life, SANDF only took its key objectives after considerable delay, and Maseru was looted by its own criminal element.

Later chapters set out earlier field intervention operations of African armies; these have included successes and failures. Tanzania's successful armed entry into Uganda in 1979 was essentially the triumph of an organised and well commanded military force against an army that had been expanded too quickly and had for domestic political reasons disposed of its best officers and non-commissioned officers. Ethiopia's expulsion of Somalia's invasion only occurred after a classic but small-scale air-land battle directed by a Soviet general and assisted by Cuban troops. The South African interventions in Angola throughout the late 1970s and 1980s saw spectacular tank, artillery and air engagements involving Angolan-Cuban and South African troops. The Uganda-Rwanda invasion of Congo (Zaire) in 1996-97 was a truly remarkable campaign in which rag-clad, often bootless, parties of men traversed some of the most difficult terrain on the continent with virtually no logistic back up. Although the opposition that they faced from the forces of President Mobutu, an unpaid, untrained mutinous rabble backed up by a small number of in the event useless Yugoslav mercenaries, was trifling, anyone assessing potential African military capabilities should bear in mind what men absolutely determined on their objective can do. Mau Mau, mounted by an ethnicity, the Kikuyu, that the British had considered the reverse of martial provides an earlier example, as do other anti-colonial liberation campaigns.

These set-piece army campaigns, however, represent only a small percentage of the actual conflict situations, symmetric and asymmetric, in sub-Saharan Africa. Looking to the future there is the grim but very real possibility of a strategic air bombing conflict between Egypt and Ethiopia if the latter restricts Egypt's water supplies from the Blue Nile. At present warfare ranges from a border war, symmetric conflict such as that between Eritrea and Ethiopia described as one with a high death toll '... because the combatants use the weaponry of the Korean war, the tactics of the first world war and the medical treatments of the 19th century',[3] to the Congo, with its 1998-99 scattered war over a vast area of country involving numerous parties and undisciplined forces not always responsive to authorities supposedly controlling them, and to the Sierra Leone asymmetric 'formless chaos' of second generation young townsmen and juveniles, not easily identifiable in streets and shanty towns, and inflamed by drink, drugs and reggae music.[4] Other conflicts have seen ineffective cease-fires, collapses of law, order and civil infrastructures, armed opposition to peace support force to control. Increasingly faction interests in one state lead to intervention to support a related faction in another, or to defend the home faction in power; inter-nation and internal conflicts merge. Most conflicts involving warlords, such as those in Liberia, have deliberately resorted to terror rather than tactical skill, with the use of torture, executions both public and protracted, check points adorned with bodies, and faction fighters in bizarre dress – carnival masks, women's wigs, shower and lavatory seat covers, together with vehicles adorned with lucky charms or chilling slogans.

Refugees and displaced persons can create problems of infinite complexity – not only the physical need of water, food, shelter and hygiene but those of infiltration by faction fighters such as the Hutu Interahamwe bent on continuing killing or other forms of warfare in camps or safety areas, or by the use of refugees or kidnapped expatriates in blackmail processes.

The insurgent factions in some conflicts may be regular military units or as in the case of some warlords such as Charles Taylor's National Patriotic Front of Liberia, NPFL, may have undergone a basic military training. In the case of the Hutu Interahamwe, their three-week training course had genocide as its aim, including videos on how to slash victims in such ways as to prevent their flight. The record established by one such trained group was 1000 killings in twenty minutes.[5] Other factions and militias have been able to recruit from men familiar with light weaponry, disaffected soldiers and policemen, ex-soldiers, ex-policemen and gendarmes, or factory guards. Armies supposedly national become revealed as the force of one faction or other, part of the problem and not its solution. In any case, men, and unfortunately also juveniles and boys as young as seven or eight, can very quickly be taught how to fire a simple and hard-wearing weapon such as an AK47 Kalashnikov rifle. The RPG-7 grenade launcher, the insurgent's pocket artillery, is almost as simple to learn and maintain. Experience in Somalia showed how the regional distribution in local military and police armouries of light weapons around the country simply facilitated the arming, after breaking open the armouries, of local factions and militia. Southern Africa is awash with weapons left over from the Soviet interventions of the 1970s and 1980s. Faction fighters with slightly more military experience have turned to mines, mortars, heavy machine-guns and cannons mounted on the back of Chevrolet or Toyota trucks, giving insurgents surprising mobility. Some forces, notably UNITA in Angola but also certain of the Liberian and Somali warlord factions, were and still are able to field artillery and armour. Further, while insurgent faction fighters can forage for food and support, return to their home areas after a foray, live off the land, or loot; professional soldier peace-keepers must have proper logistic support.

Overall conflict in Africa whether conventional national warfare or faction street fighting increasingly resembles pre-colonial warfare, bodies of men, usually but by no means invariably ethnically bonded, fighting for economic assets and resources in areas not demarcated by agreed borders, the warfare of frontiersmen.[6] These bodies of men, factions or militia often led by their respective warlords may draw on outside help; both governments struggling to survive and insurgent factions have used mercenaries or the resources of private security companies, with equipment extending to helicopters and of varying degrees of repute. Some recent fighting suggests faction fighting will centre increasingly on towns rather than rural areas, the traditional area of insurgency. In towns the sheer volume of light weaponry firepower can be more effectively deployed and may perhaps only destroy buildings and infrastructure rather than the mass killing of people. In towns, too, the opportunities of attracting media attention are very much greater. However, two new rural forms of 'economic warfare' emerged in 1998 and early 1999. In Angola the rebel UNITA's new strategy is one of compelling peasant farmers to leave their land, butchering them if they refuse to go. They are then corralled into government-held towns, besieged and their hunger used as a weapon of war with devastating effect. On a lesser but still serious scale the several Delta peoples of Nigeria are fighting amongst themselves while cutting pipelines and siphoning off fuel oil. Over 200 people were killed in May 1999 alone, Ijaws and Itsekivis.

It is in these varied and difficult contexts that peace support operations – a term covering both peacekeeping and peace enforcement - may have to be mounted. Peacekeeping itself may include peace-building, all within the frame of Chapter VI of the United Nations Charter which provides for the pacific settlement of disputes by a wide variety of peaceful measures such as negotiation, mediation, conciliation, arbitration and local judicial settlement – with if necessary and with the consent of both sides in a dispute, the presence of military support. Peace enforcement is however coercive, concerned with threats to and breaches of peace, provocation and aggression. Within the frame of Chapter VII of the UN Charter Article 41 authorises the use of political and economic pressure, and Article 42 the use of force '... such action by air, sea or land forces as may be necessary to restore international peace and security. Such action may include demonstrations, blockade and other operations by air, sea or land of forces of Members of the United Nations'.[7]

For both peacekeeping and peace enforcement operations there are two essential, indispensable requirements; firstly that the military forces committed have an UN, OAU or Regional, internationally agreed and clear, mandate covering both strategic aims, tactics, an exit strategy, and if necessary ground rules of engagement, and secondly that they have a unified command. International relations and diplomatic securing of such command and instructions lie outside the scope of this chapter; all that need be said here is that a military force which has only a fudged political compromise brief, and does not really know what is meant to be doing, will not succeed in achieving anything and will most likely worsen a conflict situation. The variety of African conflicts, their often strange and confusing first appearance forms, makes a clear mandate and instructions even more important, but the more difficult to obtain. Further, recent events suggest that in some cases where African governments have committed forces for peacekeeping the reasons for this have been far from disinterested. Governments, sometimes individual heads of state, have given their forces hidden agenda, to support or contain one faction or another, in order to develop a regional hegemony role, seek to acquire and control economic assets, secure their own borders, acquire a good international reputation or in times of internal domestic problems remove much of the military out of coup-temptation's way. Armies, too, can have their own agenda, raising the morale and prestige of the army, expectation of better equipment, or other less reputable desires including personal and political ambitions of military commanders. Forces supposedly peacekeeping but with other interests becoming evident as time passes lose credibility. At individual level there can also be difficulty should soldiers of a peace support force belong to the same ethnicity or people, across a border, among whom they are operating. Hausa, Fulani, Bakongo and many other ethnicities cross borders.

Some introduction to the rather different military requirements for both types of peace support is necessary before any assessment of the capabilities of African armies can be made.[8] Much has been written on what peace support operations should be, rather less on what such operations can mean for the ordinary soldier involved. Peacekeeping operations can include observer missions, interposition between rival factions and conflict prevention, demobilisation operations, military assistance, humanitarian relief, safe zones and guarantee or denial of movement. The governing principles are those of legitimate authority; transparent impartiality secured by contacts and absence of favouring; minimum force trained in non-lethal weaponry; procedures of rewards and penalties, curfews and check points, together with carefully prepared rules of engagement which, when desirable, leave belligerents an escape route; the securing of one's own base; credibility and mutual respect (both for the 'host' country and its customs and other units within what may be a multi-national force); and perseverance. The actual execution of operations will require coherence of mission; co-ordination with efficient liaison and communications; flexibility, including rapid availability of reserves; landmine and booby trap awareness, security of bases, logistics and locally recruited employees; concentrations of force of sizes appropriate but not provocative, somehow ensuring freedom of movement and zero tolerance of 'no go' areas without appearing to lose impartiality; the disarming of irregular forces, with perhaps their later inclusion in a unified national army; the search for concealed weapon caches, and on-going maintenance of law and order.

Peace enforcement will usually imply an identified enemy and require much larger force levels. These may have to include aircraft for reconnaissance or the enforcement of interdiction 'no fly' zones, warships for a naval blockade, the enforcement of sanctions, and direct combat unit intervention either by threat or actual use of force.

Commanders will need developed negotiation skills (for which a full knowledge of complex local land, legal and historical issues may be needed), efficient liaison, civil affairs, and public, media and community information and relations staff. Intelligence concerning the geopolitical attitudes of factions involved and their military capabilities has to be gathered. Junior military leaders need training in observing and monitoring buffer zones and cease-fire lines, negotiating skills, interpositioning perhaps under fire, the supervision of weapon surrender or decommissioning control measures in particular of key terrain, search, arrest and tactical initiative patrolling, the desirability (or feasibility) of punishment measures, together with the food, water and defence of their own personnel. In military terms, at both senior and junior command level peace enforcement requires a manoeuvrist approach with focus as much on the perceptions and attitudes of the belligerents as their material assets, and the use of manoeuvre to gain terrain, correlation of forces, and legal and moral advantage.

In sum, then, peace support operations must have consent as their aim, coercion only being used if absolutely necessary and the process being achieved by persuasion rather than force. The peace support force should be supervisory, a referee.

This is a military process somewhat alien to a soldier, who has joined an army expecting if necessary to fight for his country, or at least participate in realistic adventurous military training. The particular difficulty of adjustment, in the words of a British colonel, to 'sitting in the middle of someone else's war' is not always appreciated or understood. A soldier may not unreasonably wonder what he is doing when, as can happen, additionally civilians are openly hostile towards the peacekeeping force, or be so dependent on them that if the force attempts to leave, local civilians physically obstruct and attack it. General Sir Michael Rose, former commander of UN peacekeeping troops in Bosnia, has highlighted three elements essential for effective military performance 'weapons, doctrine and the willingness to fight or moral component'.[9] The need to provide peace support troops with the necessary weaponry is self-evident, the precise range depending on the circumstances of each intervention. However interoperability problems may arise with mixed nation forces. By no means a detail, the feeding of a multi-national force perhaps including Moslem and non-Moslem troops may also create friction. Doctrine has been summarised in the preceding paragraphs. Willingness to fight when there is no clear enemy, the moral component, needs further exposition. In the context of peace support, experience in Bosnia and elsewhere suggests the necessary ingredients may be the use of soldiers drawn from a developed political culture and where possible volunteers rather than conscripts, discipline, and thorough albeit highly expensive general military and role training, together with confidence-maintaining personal arrangements ranging from rapid casualty evacuation to pay, and support from home.[10] In Africa, this latter point, support from home, needs careful attention. Local rulers and opinion leaders in areas from which troops are recruited could hold views different from the central government that despatched the troops. The all-volunteer British and very largely volunteer (*Troupes de Marine* and Foreign Legion) French forces in Bosnia, meeting these criteria, were the most efficient in peace-keeping conditions as dangerous as general war.[11] The damage that could result from an ill-prepared military unit were well highlighted by the performance of a Netherlands conscript unit at Srebrenica.[12] General Rose summed up the lessons to be drawn as follows, 'If you want to be a good peacekeeper, first be a good war fighter'.

The moral component is one particularly affecting armies from less developed countries with low levels of education and political culture. It is not a matter affecting only African countries, the Ukrainian unit in former Yugoslavia performed so poorly and acquired so bad a record for looting that Ukrainian units were not later selected for service in the Middle East. But steadiness and probity under what can be extremely stressful conditions are essential for impartial peace support, excitability, indiscipline and loose behaviour together with over-reaction and overkill in operations destroy credibility. The West African force in Liberia and Sierra Leone, ECOMOG, acquired a very bad reputation for excess cruelty, corruption and for looting – 'Every Commodity or Moveable Object Gone' – for use and abuse of Liberian women, and for overkill both by ground troops and air to ground strikes.[13] The offenders generally but by no means invariably were Nigerian. Prior special training can only in part meet the need, but the difficulties and costs in the effective presentation of some very sophisticated but necessary peace support training on soldiers drawn from a less developed culture, and with more traditional ideas of the role and duties of a soldier, should not be underestimated.[14]

One further point needs to be made in the context of the 'moral component'. In some cases African units operating on the African continent can sometimes establish a common 'black consciousness' rapport. The most notable example has been that of the Botswana unit, in a reasonably quiet area of Somalia in 1996, whose officers and members made a deliberate effort to understand and respect Somalia's culture, personality – and language, adopting a friendly smiling style and treating the Somalis as equals.[15] The Zimbabwe unit also made similar attempts. Another asset possessed by a number of African units, through experience at home, is local level community development work, simple temporary structure building and roadways.

But there is a danger of a reverse effect likely to be corrosive on troops involved.[16] Conventional warfare, soldier against soldier, is one where often after the fury and passion of battle in which excesses do inevitably occur, adversaries can gain a measure of mutual respect, or at least empathy. Peace support work, perhaps involving huge numbers of starving and terrified refugees and providing ample evidence of wilful destruction of property, of brutal maltreatment, maiming by mines, or massacre of civilians, women and children, or as in the case of recent African conflicts professional soldiers being put in a 'kill or be killed' situation when faced with a ten year old boy holding a Kalashnikov, or if soldiers are required to bulldoze corpses into mass graves, can leave men scarred psychologically, with consequences perhaps more dangerous in Africa than elsewhere. Some soldiers may also fall to temptations of drink and drugs, particularly if the tempters come from the same rootless urban poor as they themselves.

An area difficult in any peace support operation at the best of times, intelligence and field security also presents particular problems in Africa. There may be initial language difficulties, failures to understand local customs, and almost certainly shortcoming in the training of the intelligence cycle, direction, collection, collation, evaluation, analysis, dissemination. An African peace-keeping force will be fortunate if it can include trained interrogator specialists, electronic surveillance equipment or computer data storage. In situations such as Brazzaville, Freetown, Liberia,

Lesotho (or the Hutu refugee camps in the Congo) the identification of men likely to cause violence, men out on the streets one moment who slip away to appear peaceful citizens when later an area is searched, is vital but extremely difficult – and clearly a difficulty that defeated ECOMOG. Whether African intelligence personnel could operate a system of 'spooks' (selected reliable individuals clothed in disguise from head to foot), a system in any case slow and laborious, to point out men of violence in a screening process would depend on their prior knowledge about whom to select.[17] Paid informers, in the African context, can also present risks if the informer is noticed by his neighbours as suddenly displaying wealth. While several African armies undoubtedly have signals interception expertise (in the case of Nigeria from the Civil War era), language and encryption difficulties might reduce their efforts to simple traffic analysis; it is doubtful whether any African army has the electronic warfare capacity to negate transmissions such as those in 1994 of Kigali's Radio Milles Collines with their incitements to genocide.

Funding and manpower underlie many of the problems African armies face and will continue to face in peace support operations. Inadequate funding for vehicles immobilised the OAU's first military observer group in Rwanda in 1993; inadequate funding for signals equipment virtually silenced communication between members of the OAU mission in Burundi. Will there be the funds available for the necessary manpower pre-deployment training, for the supply of food, fuel and ammunition needed to keep the force in the field perhaps for several weeks or months, for the provision, maintenance and replacement of equipment that will inevitably become needed, for the evacuation, hospital treatment and possibly invalid pensions for casualties? The costs can become astronomical and if not met disaffection can result.

Several African armies have had recent experience of peace support work – but, however, anyone associated with the military will bear in mind the rapid turnover of personnel in career structure, experience gained in earlier operations in the Middle East will now only be second-hand. Individual officers from a number of African countries including Ghana, Guinea, Kenya, Nigeria, Mali, Senegal, Zambia and Zimbabwe have been included in very recent UN missions in Angola, Iraq, Tajikistan, former Yugoslavia and Western Sahara. Ghana has provided a battalion for UN service in Lebanon, earlier Ghanaian units had served in the Middle East, and Kenya and Nigeria contributed units for operations in Croatia and Bosnia.

This recent experience would suggest that at present African armies are more suited to Chapter VI peace-keeping rather than Chapter VII peace enforcement with its complex and costly requirements. The all-African force supervising the political peace-keeping settlement in the Central African Republic, MINURCA, has proved a success; the 1,345 strong force comprised infantry company-sized contingents from Burkina Faso, Ivory Coast, Mali, Ethiopia, Senegal, Togo, Chad, with smaller numbers from three other states.

Peace enforcement has produced less fortunate results. The largest entirely African peace enforcement force, ECOMOG, operating in Liberia (from 1990 onwards) and Sierra Leone achieved some success in the former state but, to the time of writing (May 1999) has found Sierra Leone beyond its capabilities.[18] In Liberia ECOMOG's initial failures were due to its first inept commander, a Ghanaian, and until 1996 its operating, under a succession of Nigerian generals as part of the problem, being bitterly opposed to the strongest of the Liberian warlord factions, that of Taylor's NPFL. In this period, however, the force could justifiably claim to have saved a number of lives, particularly in preventing an NPFL occupation of Monrovia, a claim that could have been even stronger if ECOMOG's light artillery and air to ground strikes had avoided overkill.

The force's strength, however, was never sufficient to operate a border patrol system that could prevent arms supplies reaching the different factions. In 1996 the Abacha regime in Lagos, for its own political reasons, abandoned its opposition to Taylor and the NPFL so permitting a negotiated cease-fire and settlement, and it appointed two able generals, John Inienger and Victor Malu, to command ECOMOG. The latter in particular made a determined effort to stamp out the force's poor record for corruption and looting.

The conditions in Sierra Leone, in which a faction from the army allied with the insurgent Revolutionary United Front presented a different military problem, in many respects more of a straight ECOMOG campaign against the insurgents than a peace support operation. In Liberia more or less identifiable areas of ground had been held by the different factions and warlords. In Sierra Leone insurgents kept appearing in a wide variety of places – despite ferocious overkill, bombing, shelling and naval bombardment from ECOMOG. Three major weaknesses immediately appeared: lack of street fighting experience, the inability of many junior leaders to retain command and control of their sub-units in the confused conditions, and the absence of transport helicopters that would have facilitated rapid pursuit of small groups of insurgents before they split up to disappear in urban suburbs or forest.[19] The first two of these resulted in heavy, and often unnecessary Nigerian casualties. An additional problem was the different basic and preliminary training of the units of the force and the absence of centralised feeding and welfare amenities for units engaged in a common task, comparisons, envy and lowered morale being a result.[20]

Intervention in Guinea-Bissau, in the name of peace enforcement, provides a different example of how not to do it. Conflict between the President's government and troops disaffected, largely for economic reasons, led by the Army Commander broke out in 1998; fighting was both bloody and destructive. Senegal and Guinea (Conakry), supported by France, despatched troops with a hidden agenda in favour of the President. The force failed to end the conflict, and both the government and Senegalese troops committed excesses. A fudged settlement agreed in November 1998 envisaged a new force drawn from other West African countries. This force never appeared; in its stead 600 unarmed West African peacekeeping monitors arrived, to be brushed aside by the Army commander's forces in May 1999.

In conclusion, for the future African peace-keeping hopes must inescapably rest on external aid for training and equipment. France is sponsoring a force of 3-5,000 including French units as well as troops from Benin, Burkina Faso and Togo, and training in humanitarian assistance and the creation of safe zones.

The United States is sponsoring an African Conflict Resolution Initiative providing for an African Crisis Response Force (ACRF) of eight to ten battalions to be trained by the United States Army on a 60-day cycle with compatible signals, computers and other non-lethal equipments. Units from Côte d'Ivoire, Ghana, Ethiopia, Malawi, Mali, Senegal, Tunisia and Uganda have been or are being trained. However, a Senegalese participant commented that they had learnt nothing that they had not already learnt from the French and the objective of several governments in accepting the training offered may well have been more those of domestic threats than contributing to peacekeeping. Many other African countries have been openly reserved towards the American ACRF project. Britain has provided peacekeeping training including joint exercise experience and centring on doctrine, logistics and communications, for personnel from Angola, Botswana, Lesotho, Malawi, Mozambique, Namibia, Tanzania and Zimbabwe.

Two further possible useful developments might be an international military peace support staff college training to agreed procedures, and recognition by smaller contributing countries that a peace support force based on a coalition must have, for efficiency, style and co-ordination, a major power 'Framework Nation', as for example Britain in the Kosovo Kfor.

It remains to be seen whether all these projects and the training provided will make a successful contribution to peace-keeping. The difficulties, political, economic and military, remain massive.

Notes

1 The detail that follows is taken from the International Institute for Strategic Studies (1997), *The Military Balance 1997/98,* Oxford, OUP, pp. 230-63. After call-up of reserves and further drafting Ethiopia and Eritrea were both fielding armies of over 150,000 in the early 1999 fighting. For comparison, the strength of the post Cold War British Army is 115,000 and the French Army is reducing by stages to 136,000.

2 For example, *The Times*, 14 May 1999, notes that Zimbabwe forces serving in the Congo 'have taken heavy casualties from disease, chiefly AIDS and malaria in an environment that is regarded as an ideal hothouse for deadly tropical diseases'.

3 *The Economist*, 8 May 1999, p. 73. The Ethiopians are however bringing their Sukhoi 27s with Russian pilots into the fighting.

4 A term coined by Professor René Le Marchand at the Triangle Institute for Security Studies conference 'Conflict in Africa', Chapel Hill, North Carolina, 5 February 1999. For this analysis of Sierra Leone's insurgents, see Ibrahim Abdullah and Patrick Muana (1998), 'The Revolutionary United Front of Sierra Leone' in Christopher Clapham (ed) *African Guerillas*, Oxford, James Currey, xi, pp. 173-191.

5 *The Times*, 4 March 1999, article by Linda Malvery, p. 21.

6 Readers may need to be reminded that pre-Colonial Africa south of the Sahara was a vast region of over 5,000 polities: states, demi-states and acephalous societies with only in a few cases any clearly demarcated borders. Warfare was waged over the economic assets of the time, stock, grain, water-holes, women.

7 The text of Article 42 is set out conveniently in the British Army's *Field Manual Volume 5. Operations Other than War Part 2 Wider Peacekeeping*, London, HMSO, 1994, pp. 4-10. The term 'Wider Peacekeeping' has since been replaced by 'Peace Support'.

8 The exposition that follows is drawn from *Wider Peacekeeping*, ii, iii.

9 *The Times*, 26 March 1999, p. 4.

10 Senegalese soldiers, in total some 100, demonstrated on their return from peacekeeping in Bangui on 8 April 1999, blocking a Dakar main road and

alleging non payment of allowances. It was apparently the third of such demonstrations and an indication of discontent, BBC *Monitoring Reports, Africa*, 10 April 1999.

11 The British battalion in Gorazde, in the midst of violent Serb versus Moslem warfare, suffered men taken hostage; soldiers were obliged to live under cover in shelters without electricity for lights, hot water or food and on short rations for four weeks. Despite an attempt by the Moslems to use the British battalion's base as a shield, the battalion was able by extremely hazardous interpositioning to arrange a route for food supplies into the town and escorted some 70 convoys bringing in 8,000 tons of food.

A Ukrainian conscript unit, also part of the garrison, was overrun. An account of these operations, in which the British battalion fought 60 separate combat operations, some lasting for over five hours, and fired more than 10,000 rounds appears in *Y Ddraid Goch, The Journal of the Royal Welch Fusiliers*, March 1996. Of interest also is the home support factor, in this case a visit by the Queen to the soldiers' wives and families in Wales.

12 The Dutch battalion, which the UN command refused to support from the air, was obliged to give in to one side, the Serbs, even to the extent of assisting the Serbs in deporting the Bosnian Moslems, some 8,000 being subsequently murdered. A film of these proceedings was destroyed in mysterious circumstances, 'Investigating Srebrenica', *Transition*, October 1998, pp.16-19.

13 Two reports may be cited. The BBC 9.00 pm television news bulletin of 1 March 1999 showed film of brutality in Sierra Leone. The *Daily Telegraph* of 19 February 1999 reported that 100 ECOMOG soldiers had been arrested and charged with the summary execution of civilians and excessive use of force in Freetown.

There had been numerous earlier reports of such behaviour during the Liberian operations.

14 In special training for peace support work in Kosovo, for example, men of the British Army's Irish Guards were trained on virtual reality computers which with satellite imagery and maps replicated the precise terrain and driving conditions in Kosovo, soldiers being able to drive up and down mountains by computer. Individual soldiers were also being taught the correct body language and facial expressions for negotiations and the defusing of potential problems, *The Times*, 22 February 1999, p.14.

15 Orth, R. (1996), 'African Operational Experiences in Peacekeeping', *Small Wars and Insurgencies*, 7, 3, Winter, p. 313.

16 Colonel A. Duncan in 'Operating in Bosnia', *IBRU Boundary and Security Bulletin*, 2, 3, October, 1994, p. 47, noted that British units serving in Bosnia had psychiatric nurses available to help troops cope with such experiences and their services were increasingly needed.

17 The system was tried with some success by the British during the Mau Mau period in Kenya; there were, however, a number of cases of personal vendetta and settling of old scores.

18 The original August 1990 ECOMOG force in Liberia comprised 800 Nigerian troops, 800 Ghanaian, 500 from Guinea, 300 from Sierra Leone and 100 from Gambia. Later the Nigerian representation was heavily increased and units from Senegal, Tanzania and Uganda all served briefly.

19 The cease-fire agreement reached on 18 May included the illustrative clause … 'to establish safe corridors for the supply of food and medicine to ECOMOG soldiers behind RUF lines and to RUF fighters behind ECOMOG lines', BBC *Monitoring Reports Africa*, 20 May 1999.

20 See, for example, the observations of General Olurin, one of ECOMOG's commanders, quoted in Francis Vib-Sanziri (1998), 'Managing and resolving conflicts on the African continent; a proposed approach', in *Low Intensity Conflict and Law Enforcement*, 7, Summer, 1, p. 110.

Part Two
The Interveners

4 Tanzania's Military Intervention in Uganda

Oliver Furley and Roy May

Introduction

The intervention by Tanzania in using her army to overthrow Idi Amin in 1978 raises a number of questions, not only about inter African relations but also about Tanzanian regional policy and political attitudes; it could also lead into the debate about the nature of militarization and militarism in Africa. It also revealed that Africa, in the shape of the OAU, and indeed the international community in the UN, was not yet ready to accept the idea of a justifiable intervention against an African sovereign state, however great the need appeared to be.

The first crucial question that needs to be answered is how Tanzania had the military capacity to carry out the substantial military operation as well as other actions that will be referred to later in this section. In 1961 the Tanzanian army numbered some 4,000 troops organised on the British model but following the 1964 mutiny, Mathews (Keegan 1983) argues that it was decided that the British model was elitist and inappropriate for a socialist African state and it was therefore re-organised as the Tanzanian People's Defence Force (TPDF). Since then the army grew to 38,000 by 1983 (though it was close to that figure in 1978), organised in two divisional headquarters with 8 infantry brigades each of three battalions, a tank battalion, two field, two anti-aircraft, two mortar and two anti-tank artillery battalions, a surface to air missile battalion and two signal units. These troops were well armed at the infantry battalion level with Soviet battalion weapons, AK47 rifles and RPG7 grenade launchers. It is notoriously difficult to estimate equipment but Mathews (Keegan 1983) suggests that in 1977 they included 30 Chinese type 59, 30 type 62 and 36 British Scorpion tanks. SIPRI (1978) (Stockholm International Peace Research Institute) recorded that 350 Soviet T.54 main battle tanks were delivered in 1978. Mathews also suggested that there were large numbers of armoured reconnaissance vehicles, armoured personnel carriers, a range of 76 mm, 122 mm and 130 mm guns, 82 mm and 120 mm mortars, 50 BM2l rocket launchers and unspecified numbers of anti-aircraft guns. There were also SAM-3, SAM-6 and SAM-7 anti-aircraft systems.

This range of equipment and large armed forces need to be placed in a comparative context to attempt to assess its significance. Brayton (Baynham 1986) suggest that in 1983 out of 50 African armies 37 were smaller and only 9 significantly larger (Libya, Somalia, South Africa, Sudan, Algeria, Egypt, Ethiopia, Morocco, Nigeria); given the nature of some African micro-states, this may not be surprising, but he goes further and, by using data from the United States Arms Control and Disarmament Agency in 1980, makes an assessment of Military Expenditure (Milex), Milex as a percentage of GNP, Milex per capita in constant US $, and armed forces per 1,000 of the Population. In all of these, Tanzania rated reasonably high with a Milex of $148m, rankcd 8th of the 46 in the survey. The Milex/GNP of 4.2% was equal to that of Nigeria and South Africa as 7th of 46 countries and against an African average of 3.1%. The Milex per capita figure showed that Tanzania at $8 was 17th against the African average of $6 while the figure for the armed forces per 1,000 of the population was 16th on the list but above the African average of 3.3.

What now has to be assessed is what use did Nyerere make of these rapidly increasing armed forces? Now while the TPDF roles included those of 'nation building', such things as rural development including at times 'repressive enforcement of the *Ujaamas* (or commul villages)' (Mathews 1983) it also took on tasks against crime and smuggling; however it did start playing a role outside Tanzania. Tanzanian troops were sent to the Comoros in 1975 to support the regime of Ali Soilih and to help to train his forces. In 1977 some 400 troops were sent by Nyerere to support the new radical government of Albert René in the Seychelles. These troops were to play both a training role and a protective role for René, indeed it is suggested that a mutiny in 1982 was put down by Tanzanian soldiers.

A more substantial force was used in a supportive role to the Frelimo government in Mozambique; there had been a historical connection of support for Frelimo before independence but, after a serious threat from guerilla forces in the Cabo Pelgado region, forces were committed by Tanzania of some 1,500 men organised in two battalions. These troops stayed till 1979 when a combination of domestic pressures and an improvement in Mozambique led to their withdrawal. It can also be noted that, after the deposition of Amin in 1980, Tanzanian troops were sent to support the Zambian government during the troubles of 1980, the troops being deployed in patrolling the copperbelt.

This use of the TPDF on foreign ventures has to be put in the context of a general growth and use of African armies and military outside national territory. Foltz (Foltz and Bienen 1985) suggested that two patterns of cross border activity have increased in this period; the transfer of arms by African states to dissident groups and direct invasion or deep penetration raids. There are many examples of the former with the actions of South Africa and Libya prominent but with Tanzania, Sudan and Zaire notable amongst the others. The latter would include South African invasion into frontline states (those borderline states supporting anti-apartheid guerillas in South Africa), Angola into Zaire, Somalia into Ethiopia and then Tanzanian intervention into Uganda. Foltz also refers to a more significant trend, 'the ability of a few states to loan - or rent - troops to other African regimes in trouble'. This point, and the wider one of the use of African armies in pursuit of foreign policy objectives, has been analysed by Hughes and May (Baynham 1986) where 29 cases of the use of armies outside national boundaries are analysed. Of this 29, 18 were in the category of regime-supportive, where that support is to provide military assistance to a threatened government, as with Guinea sending troops to support President Stevens in Sierra Leone in 1971 and 1977, and in the 4 Tanzanian cases quoted in this chapter (Comoros, Seychelles, Mozambique, Zambia). 6 of the 29 cases appear to be regime-opposing, seeking the destabilization or overthrow of the government, viz. Zairean troops fighting alongside Holden Roberto's FNLA in the mid 1970s and the Tanzanian invasion of Uganda. The final category is state-supportive; these number 5 and would include the African members of the UN forces of the Congo and the various OAU forces in Chad. The conclusions of this survey show that civilian regimes are more likely to use national armies on external missions than military regimes, that radical countries engage more frequently in such acts than moderate countries and that the most interventionist states have been the most impoverished (Tanzania and Guinea). It is in this context that we wish to examine the actions of President Nyerere in 1978.

Nyerere's Stand Against the Amin Regime

Ever since the military coup in Uganda by Idi Amin in 1971, Nyerere had been foremost in Africa in expressing his revulsion against the military regime of a 'usurper' who had overthrown a democratically elected government. He was horrified by the frequency of military coups in Africa, and had experienced a severe crisis in the army mutiny in Tanzania in

1964, when he 'disappeared' for several days at the height of the tension. This was followed by a very determined effort to transform the Tanzanian army into a 'people's army' (TPDF), with new types of training and discipline focused on politicisation and education regarding an army's proper role.

Nyerere refused to acknowledge Amin as a legitimate head of state, and his refusal to meet him and shake hands with him at the formal conference level meant that the East African Community was doomed, as the constitution required the three heads of state to meet and agree on the annual budgets. This, together with quarrels between Tanzania and Kenya which led to the closing of their border) meant that the EAC could not survive. Meanwhile; it took a long time for international opinion to come round to Nyerere's view and take a critical line against the obvious tyranny of Amin's rule. Only in 1977 did the Commonwealth Heads of Government meeting at last make a unanimous statement condemning Amin's rule. The Organisation of African Unity (OAU) refused to do so, on the grounds that this would be interference with the internal affairs of a member state. It even accepted Amin as its chairman for one year. Of Uganda's other neighbours, Zaire remained silent, and Sudan was inclined to be friendly to Uganda now that the latter had a Moslem ruler and appeared to be making some progress to turn itself into a Moslem state. Even Kenya, then a comparatively democratic state, was cautiously friendly to Uganda, in many ways preferring Amin to the avowedly socialist policies of his predecessor, Obote. In October 1978 the US government did agree to an oil embargo on Uganda in protest against the régime, and accordingly Caltex, Esso and Mobil ceased trading in Uganda. Kenya, however, did not agree to pressure to cut off other supplies, always quoting the agreement safeguarding the access to ports for the African inland states. Kenya in fact kept up a valuable trade with Uganda, especially after Daniel Arap Moi succeeded Kenyatta as President in 1978. Britain was another country that helped to prop up the Amin régime in spite of widespread revulsion against the reported violations of human rights.[1]

Tanzania, however, was in many ways committed to opposing Amin. The commitment was deeper than merely a legalistic objection to a usurper who had achieved power by a military coup, nor was it just a moral stand against tyranny, or an ideological stand against right-wing militarism. Nyerere harboured his friend Milton Obote, the deposed President of Uganda, in his country, and allowed Ugandan exiles to undergo military training at secret camps. As early as 1971 there were skirmishes into Uganda by these guerilla forces, and Amin was already making claims to part of Tanzanian territory, namely the Kagera Salient to the south-west of Uganda below the existing border. The Kagera River might indeed have proved a more natural border between the two countries, but it was a staunch principle of the OAU that the former colonial boundaries must be adhered to. Next year, amid rumours of plots to invade Tanzania by Uganda and of possible British intervention in Uganda to protect the Asian community who were being expelled, Nyerere agreed that the Ugandan exiled force could stage an invasion of Uganda from his country. The idea was that this small force would spark off a mutiny or a rising in Uganda to overthrow Amin. The invasion in September 1972 was a fiasco, and the hoped-for rising did not take place.

The result was that Nyerere drew much criticism in the OAU for allowing such an attack to be staged from his country. Nigeria, Guinea, Libya and Egypt all condemned him for going against the OAU charter which stressed non-interference in the internal affairs of member states.

Colonel Guadhafi went further, and sent 400 Libyan and Palestinian troops to bolster Uganda's army, together with supplies and a MIG fighter. There followed a period of years when Nyerere did his best to patch up relations with Uganda. In October he signed the Mogadishu Agreement between the two countries, pledging peace and agreeing that subversive forces be not allowed to operate in one country against the other. However, he would not agree to expel Obote from Tanzania, and from 1974 to 1978 Amin quite frequently made false allegations that Tanzania had invaded Uganda. Nyerere did not react, and the 20,000 or so Ugandan exiles in his country turned more to civilian pursuits, though Obote kept up a small amount of guerilla activity in Uganda.[2]

The Attack on Tanzania

It was a very uneasy peace between the two countries. Amin continued to accuse both Tanzania and Kenya of subversion attempts, and he was suspicious of the agreement between Tanzania, Rwanda and Burundi for a Kagera River Basin Development Project. Though earlier on Uganda had withdrawn from this, Amin now felt he was being cut out. Moveover, he was faced with growing disaffection among his henchmen in Uganda. The split was mainly with Vice-President Mustafa Adrisi, a Lugbara Moslem, who led the resentment of many army officers against Amin's promotion of and reliance on non-Ugandan 'Nubians' or Southern Sudanese, often recruited in Sudan or northern Zaire. In April 1978 an attempt was made to assassinate Adrisi in a fake car crash, and although he survived with injuries, he was stripped of his offices. Other dismissals were made, such as Brig. Moses Ali, Minister of Finance, Kassim Obura, Chief of Police, and Lt. Col. Nasur, Commander of the Mechanised Regiment. These dismissals simply exacerbated internal power struggles within the army, and later in 1978 a mutiny was reported among the Lugbara soldiers in support of Adrisi. Amin then plotted to kill off dissident troops by sending them on a special mission to Masaka supposedly to deal with a mutiny, but it was a trap in which some 200 of them were killed on October 25 to 27 by Lt. Col. Juma Ali's troops.[3]

While Amin had clearly been building up forces with a view to attacking the Kagera Salient as a diversion from the general tense situation at home, this army unrest must have made up his mind to launch a full-scale attack. On October 27 Amin was presented with a memorandum from the southern and western commands, containing twelve demands to be met by midnight on November 1. Amin ordered his loyal units to invade Tanzania 24 hours before this deadline.[4]

He had already accused Tanzania of invading Uganda on October 11, and even said they had got as far as Mbarara. Ben Mkapa, Tanzanian Foreign Minister, replied that this was 'absolute nonsense' and complete lies. Then Amin claimed Tanzanian troops were backed by Cubans, that they had taken Mutukula just inside Uganda and were advancing with tanks and heavy weapons, while others were sailing across Lake Victoria to Entebbe and Kampala. Tanzania issued denials but did report that on 27 October three Ugandan planes bombed Bukoba; otherwise no news was issued, even though there had been skirmishes across the border by Ugandan troops as early as 9 October.[5] A Tanzanian journalist recalls this time when as a schoolgirl she had to be evacuated when a Russian MIG16 narrowly missed their dormitories along the shore of Lake Victoria.[6] While Radio Uganda continued pouring out false stories of Tanzanian incursions, implying that Amin's offer of friendship was spurned and his patience was being tested to the limit, Tanzania apparently did very little to prepare for any military escalation of this crisis. When serious fighting broke out on 25 October, Tanzanian troops had to withdraw at first because requests for reinforcements were ignored.[7] On 30 October, a full-scale invasion took place, with little resistance, so that the Kagera Salient was very quickly conquered. Some 710 square miles of territory were occupied, and several hundred Tanzanian civilians were taken prisoner and sent to Uganda. Up to 3,000 Ugandan troops were involved, and they went on a spree of pillage, looting and rape in the captured area. The damage caused was severe and it is reckoned some 1,500 Tanzanian civilians were killed. Curiously, the Ugandan army blew up the only bridge across the river (with help from European experts from the Kilembe Copper Mines) and did not consider going further south. But Uganda now clearly intended to stay. The government announced it had pushed the border to Kagera river, annexing this territory, in retaliation for the Tanzanian 'invasion'. The new territory would be administered as a Ugandan district. As a final insult, Amin underlined the personal animosity and dislike between himself and Nyerere by one of his usual humorous, self-publicising gestures. He challenged Nyerere to a boxing match to settle their differences, with Mohamed Ali as the referee.[8]

The Tanzanian Response

Nyerere, often said to be one of the most peace-loving of leaders and 'one of [Africa's] most influential and unwarlike statesmen' - though we have indicated our reservations on this view - kept quiet in face of the early provocations, even the bombing of Bukoba, but he now reacted with intense urgency, giving the repulsion of Uganda absolute priority, letting the situation in Rhodesia and South Africa take second place in his preoccupations for the time being.[9] He ordered an all-out war effort, and sent reinforcements to the war zone as quickly as possible, though the huge distances involved and the absence of usable road and rail links made it a slow process, especially for the tanks, artillery and armoured personnel carriers (APC's) which would need to be mustered. The Tanzanian people were warned that the campaign to push Uganda out might not be over quickly but could take weeks or months. People's militia units around the country were activated and required to report each day after work for training. Meanwhile little news was supplied to the nation – journalists were banned from the war zone, even those from the government's own national news agency, and this tendency was a feature of Tanzania's war.[10]

Nyerere's sense of outrage and indignation was made very clear. In response to overtures from other countries, he asked his 'friends' not to mediate, for he wanted to fight 'until this snake is out of our house' as he put it. He did appeal to Kenya to cut off oil supplies. This was turned down, though Kenya did appear to limit these supplies. Libya's minister for information, Mohamed Zuwai, went to Dar with a message from Col. Guadhafi calling for a 'brotherly solution' to end the fighting. Nyerere reacted sharply and refused any idea of mediation, asking if Uganda's action could be described as 'brotherly'.[11] According to Avirgan and Honey, Nyerere however did collect one ally in his campaign. President Samora Machel of Mozambique had been angered by Zambia's reopening of its border with Rhodesia, without consulting the Frontline Presidents, of whom Nyerere was chairman. Nyerere flew to Beira on 2 November to meet Machel, and they agreed on a 'second front' analysis of Amin's invasion. Amin had ties with Ndabaningi Sithole, the African nationalist in Rhodesia who was now collaborating with Ian Smith's white minority government. Sithole had troops training in Uganda. Amin's invasion, therefore, could be construed as a second front to divert Tanzania's attention from the main campaign to liberate Rhodesia – the Zimbabwe liberation struggle. Nyerere promised Machel he would not slacken his support for this struggle, even though the battalion of Tanzanian troops stationed on Mozambique's Rhodesian border would be withdrawn and sent to the 'second front'. Machel offered to send a battalion of Mozambican soldiers to Tanzania to fight on this front as a gesture of solidarity.

'The Mozambicans were dispatched to Tanzania in a matter of days and were immediately sent to Kagera. Not a word of their presence ever appeared in the Tanzanian press, and one of the very few bits of evidence that there were Mozambicans in the Tanzanian ranks was a copy of the Mozambican newspaper *Noticias* left inadvertently behind in the lounge of the Mwanza airport.'[12]

Except for about 1,000 Ugandan guerillas in support of Obote, no other nations appeared to contribute men to Tanzania's campaign and this is the only reference to the Mozambicans; what part they played is open to doubt. The Uganda guerilla force recruited many more as the campaign progressed.[13]

In November, it did not take the Tanzanians long to recapture the Kagera Salient. Once they had crossed the river by temporary bridges and got their tanks and vehicles over, there was little opposition at that point. Nyerere came to see the situation, and was told the region could not be considered secure because Ugandan forces in Mutukula just across the border held a commanding position from which they could easily attack again.

Punish the Aggressor

Would the war end there? Would Tanzania be content, having regained her territory? Neighbouring countries and other African states feared not, and this period sees urgent efforts in Africa to mediate between the two sides. Much international pressure was put on Amin in the first place, by the OAU, with President Numeiry of Sudan as chairman, and by General Obasanjo of Nigeria, who did persuade Amin to say he was pulling back his troops. Numeiry visited Uganda, Tanzania and Kenya in December, and claimed he had persuaded both combatants to withdraw from the border. Kenya offered to mediate, and a special committee of the OAU was set up to do so. It is clear that the war caused acute embarrassment in the OAU, for here were two Black African countries openly at war with one another after some seven years of 'cold war' between them. Moveover, one of them was a frontline state in the struggle against South Africa. Nigeria was strongly critical of the fighting as a diversion from the main task directed against South Africa and Rhodesia. The *Tanzania Daily News* countered this with the charge that Amin was in league with Rhodesia's Ian Smith, creating a second front in Tanzania, as the Nyerere-Machel meeting had suggested. Condemnation of Uganda's invasion of Tanzania was expressed by Britain, the Scandinavian countries, Canada, Jamaica and Guyana but by none of the African countries except Zambia. Many of the African countries, notably Sudan, Tunisia, Ivory Coast, Guinea, Mozambique, Ethiopia and Algeria, instead appealed for peace. Libya offered to mediate. The US Secretary of State, Cyril Vance, expressed support for Tanzania, and called on Uganda to withdraw from Tanzania. Amin responded by accusing the US of interference, with the aim of creating a second Vietnam. He suggested that the British Prime Minister, Mr Callaghan, should mediate – even though shortly before this he had accused Britain of complicity in Tanzania's 'numerous invasions'. Probably in response to Numeiry's pressure, Amin did order withdrawal from Tanzania and dropped his previous demand for a written guarantee that Tanzania would never again invade or arm Ugandan exiles in Tanzania.[14]

Nyerere's response to this pressure from the OAU and from other African states for mediation to settle the issue peaceably was one of anger. He was burning with indignation at the loss of life and the devastation in the Kagera Salient. He had recovered the lost territory in swift campaign, but instead of winning praise and sympathy from the fellow members of the OAU, his action had caused consternation and intense pressure for mediation. He told the OAU special committee, led by Philip Obang, that he expected the OAU to condemn the illegal invasion by Uganda. That was an essential first requisite before mediation could take place. It would restore or rather confirm the moral position of Tanzania. Nyerere, one feels, saw this as a vital justification for him personally throughout the war, as the leader of Tanzania. He laid down three conditions before he would consent to any mediation:

1 The intervening third parties must first condemn Uganda's aggression;
2 Uganda must abandon all claims to territory on the left bank of the Kagera River.
3 Uganda must agree to pay full reparations for the devastation caused by its October invasion.

In addition, he made a comment showing that the restoration of the pre-war position would probably not be enough. 'Even if Amin gives these assurances', he added, 'we cannot believe his words and we must strengthen our forces to defeat him once and for all'. Amin's reply was also significant and referred to another essential factor in the long-term situation: there would be no peace while Tanzania was sheltering Obote and fostering his military adventurism.[15]

Obote was merely one factor in what was now becoming a transformation in Tanzania's aims. On 17 November Nyerere said 'Our duty is to push this aggressor out of our country but that is no longer the problem. The problem is what next?' Tanzania had no intention of occupying Uganda, but 'Amin has committed these acts of aggression against Tanzania. Supposing he withdraws or is pushed back to the border, do we then say fine and he gets away with it?' The charter of the OAU had been violated and he demanded to know what Africa was going to do about it. 'Is Africa asking Tanzania to pay for these massacres and the wanton destruction of property? Africa would be setting a dangerous precedent if it allows matters to end there'. Nyerere was moving from mere recovery of territory to the aim of 'punishing' Amin, and this could involve teaching him a lesson by serious incursions into his own territory. Pushing him back over the border was not enough. If he remained in power, he would very probably attack Tanzania again. According to David Martin of the *Observer,* Tanzanian officials believed the *removal* of Amin would be a service to the rest of Africa and mankind (not to speak of Uganda). One said that he thought Tanzania would limit itself to wiping out Amin's southern army units, then would leave it to the exiled Ugandan forces plus internal dissident forces to settle the matter.[16]

The first moves into Uganda were made by the Tanzanian troops late in January 1979 when they attacked Mutukula, the strategic point on high ground overlooking the Kagera Salient. Mutukula was taken without difficulty, and the town was totally destroyed, with many of the civilian population killed. Bulldozers flattened what remained. This was indeed 'punishment', but Nyerere was horrified by the civilian deaths and destruction of civilian property. He issued an immediate order that from that moment a sharp distinction must be drawn between civilian and military lives and property, and that the greatest care must be taken to protect anything non-military.[17] This was a very important element in the following seven months' campaign in Uganda: both for humanitarian and political considerations civilian lives and property had to be spared. The civilian population must welcome the 'invaders', as 'liberators', otherwise part of the justification for action was removed. It was also an essential part of the plan by the Ugandan exiles' force to win over the population as they advanced through Uganda. They crossed the border with only about 900 men to assist Tanzania's force and if they were to play a major role they needed to recruit new volunteers along the way. It was hoped that the original incursion would spark a popular rising, thereby justifying the Tanzanian intervention. (The latter capture of Masaka and Mbarara proved exceptions to this policy, however, as it was accompanied by much seemingly deliberate destruction.)

Nyerere had already played a part in rallying and organising the many groups of exiled Ugandans. At Christmas 1978 there was a secret meeting of many of these groups in Nairobi, and Nyerere urged them to drop their rivalries and unite to oust Amin. He did not intend Tanzanian troops to be regarded as an occupying force if Amin was ousted: if Tanzanian intervention did in fact lead to Amin's fall, it must certainly be with the popular support of Ugandans, otherwise it would appear to be a 'conquest', perhaps with a puppet government installed, to create a satellite for Tanzania. Here Nyerere faced a severe difficulty, in that he had harboured Milton Obote, the former President of Uganda, for so many years. Was Tanzanian intervention merely to reinstate Obote? If so, it would be very much opposed by some of the exiled groups and in many areas of Uganda – particularly those areas in the south through which Tanzania might advance. He therefore stressed very strongly that he did not wish to impose any leader on Uganda, and he asked Obote to make a statement saying that he did not claim Ugandan leadership but appealed to Ugandans to rise.

Obote was extremely cautious at this time and would not go to Nairobi, but Nyerere persuaded him to send a representative. At the meeting a united front was declared, with no name as yet for security reasons, and the question of leadership was not resolved. There was still a long way to go before the Moshi meeting in March put the front on a more satisfactory footing.[18]

On 13 January Obote broke his long silence which he had kept for eight years and spoke out, calling on Ugandans to launch their own military struggle against Amin, and denying that Tanzania was planning to impose him or any leader on Uganda. He gave a detailed account of the army mutinies in Uganda which led Amin to invade Tanzania as a diversion from that serious crisis. As for Obote's participation in this, he declared his 'fundamental right as a Ugandan to join hands with other Ugandans and put up resistance to a reign which takes pride in extensive and wanton killings of its citizens ... the main force for change must be organised from within – there should be no wishful thinking that there are foreign troops who will liberate the people of Uganda'.[19] Obote stressed that he had no office to gain or re-gain, and Tanzania was not helping him to do so. Tanzania was not playing the role of king-maker, as he repeated in a BBC TV interview. These statements were sanctioned by the Tanzanian government, and were backed up by daily radio broadcasts to Uganda from Dar es Salaam, calling on the people to rise.[20] In effect, Nyerere's stance could well have been drawn from the political theories of the philosopher John Locke, whose basic tenet was that a tyrannical rule had broken the original contract between a ruler and his subjects to give them protection and rule justly; therefore his subjects would be justified in overthrowing him. Evidently some African states took the same view. Mozambique supplied a battalion of soldiers plus a token shipment of arms. Zambia and Angola, Tanzania's other fellow frontline states, also sent arms, so did Ethiopia. Algeria sent three shiploads of arms, though she did not admit it publicly for fear of angering other Muslim Arab states.[21] Libya, a state which had already aided the Amin regime and would soon do so again, naturally took a hostile view of Tanzania's action. In February, the Secretary for Foreign Affairs in a letter to the UN Secretary General protested that the Tanzanian invasion was,

> A matter of great danger to the peace and security of Africa. He stated that it was necessary and urgent to act in order to bring about a peaceful evacuation of Tanzanian troops, and expressed the hope that the Secretary General would act promptly, guided by the principle that no state had the right to overthrow the regime of another by force or any other means.[22]

The OAU reacted in the same month by seeking a peace accord through a meeting of the Reconciliation Committee in Nairobi on 21 February 1979, and as the war progressed it was clear that one of the chief concerns of African states was that this war was a diversion from the more important matter of securing the downfall of apartheid in South Africa. A Summit Meeting of the Frontline States in Luanda on 4 March 1979 issued a communiqué: Amin's attack 'served the objective of the enemy of the frontline states, for the aggression could only be designed to force Tanzania to divert resources from the liberation struggle against the minority racist regimes to the defence of its sovereignty and territorial dignity'.[23]

The Tanzanian Army on the Move

At first, Nyerere was hesitant about proclaiming the exact role Tanzania was playing. After claiming that Ugandan troops had made fresh incursions into Tanzania, the government-owned 'Tanzania Daily News' finally admitted that Tanzanian troops had crossed into Uganda. Nyerere warned that if there were further attacks on Tanzania the ensuing fighting would take place in Uganda, not in Tanzania. At the same time, Tanzania 'had no intention of occupying any part of Uganda'. The first thrust was successful, and when Rashidi Kawawa, Minister of Defence, visited the Mutukula area he saw the captured collection of two Ugandan tanks, six APCs, three Landrovers, plus Jeeps, trucks and weapons. But foreign reporters were barred from the war zone, so it was impossible to get independent confirmation of the claims made by either side.[24] The Tanzanian army in fact found that vehicles and equipment left behind by retreating Ugandan soldiers were a very useful, almost vital, supplement to their own weaponry and transport. It is said that the Ugandan troops never walked; they rode everywhere in trucks, and they were backed by Russian-made 122 mm howitzers and BM-21 rocket-launchers, as well as Russian tanks and APCs. Standards of training and discipline in the Ugandan army were notoriously poor, and sometimes they did not make the best use of the elaborate equipment they had. The Tanzanian army, by contrast, was well trained and had good morale and discipline. The army was well equipped as we have seen, though it was difficult logistically to move some of this along such long lines of communication. Troops and supplies were sent by rail to Mwanza, then ferried across Lake Victoria to Bukoba, then taken by truck to the front, a journey of some 2,300 km in all at the beginning of the campaign, and almost 3,000 km when the Sudanese border was reached in

June.[25] Perhaps because of this the Tanzanians based their advance on the speed of marching soldiers, not attempting armoured clashes, and this helped to keep their casualties low. This concept is said to owe much to Tanzanian contacts with Frelimo, the revolutionary party in Mozambique.[26] Another factor limiting the speed of advance was food supplies. Dar-es-Salaam kept the army well supplied with military needs, but could not afford to supply food to units in Uganda (some 10,000 men to start with) and expected them to rely on local resources. With a willing population, this was no great problem, though as the campaign moved north it could cause resentment.[27] In some areas it was the Tanzanians who had the food, while the local population was semi-starving; they sometimes won over the population by hand-outs of food. Contact with the local population was of course maximised by the fact that Tanzanian soldiers walked almost throughout the seven-month war. There was a parallel in the way British troops had to fight in the Falkland Islands, 'yomping' through marshes and mud. But unlike the Falklands, the air force could not help much, and air strike power, with one or two exceptions such as strikes at the airport of Entebbe, was little used, as was air transport. The only lifts the Tanzanians got were usually in captured Ugandan vehicles. When they took Fort Portal, they came in a Landrover, three Ugandan tanks and various vehicles, cars and bicycles. When they took Kampala, people were surprised to see them walking into the town, not riding in tanks or trucks.[28]

The initial thrust into Uganda had proved easy, which encouraged Nyerere to commit himself to a more serious invasion, to go at least as far as the larger towns of Masaka and Mbarara. Both of these were easily taken at the end of February. Even then, it seems the Tanzanian government was loathe to claim a victory for its own troops, and tried to credit the Ugandan exiles' force with the victories. It was also expecting the capture of these two towns would spark off the hoped-for popular rising that would relieve the Tanzanians of future participation. There was some justification for this hope: by February some of the Uganda units had linked up with sabotage groups and Uganda admitted that fighting within the army had spread to Nile Province, Eastern Ankole and around Kampala.[29] The Ugandan exiles' units were now playing a prominent part in the fighting, especially in the capture of Masaka, under Col. Tito Wini, Lt. Col. Oyite Ojok and Major Oboma, while other forces assembled in Tanzania and western Kenya were led by Col. Maruru, former commander of the air force, carrying out raids in Uganda. One raid, said to be carried out by the Save Uganda Movement (SUM) temporarily occupied Tororo, the town twenty miles from Uganda's eastern border with Kenya, and some of

Amin's troops joined the guerrillas. The raid was soon repulsed, and drew criticism from other anti-Amin forces as an unco-ordinated and premature move.[30]

Mediation Attempts Harden Nyerere's Line

Meanwhile the capture of Masaka and Mbarara and the devastation caused there made African states once again press for mediation. Amin had already appealed to the UN Security Council to meet, saying Uganda was suffering an invasion but that he claimed no Tanzanian territory. He also appealed to the Palestine Liberation Organisation and all 'friendly' countries to assist, saying Uganda was holding back on going on the offensive, waiting for the outcome of the meeting of the OAU reconciliation committee.

This body had met in Nairobi in February to try to achieve a ceasefire. An OAU four-man delegation visited Uganda and Tanzania, but Nyerere treated the mediation efforts 'with little short of scorn', as one paper put it. His attitude was still one of the injured party demanding recognition and compensation. His conditions for peace were that the OAU should condemn Uganda's invasion; Amin must renounce all claims to Tanzanian territory and must agree to pay compensation for loss of life and property, and cease using Tanzania as a scapegoat for his internal problems. He told the OAU delegation that 'there could be no question of neutrality on the part of the OAU'. The OAU must be the prosecutor: this was central to Nyerere's case. President Moi of Kenya appealed to both sides for a ceasefire, and Libya sent its foreign minister, Ali Tureiki, to Uganda and Tanzania. Uganda of course readily accepted Libya's proposal, but Nyerere insisted mediation must be by the OAU. He declared in a broadcast on 28 February that he would be 'very happy' if Amin were overthrown, but his government did not aim to oust him: the war could end immediately if his four conditions were met.[31] By this time however, any diplomats and observers thought otherwise: Nyerere had committed his army to involvement in Ugandan affairs; the Tanzanian forces, then put at 17,000, had played a vital part in the capture of Masaka and Mbarara and furthermore, the Ugandan exiled force, mostly Obote's followers and now thought to number some 3,000, were still quite inadequate to hold the liberated areas and march on Kampala. There could hardly be a withdrawal of Tanzanian troops until the vital target of Kampala was taken.[32] If they withdrew, Amin might rally and get extra help. 'What finally convinced

Nyerere to go on was the realisation that to retreat back to Tanzania would leave several million in southern Uganda at the mercy of Amin', claim Avirgan and Honey, though they stress that the Tanzanian army hence forward tried to keep in the background, as a back-up force for the Ugandans to liberate Kampala.[33]

A New Dimension: Libyan Troops

This was not always possible. Amin's army had already been helped by Libyan and PLO 'advisers', some of whom had been killed in the fighting. But early in March Col. Gadaffi decided Amin needed drastic help if he was to survive. He therefore flew in some 2,500 to 3,000 Libyan troops, along with six Mirage and seven Mig-21 fighters, and later a Russian Tupolev-22 high-altitude bomber. There were reports too that contingents of troops arrived from Zaire, and some from Morocco, though Morocco denied this and we do not hear of them again.[34] The result was that Amin's forces were given new hear, and it was a setback for Tanzania. The Libyans were reported to have virtually taken control of Uganda's military operations, and they were using Libyan 122 mm long-range artillery which matched the Tanzanian artillery. The Tanzanians were within thirty miles of Kampala, yet the hoped-for popular rising had not really taken place. Amin had secured a three million pound loan from the Arab Economic Fund, and the troops supporting him now were mostly foreign – Sudanese, Palestinians and Libyans. 'It is uncertain whether the Tanzanians have the will, politically or militarily, to push on to Kampala', speculated the Guardian on 8 March.

A sharp reversal and one of the few major battles of the war helped to resolve the issue of further Tanzanian participation. From Masaka, the only main route to Kampala was the coast road by the lake, passing the small town of Lukaya, then proceeding by a causeway through a swamp. Tactically therefore it was risky to advance by that route, but it fell to the Tanzanians to do this. They took Lukaya, but then the full effect of Amin's Libyan reinforcements was felt for the first time. They attacked from north of the swamp with their 'Katushka' rocket launchers, and recaptured Lukaya. It took some severe fighting by the Tanzanians and Ojok's Ugandan liberation forces to restore the situation, in a battle in which 400 of the enemy were killed, including some 200 Libyans. Similarly, the Tanzanians met with a sharp reversal in the other thrust of this drive to the north, further inland starting from Masaka. It was however a less significant battle than Lukuya, in which the Libyans had played an important part. The Libyan factor must have played a big part in galvanising Nyerere's willingness to see the campaign through and help the Ugandan liberation forces complete their victory. They could not do without the Tanzanians.[35]

Another factor in this galvanisation was the resolution, temporarily at least, of the rivalries and factions among the various Ugandan liberation groups – a resolution which Nyerere instigated and organised. He always insisted that he was not fighting to replace Obote, but a weakness in his case so far was that there appeared to be no other leader in the offing, and that most of the Ugandan liberation force were Obote's followers. However, he was now able to bring all the rival groups of exiles together at Moshi in Tanzania. One hundred delegates from eighteen factions met in March, and were given the task of forming a council to administer the liberated areas, forming a transitional government and after Amin's fall, organising democratic elections – in which Obote would have an equal chance with others. Nyerere in fact excluded Obote from the meeting. (Others say Obote thought it wise to keep away.) Not only did Kenya and Britain voice concern that Obote might be re-installed as a result of the Tanzanian intervention, but Nyerere also realised that many of the liberated areas of Uganda were strongly against Obote. He was therefore anxious that an exiled government be set up with a more 'neutral' figure as leader. It is not the place here to go into the extremely convoluted politics of the Moshi meeting, but when Professor Yusufu Lule, a former Principal of Makerere University College in Kampala and a comparatively neutral figure, emerged as the elected leader and chairman of the executive council, this may have been a great relief to Nyerere. The Ugandan National Liberation Front (UNLF) was set up, with the forces united under the title of United National Liberation Army (UNLA). Nyerere had made the uniting of the exiles under an acceptable leader a condition for his continuing drive into Uganda. He had now achieved that, or rather the exiled groups by a superhuman effort did it for him.[36]

Amin Defeated: Tanzania's Goal Achieved

The day after the conference, Colonel Gadaffi issued a threat to join the war on the side of Amin unless Tanzanian troops withdrew from Uganda in 24 hours. Nyerere's answer showed the strength, as he saw it, of his moral position. In a broadcast to the Tanzanian people, he said he was helping

Ugandans to remove a fascist dictatorship, which Ugandans had the right to do. President Moi of Kenya too urged that Tanzania ought to withdraw, now that the conflict was being 'internationalised'. Nyerere spurned this plea and instead said Kenya was being obstructive in allowing Libyan planes to land and refuel in Kenya. He asked Kenya not to allow a convoy of 50 trucks of arms from Mombasa to go through to Uganda, a request which Kenya, as before, refused.[37]

Fresh units of Libyans were reported to have reached Uganda, but with both Tanzanians and the UNLA advancing on Kampala, and Tanzanian planes causing havoc in attacks on Entebbe airport, the end was in sight. Amin fled east and then north, and his army was disintegrating. Entebbe was quickly captured by the Tanzanians, with between 120 to 400 Libyans killed. Amin's soldiers had fled. When Kampala's turn came, UNLF and Tanzanian units approached from various directions, but Nyerere urged extreme caution. He wanted to minimise bloodshed, but there were also political considerations. First it would be best if the Ugandans were seen to be the liberators of this capital city, with Tanzanians only in a supporting role. Secondly, he did not want to trap and kill a lot of Libyan troops in the capture of the city because of the obvious international repercussions. So an escape route was to be left open for them along the road east to Jinja.[38] In the end, the Tanzanians of the 19th Battalion of the 208th Brigade took a prominent part in the 'walk-in' to Kampala, along with Lt. Col. Ojok's UNLA units, and crowds were soon thronging around troops who were very obviously Tanzanians. By 11 April, the city had fallen, with only minimal opposition.[39]

Yusufu Lule was soon installed as President and his provisional government was established. He thanked the Tanzanians and made it clear that they would be staying in Uganda for some time. He 'formally welcomed Uganda's allies, brothers and friends to this country'. In fact it took the Tanzanians and UNLA nearly another two months to complete the cleaning up process against Amin's troops. Amin fled the country, and by 3 June 1979, the war was over.

The war had been a very expensive affair for a poor country like Tanzania, costing some $500 million, one source estimates. Considering it lasted seven months it was not expensive in casualties. The Tanzanians lost 373 soldiers. Of these, only 96 were killed by the enemy, the rest died in accidents. The UNLA lost about 150 men, most of them drowned on a raid across Lake Victoria. The Libyans lost c. 600 and Amin's army, c.1,000. In addition, 1,500 Tanzanian civilians were killed in the Kagera Salient, and during the war about 500 Ugandan civilians died.[40] Tanzania's role in the settling of the peace in Uganda was of course by no means over, but we are mainly concerned here with military intervention.

The Verdict on Tanzania: International Reactions

The new government of Uganda was quickly recognised by many nations, which could be taken at least as an acceptance of Tanzania's intervention. In a broadcast, Nyerere stressed that Tanzania's main task had been to 'punish dictator Amin', but that this had been the work of Ugandans not Tanzanians. 'The aim of uprooting Amin was not our task; it was the task of the people of Uganda and they alone could make arrangements and declare "we do not want this man, we are uprooting him to replace him with another to lead us".' He denied he had contravened international law; it was Amin who had done so: 'Tanzania decided to act as the policeman. We entered and punished him'.[41]

Whatever other countries might think of the gloss that Nyerere put on Tanzania's action, many quickly backed up the result by welcoming and recognising the new government. Zambia was the first, followed by Mozambique, Botswana, Gambia, Rwanda, Guinea, Angola, Malawi and outside Africa by Britain, Canada, Australia and the USA. The *Times* of Zambia (13.04.79) said it was a triumph for Ugandans: 'It is also a triumph for President Nyerere's wisdom and keen sense of timing. As a man of peace the decision to support a war must have been a hard one. But he recognised the wider evils that would stem from Amin being allowed to stay in power. His courage and foresight have earned him the gratitude of Africa at large.' Opinion in the West tended to follow this line, though with some doubts about the legality. They still clung to the idea – historically incorrect – that Nyerere was basically a non-interventionist. The *New York Times* said it was the end of a nightmare, which now removes any misgivings about Tanzania's role: 'There is an irony in the part played in Amin's downfall by Tanzania and its President Julius Nyerere. Mr Nyerere, one of Africa's respected leaders, is also one of the least militaristic. Yet Tanzania has set a disturbing precedent. What has been done this time in a good cause, and with considerable provocation, might as easily be done by others in difference circumstances.' British papers expressed the same approval and reservations. The *Daily Telegraph* (12.04.79) said a strong taboo, rigidly upheld by the OAU, had been broken. For the first time one African state had invaded another and deposed its ruler. 'Most remarkably it has been broken by a man, President

Julius Nyerere of Tanzania, who has always posed as a kind of plaster saint of African politics'. Colin Legum in the *Observer* (15.04.79) pointed to confusions in the application of international law. Nyerere's action had been directly against the principles of the UN and the OAU, but there was bound to be debate about international responsibility 'where a paranoiac mass murderer can shelter behind the international convention of military non-interference in the sovereign affairs of states'. Thus Nyerere and the rest of the world had condemned Somalia when it sent an army to Ogaden province in Ethiopia the year before. On the other hand, the UN failed to agree to condemn Vietnam for invading Kampuchea to overthrow the Pol Pot regime, so the principle was unequally observed in practice. An international lawyer has tried to put Tanzania's intervention into one of the legal categories which might be permissible – self-defence; intervention in a civil war; a war of national liberation etc. – but failed. However, she admits the international community accepts that Tanzania did right. 'Morally, politically, economically and strategically the Tanzanian action seemed the correct response to the situation within Uganda. What it has served to do also is to point to the distance between simplistic legal categorisation of the permissible and impermissible uses of force and complex political realities'. If Tanzania was condemned by international law, then it was international law that needed amending.[42]

Needless to say Nyerere's critics still condemned his intervention. Libya did not relent, neither did Nigeria and Sudan. The OAU itself never managed to condemn Amin's action as Nyerere wanted. The OAU Ministerial Council meeting in Nairobi in the spring of 1979 refused, and quoted the OAU charter at Nyerere. The OAU Defence Commission Conference in Addis Ababa in the summer was divided between those applauding Tanzania and those who only gave it qualified support and were concerned about the wider implications. There were also feelings that Nyerere was 'the arrogant custodian of the Pan African conscience'.[43] At the 16th OAU Summit Conference in Liberia, Nyerere left only twelve hours after it opened, after a bitter clash with President Numeiry of Sudan over the Ugandan issue. The conference agreed only to examine and revise the Charter, to try to avoid similar crises in the future. Further Nyerere never obtained the financial compensation he sought from African countries to set against the huge cost of the war. It is reckoned that the war cost some $500 million on war expenditure and $100 million on the provision of support to Uganda. This was at a time when the world oil prices were about to double (1979-1980). Nyerere once told Colin Legum that 'before embarking on that operation I had no idea of the cost of a military operation ... I wonder, if I knew at the time what the cost would be, whether I would have had the courage to undertake it.' The *Economist* judged that 'it finally bankrupted Tanzania'.[44]

Tanzania's is 'a seemingly incongruous record, given President Nyerere's gentle and anti-militaristic reputation'.[45] Yet the military build-up of the 1970s and the record of intervention may support Mathew's assertion that President Nyerere's ambition was for something approaching a hegemonic role in East Africa.[46] Given the provocation by the occupation of the Kagera Salient, the brutal behaviour of the Ugandans, the inability of the OAU to deal with the matter and the predisposition to intervene, as demonstrated by the early part of this chapter, this intervention was not as surprising as some more superficial accounts would suggest. At the end of the war, many Ugandans were of the opinion that the Tanzanian troops outstayed their welcome. At first, they had been well-behaved and they were welcome, but the honeymoon was short-lived. There was one serious incident when Tanzanian troops attacked civilians at the Kajansi Trading Centre near Kampala in January 1980, said to be an effort to destabilise the regime of Godfrey Binaisa, who had taken over as President when Lule was ousted.[47] Further as they progressed through to Kampala, Tanzanians indulged in much looting and caused much damage. Coming from very poor rural communities themselves, they were astonished at the comparative wealth and material possessions of Ugandans, and felt angry that they had been obliged to come and 'rescue' a population who were better off then themselves.[48] How long should the Tanzanians have stayed? In political circumstances which are outside the scope of this chapter, it appeared that Nyerere gave considerable support to his friend Milton Obote, who arrived back in Uganda in May of that year, and won the elections in December (many allege fraudulently) to become President for the second time. Tanzanian troops assisted in no small measure: at the time of the elections they were guarding the towns of Masaka, Mubende, Fort Portal and Mbale, while Ugandan troops guarded Kampala. Tanzanian advisers to Obote apparently stayed on until as late as 1984.[49] Nyerere's recent death, in October 1999 and the appearance of numerous obituaries, afford a second opportunity to assess world opinion about this particular venture in his career. The surprising feature of the obituaries is how little is referred to; it is evidently regarded as just one of the manifestations of his general record of support for humanitarian and liberation causes. 'Julius Nyerere: the Conscience of Africa' was the heading of one obituary, which mentioned the invasion but without comment.[50] It was linked with his backing of the liberation movements in Mozambique, Angola, Zimbabwe,

Namibia, and the fettering of apartheid in South Africa [though as we have seen it was in fact a very different enterprise].[51] As praise was heaped upon him by the UN, the OAU, and, among others, Madeleine Albright, US Secretary of State, who called him 'one of the century's great freedom fighters ... [who] set a standard for humanitarianism in the world', the unique character of the Uganda invasion was lost sight of. Tom Porteous in *The Independent* however draws attention to the issue that the invasion raised which has most relevance to African today: condemned at the time by the OAU, 'it showed Nyerere as a risk-taker who was prepared to put his humanistic principles above the slogan of 'territorial integrity' behind which so many African dictators sought – and seek – to conceal the determined pursuit of their self-interest and self-preservation at the expense of their people'.[52] In the age of intervention in present-day Africa, Nyerere's invasion would not have attracted so much criticism as it did then. It marked a mile-post in the history of Africa.

Notes

1 Furley, Oliver (1989), 'Britain from Uganda to Museveni: Blind Eye Diplomacy', in Kumar Rupesinghe (ed). *Conflict Resolution in Uganda*, James Currey, London.

2 A good account of these events is in Avirgan, T. and Honey, M. (1982), *The War in Uganda. The Legacy of Idi Amin*, Tanzania Publishing House Ltd, Dar es Salaam.

3 Otunnu, Omara, A. (1987), *Politics and the Military in Uganda 1890-1985*, Macmillan, London, pp. 140-141.

4 The Observer, 5.11.78.

5 *Africa Confidential,* 15.12.78, *Africa Research Bulletin*, 1-31 October 1978, *The Times*, 13, 14 and 27.10.78.

6 Vicky Ntetema, 'Nyerere: a Personal Recollection', BBC Online Network 14.10.99.

7 Avirgan and Honey, op. cit., pp. 58-60.

8 *The Daily Telegraph*, 4.11.78.

9 *The Sunday Times*, 5.11.78. Nyerere, along with President Kaunda of Zambia, had actually 'considered themselves at war with South Africa, and saw the military option as a short-cut towards majority rule', in this campaign by the Frontline states to bring down the apartheid system in South Africa and white rule in Rhodesia. Edward Heath (1998) *The Course of my Life. My Autobiography*, Coronet Books, Hodder and Stoughton, London, p. 478. The Frontline states were Angola, Botswana, Mozambique, Tanzania and Zambia. Of these, Tanzania was regarded as the leader, providing bases and training camps for southern African guerillas.

10 *New Africa*, December 1978, p. 23.
11 Ibid., and *The Observer*, 5.11.78.
12 Avirgan and Honey, op. cit., p. 66.
13 According to A. B. Kasozi, Obote's group had 700 men, growing to 5,000 by June 1979. Museveni's FRONASA group had 300, or 3,000 by the time they reached Kampala. But the third group, the Save Uganda Movement, lost 140 drowned in Lake Victoria in a disastrous invasion by boat. *The Social Origins of Violence in Uganda, 1964-1985*, McGill-Queen's University Press, Montreal and Kingston, Canada, 1994, p. 127.
14 *Africa Confidential,* 15.12.78, *Africa Research Bulletin*, November 1-30, 1978, and *The Daily Telegraph*, 3.11.78.
15 *Africa Research Bulletin*, December 1-31, 1978.
16 *The Observer*, 5 and 9.11.78.
17 Avirgan and Honey, op. cit., p. 70.
18 *Africa Confidential*, 14.3.79, *Africa Research Bulletin*, February 1-28, 1978.
19 *Africa Confidential*, 31.1.79, *Africa Research Bulletin*, January 1-31, 1979, *The Observer*, 14.1.79.
20 *New African*, March 1979, p. 50.
21 Avirgan and Honey, op. cit., pp. 76-77.
22 *UN Year Book*, Vol. 33, 1979.
23 Ibid., p. 262.
24 *Africa Research Bulletin,* January 1-31 and February 1-28, 1979, and *The Guardian,* 27.1.79.
25 Prunier, G. A. (1984), 'Tanzania's ambiguous Ugandan victory', *Cultures and Dévelopement*, Vol. XVI, 3-4.
26 Keegan, J. (1983), *World Armies*, 2nd Edition, Macmillan, London, p. 575.
27 Foltz, W. and Bienen, H. (1985) *Arms and the Africans*, Yale University Press, New Haven, p. 112.
28 Eye-witnesses, Uganda Church Association Newsletter, November 1979.
29 *The Observer*, 18 and 25.02.79, and *The Guardian,* 24 and 28.02.79.
30 *New African*, April 1979, p.18-19, and *The Daily Telegraph*, 3.3.79.
31 *Africa Research Bulletin*, February 1-28 1979, *The Guardian,* 1.3.79.
32 *The Financial Times,* 28.02.79, and *The Observer,* 11.03.79.
33 Avirgan and Honey, op. cit., pp. 86-87.
34 Omara Otunnu, op. cit., p. 141, *Africa Research Bulletin,* March 1-31 1979, *The Observer*, 4.03.79.
35 Avirgan and Honey, op. cit., pp. 89-93, *Africa Research Bulletin*, March 1-31, 1979.
36 *Africa Research Bulletin*, March 1-31 and April 1-30 1979, Avirgan and Honey, op. cit., Chapter 5 on 'The Moshi Unity Conference', *The Guardian* 21.03.79.
37 *Africa Research Bulletin,* April 1-30 1979, *The Daily Telegraph*, 28.3.79, *The Guardian*, 2.4.79, *The Observer*, 3.4.79.

38 Avirgan and Honey, op. cit., pp. 124-5, *The Observer*, 8.4.79.
39 *Africa Research Bulletin*, April 1-30 1979, *New African*, May 1979, p. 13, *The Guardian,* 12.4.79. Avirgan and Honey give a vivid account but clearly it derived from accompanying the Tanzanians only, pp. 125-145.
40 Avirgan and Honey, op. cit., p. 196. *The Observer* of 22.07.79 puts Tanzanian losses in soldiers at a much higher figure: c. 2,000 men.
41 *Africa Research Bulletin*, April 1-30 1979.
42 Burrows, Noreen (1979), 'Tanzania's Intervention in Uganda; Some Legal Aspects', *The World Today*, July.
43 *New African*, July 1979, pp. 18-19.
44 Svendsen, K. E. (1995), 'Development strategy and crisis management', in Legum, C., and Mmati, G. (eds), *Mwalimu: the Influence of Nyerere*, James Currey, London, p. 115 and Legum, C. 'The goal of an egalitarian society', ibid., pp. 191-192, and the *Economist*, 23.10.99.
45 Hughes, A. and May, R. (1986), 'Armies on Loan' in S Baynham (ed) *Military Power and Politics in Black Africa*, Croom Helm, London, p. 181.
46 Keegan, J., op. cit.
47 Bwenjye, F. A. (1985), *The Army of Uganda, from Amin to Obote*, Regency Press, London, pp. 173-175. His account is written strongly from the Democratic Party's point of view.
48 Interview with Henry Gombya, freelance journalist, London, 9.11.99.
49 Kasozi, A. B., op. cit., pp. 144 and 129.
50 BBC Online Network, 14.10.99.
51 Panafrican News Agency, 14.10.99.
52 *The Independent*, 15.10.99.

5 Angola

Norrie McQueen

Historically, Angola lies at the centre of a particularly complex architecture of international intervention, both intra-African and more broadly global. Over the years the interplay between its geographical location and the political contests fought out within its borders has generated extensive external intervention both *in* and *by* Angola. To the south the border with South Africa (more particularly that with South West Africa/Namibia) placed Angola within the crucible of the Apartheid state's final fight for survival. To the north the political hostility and economic covetousness of Mobutu's Zaire brought corresponding problems in the first two decades of the Angolan state. Most damagingly, following the unravelling of détente in the late 1970s, these regional entanglements quickly became enmeshed in broader global rivalries.

One side effect of two decades of continuous conflict was that by the mid-1990s the Luanda regime had acquired probably the largest and most heavily equipped armed force in Africa. An army of about 110,000 was supported by the most advanced artillery and armour to be produced in the eastern bloc before the collapse of the Soviet Union. The Angolan airforce, similarly equipped, remains immensely powerful, despite the end of the cold war and the eastern bloc armament production which went with it. While this formidable military might has proved incapable of resolving the war within Angola's borders, it has given Luanda the capacity for extensive foreign intervention. In short, the very stalemating of the civil war has provided the government with both the motive and the material to extend the battleground beyond the national frontiers. In addition to these immediate geographical and political circumstances, what might be described as a certain 'proclivity' for the idea of intervention was acquired by Angola as a result of its particular colonial experience. Uniquely in sub-Saharan Africa, the five Portuguese-speaking states (Mozambique, Guinea-Bissau, Cabo Verde and São Tomé e Príncipe in addition to Angola) formed a distinct, self-supporting group. United in part (and ironically) by the language of the colonial power, the five came to independence within months of each other after the Portuguese revolution of 1974. In addition, all five professed a similar Marxist ideology, which they had adopted and consolidated through mutual influence and collective diplomatic action during the long years of anti-colonial struggle.

It is possible to identify four phases in Angola's military involvement abroad. Firstly, even before independence, South Africa sought to stiffen Portugal's anti-guerrilla campaign during the long anti-colonial war between 1961 and 1974. Then, secondly, at the time of its independence, Angola found itself between two large, very different, but essentially conservative states: South Africa and Zaire. This pivotal geographical position meant that internal conflicts in Angola could not remain immune from external manipulation. Next, although Angola came to independence at the high tide of détente between the superpowers in the mid-1970s, the 'second cold war' already loomed on the horizon of world politics; what had been essentially regional issues around the time of independence become wholly global within a few years. The Angolan 'civil war' was co-opted by the superpowers in pursuit of the larger contest in the global South. The fourth, final, phase came with the end of the cold war. Despite the passing of superpower involvement and interest, Angola remained locked in an insoluble internal conflict. Although external interference had supplied and driven the conflict in the 1980s, real internal ethnic and regional issues had always been present. The momentum of violence continued, fuelled now by purely Angolan animosities. The conflict was sustained by the paradoxical 'curse' of Angola's great natural wealth. The simultaneous and in some ways similar civil war in Mozambique had been resolved with the help of outside mediation in the early 1990s, in large part because of the absence of obvious spoils left to fight for. This was not the case in Angola. Oil revenues financed the Luanda regime's war effort while the illicit trade in diamonds underwrote its opponents. Moreover, throughout the post independence period the Luanda regime was not simply 'subject' to external involvement, it has, at a number of key points in regional politics, sent its forces abroad. These interventions have had various degrees of success. All of them, however, were essentially external projections of Angola's continuing internal conflict. Perhaps nowhere else in Africa has the fragility of the domestic-external dichotomy in security issues been better illustrated than in Angola - whether in the importation of foreign forces or the exportation of its own.

The 'Culture' of Intervention: From the War of Liberation to the Establishment of the MPLA State

Long prior to its independence, the regional importance of Angola had brought military involvement by South Africa. During the thirteen years of spasmodic anti-colonial war Pretoria maintained a discreet but significant presence in support of Portugal. From its bases in South West Africa/Namibia the South African Defence Force (SADF) aided the anti-insurgency effort by providing the Portuguese with helicopter transport, surveillance flights and general logistical support. This involvement had become sufficiently institutionalised by the late 1960s for the creation of a joint South African-Portuguese command centre at the strategic south-western outpost of Cuito-Cunavale.[1] On the eve of independence in 1975, however, South African involvement accelerated dramatically. While South Africa appeared willing to reach a *modus vivendi* with Mozambique, its other new neighbour in the east, Angola was perceived as more of a threat. While Mozambique was thought to be 'functionally integrated' with South Africa (through its ports, railways, migrant labour and trade flows), Angola, which was potentially much richer and therefore less dependant than Mozambique, posed more of a challenge. Moreover, on the eve of independence in Angola, in contrast to Mozambique, there were available alternatives to the Marxist guerrillas awaiting the transfer of power. As Portugal lost both the will and capacity to shape events in Angola in the months leading up to its withdrawal in November 1975, Pretoria attempted what was designed to be a decisive intervention against the Marxist Popular Movement for the Liberation of Angola (MPLA: *Movimento Popular de Libertação de Angola*), which held Luanda. Limited South African incursions into southern Angola had taken place from mid-1975, initially focused on the Cunene Dam, which supplied part of Namibia's power requirements.[2] In October, however, a major invasion of around 2,000 SADF troops in an armoured column was launched. 'Operation Zulu', as it was called, brought together a ragbag of anti-MPLA forces including right- wing Portuguese settlers and renegade elements of the colonial army.[3] Under this South African umbrella - and more prominently *behind* it, laying claim to the territory it advanced through - was the smaller of the MPLA's internal rivals, Jonas Savimbi's National Union for the Total Independence of Angola (UNITA: *União Nacional para a Independência Total de Angola*). The South African drive from the south eventually reached the Queve river, about 200 kilometres south of Luanda.[4]

UNITA's ally against the MPLA, the numerically larger National Front for the Liberation of Angola (FNLA: *Frente Nacional de Libertação de Angola*) also had a presence in the South African column. The more substantial FNLA threat, however, was from the north, and this too involved a significant element of foreign intervention: two battallions of Zairean regulars.[5] This combined force, with some former Portuguese army troops and a sprinkling of (largely useless) white mercenaries pushed towards Luanda, reaching almost to its outer suburbs on the very eve of independence. The bases of Zaire's interest in Angola at this time were varied. The FNLA leader, Holden Roberto, was related to Zairean president Mobutu Sese Seko by marriage and relied on the resources of the Zairean state in his war with the MPLA. Beyond family and ethnic affinities with the FNLA, Zaire had more directly material interests in the outcome of the struggle for the Angolan state. Both Zaire and the Republic of Congo (Brazzaville) had long cast covetous glances at Angola's oil-rich Cabinda enclave which cut into their territories from the Atlantic coast. Portugal's first post-revolutionary president, the conservative General António de Spínola, sought to co-opt Mobutu into the search for a 'solution' to the Angolan question, which would marginalize the MPLA. According to some reports this would involve a free hand for Zaire in Cabinda.[6] In the event it was yet another foreign intervention that saved the situation for the MPLA: the arrival of thousands of Cuban combat troops. The Cubans and the MPLA army (FAPLA - *Forças Armadas Populares Angolanas*) quickly scattered the FNLA in the north and gradually pushed the South Africans back to Namibia in the south.[7]

This early flurry of foreign intervention set the terms of the Angolan civil war until the end of the 1980s. The FNLA quickly ceased to be a significant element in the Angolan equation. UNITA, on the other hand - with direct South African support and growing American backing - grew in military strength and diplomatic significance.[8] Angola declined into a state of apparently permanent, externally supported civil war. While American treasure and South African intervention sustained UNITA, the Soviet Union and Cuba provided the same for the MPLA. Now, simultaneously, with this intervention of foreign military forces in Angola, Luanda began to see the possibilities of intervening itself beyond its frontiers in pursuit of its war aims. Although there is no clear evidence that Angolan combat troops were ever committed, the MPLA extended considerable military assistance to the South West African People's Organization (SWAPO), the main Namibian nationalist guerrilla movement. Training centres and refugee camps were established and military lines of supply installed through southern Angola. Increasingly, the respective justifications for Angola's support for SWAPO's armed struggle and South Africa's interventions in southern Angola became circular, with Luanda justifying itself on the basis that a strong SWAPO would reduce South Africa's capacity for intervention in Angola, and Pretoria claiming that its incursions into Angola were simply a consequence of the MPLA's support for SWAPO.

A similar cycle of confrontation was present in the north. With the FNLA more or less defunct, the Mobutu regime now sponsored UNITA, which had begun pushing beyond its ethnic heartland in Angola's central plateau to fill the geo-ethnic space vacated by the FNLA. The MPLA, for its part, nurtured the remnants of the secessionist forces from the Congo (Zaire) province of Katanga. This so-called 'gendarmerie' had in fact been the military force behind Moise Tshombe's short-lived separatist state established following the Congo's chaotic decolonization in 1960. Following the collapse of the secession these forces sought refuge with the Portuguese in northern Angola, Portugal having in common with other imperial-minded European states been sympathetic to Katanga. By the time of Angola's independence Mobutu's brutal centralism made these refugees - now well into their second generation - natural allies of his MPLA opponents. They soon formed a distinct elite - the 'Katangan Tigers' - within FAPLA. When secessionist pressures broke through again in the old Katanga province (now renamed Shaba) in 1977 and 1978, Luanda was happy to facilitate the cross border movements of these forces which were now, strictly speaking, as much Angolan soldiers as foreign separatists. To both south and north, therefore, the interplay of Angola's civil conflict and those of its neighbours became militarily intermeshed.

The Lusophone Connection and the Culture of Multilateralism

The other element that we suggested might have contributed to a propensity for foreign intervention on the part of the MPLA was its distinct, shared colonial experience. The co-ordination of the anti-colonial movement throughout Portuguese Africa had many and complex cultural roots, but it first took institutional form in 1961 when the Conference of Nationalist Organizations of the Portuguese Colonies (CONCP: *Conferência das Organizações Nacionalistas das Colónias Portuguesas*) was established in Algiers. For thirteen years the CONCP provided the basis for a joint diplomatic campaign against Lisbon's African policies on the part of Frelimo (*Frente para a Libertação de Moçambique*) in Mozambique and the PAIGC (*Partido Africano para a Independência da Guiné e Cabo Verde*) in Guinea-Bissau and in Cabo Verde. Later the CONCP 'adopted' and nurtured the liberation movement in São Tomé (MLSTP: *Movimento para a Libertação de São Tomé e Príncipe*). The influential diplomatic support of its sister organizations in the CONCP was of considerable value to the MPLA, particularly in the rest of Africa, when it was fighting for ascendancy in Angola during 1975. The group identity which was at the same time both reflected in and nurtured by the CONCP carried on in the post-independence period with the creation of the (organization of) African Portuguese Speaking Countries (PALOP: *Países Africanos de Língua Oficial Portuguesa*) in Luanda in 1979. There was never any serious consideration of the CONCP or PALOP assuming a significant military dimension. Nor were all the Portuguese-speaking states equally enthusiastic about the continuation of the link.[9] But a culture of multilateralism had been planted by the CONCP.

The most tangible example of this came in 1978 when a force of about 1,500 Angolan troops was sent to São Tomé e Príncipe at the request of the MLSTP regime there. The archipelago, some 240 kms out in the Atlantic, is the smallest of the PALOP states with a population assessed by a Portuguese minister at the time of independence as barely enough to fill a football stadium - around 110,000. São Tomé's nearest landfall on the continent is Gabon, and the tension between its Lusophone history and culture on the one hand and its proximity to Francophone neighbours on the other was evident even before independence.[10] This tension was reflected in splits within the governing MLSTP. These factional divisions then became entwined with perceived threats from the outside. In 1978, in the third year of its independence, something of a panic descended on the country over intentions of both South Africa in pursuit of strategic 'assets' in its campaign against Angola, and France after a recent mercenary-led intervention in the Comoros.[11] Since independence São Tomé e Príncipe had developed particularly close links with Angola, at least in part as a counterbalance to Gabonese (and more broadly Francophone) influence. It had been one of the first African states to recognise the MPLA regime in Luanda while the threat from the FNLA and South Africa was at its height at the end of 1975. Its oil requirements were met on preferential terms by Angola and, reflecting the duality of its regional identity, its two air-links with the outside world were *via* Libreville in Gabon, (which was geographically rational) and Luanda (which was not). Additionally, the São Tomé president, Manuel Pinto da Costa, had a good personal relationship with his Angolan counterpart, Agostinho Neto, up to the latter's death in 1979. The vulnerability imposed by its microstate status was a sensitive issue in São Tomé, however. The external perception that its place in the international system could only be comprehended in terms of its relationship with its larger neighbours clearly irritated its leaders. In 1977 the prime minister, Miguel Trovoada complained that '(a)fter our independence it was said and written that we were going to be "Gabonized" now there are some Cuban technicians here, that we are "Angolanized". We are neither Gabonese nor Angolans, and what is good in Libreville or Angola is not necessarily good in São Tomé'.[12]

Whatever the broader political setting in which it took place, the presence of the Angolan contingent from 1978 (which was about three times the size of São Tomé's own paramilitary force) was a stabilising element and reassured the nervous MLSTP regime. By the mid-1980s, however, the ideological map of Africa was changing and São Tomé was following its one-time Marxist partners in the PALOP group in their *abertura* (opening) to the west. The threat of neo-colonial conspiracy, real or supposed, was not now so potent. Military assistance (though not intervention) was now being sought by the MLSTP from Portugal and the United States. The continued presence of the Angolans (as well as the small number of Cuban technicians who were also in São Tomé) was no longer either strategically necessary or politically desirable. Overall, however, the intervention had been a successful one for Angola as well as São Tomé. Luanda's involvement was not purely altruistic, whatever the rhetoric of revolutionary solidarity in which it was dressed.[13] It was far from certain that the security concerns of the MLSTP government were unfounded. The Angolan presence had deterred any mercenary-led intervention which might have been considered, whether by Pretoria or by the predominantly conservative forces of political *francophonie*. In this way the principal regional patrons of the MPLA's internal enemies were blocked out of a potentially important strategic base, and the radical Lusophone identity of São Tomé safeguarded. For the MPLA the intervention had a clear justification as an exercise in strategic pre-emption.

The Intervention in the Republic of Congo (Brazzaville)

Whatever its underlying objectives in terms of Angola's internal conflicts, the intervention in São Tomé e Príncipe could in many respects be characterized as a 'peacekeeping' operation. Its immediate purpose was to stabilise a highly febrile domestic environment through an act of 'preventive diplomacy' - the deterrence of physical incursions from the outside. The essential 'Angolan' interests involved in the subsequent intervention in the Republic of Congo were much more obvious. Successive regimes in Brazzaville had maintained largely co-operative and cordial relations with Luanda from the time of Angola's independence until the early 1990s. In part this was the result of a natural balancing of power against their common neighbour, Zaire. But between 1979 and 1992 there was also a distinct ideological affinity between the MPLA and the professed Marxist president of Congo, Denis Sassou Ngeusso. The coming to power of the new Congolese president coincided closely with that of Eduardo dos Santos in Angola who succeeded Agostinho Neto after the latter's sudden death in 1979, and the two new heads of state enjoyed a good relationship. In 1992, however, succumbing to the broad trend of democratization in sub-Saharan Africa, Congo held its first open election. This resulted in the defeat of Sassou Ngeusso and his replacement by Pascal Lissouba. There was in truth little ideological significance in the change of regime, the regional dimension was probably more significant in the supplanting of a Sassou Ngeusso, a northerner, with Lissouba who was from the south of the country. But the implications for Angola and the external spillage of its war with UNITA were important. Under the new regime UNITA, hitherto firmly excluded from Congo by Sassou Nguesso, was able to extend from Zaire the trading activities which largely funded its war. It was also able to establish alternative supply lines into northern Angola from the Congolese port of Point Noire (through which, ironically, Cuban troops had rushed to the defence of the MPLA in late 1975). The basis of the Lissouba-UNITA relationship appears, as is now common in the region, to be based on mutually lucrative commercial relationships.[14]

By the second half of 1997 a number of factors had come together to push Luanda into military intervention in Congo. Firstly, the Mobutu regime in Zaire had just been overthrown by the coalition of forces under Laurent Kabila, and there was a real expectation in Luanda that UNITA would now be excluded from what had been its main foreign *entrepôt*. It was all the more important now to shut down any alternatives that might be developed. Secondly, the cease-fire within Angola, which had been a central part of the 1994 Lusaka peace agreement, was generally holding.[15] However, the Luanda regime was increasingly frustrated by UNITA's endless evasions in the implementation of the long-term political and military requirements of the accord. It was deeply suspicious that the cease-fire was being used by UNITA to re-organize and re-equip for yet another resumption of the civil war. Additionally, it had not only been UNITA that had benefited from Lissouba's presidency. The desultory and fissiparous campaign by the Cabindan Liberation Front (FLEC: *Frente de Libertação do Enclave de Cabinda*) which had been going on since before Angola's independence, had smouldered back into life with the availability of new rear bases and supply routes. At the same time, the absence of immediate military pressure on the Angolan army inside the national territory because of the cease-fire permitted Luanda a certain latitude in the use of its forces (now the supposedly integrated FAA: *Forças Armadas Angolanas*, which had replaced FAPLA as part of the peace agreement). The Republic of Congo's second democratic election was scheduled for 1997, and Luanda clearly hoped that Sassou Ngeusso would return to power. However, the tensions of the campaign triggered widespread violence. After his defeat in 1992 Sassou Ngeusso had returned to his power base in the north where he surrounded himself, warlord fashion, with his own private army, his so-called 'Cobra militia'. Following an assassination attempt by Lissouba supporters in May 1997 he moved to Brazzaville, where, with his militia, he posed an obvious challenge to the authority of the government and its own semi-private forces. Fighting between the factions broke out in early June and intensified over the following weeks.

Luanda was now faced with a dilemma. The electoral process in Congo was obviously at an end. An attempt at mediation by the Gabonese president, Omar Bongo, had come to nothing. Although under military pressure, Lissouba still had the resources of the state at his disposal. The general chaos could provide an opening both for the extension of UNITA's presence in the country, turning it into a full substitute for the supposedly 'lost' Zaire (now the Democratic Republic of Congo). By the same token, FLEC's separatist campaign might now become more than the mere irritant it had been for most of the post-independence period. Consequently, on 12 October an Angolan infantry force of about 1,500 backed by heavy armour entered Congo from Cabinda and moved on the southern towns of Loudima and Dolisie. Simultaneously, Lissouba was reported to have enlisted UNITA fighters to his cause.[16] Three days later, with Angolan air support, Sassou Nguesso's forces took Brazzaville. The Angolans, whose numbers had now increased to about 3,000, then clinched his victory by taking (and comprehensively looting) Pointe Noire.[17] Pascal Lissouba fled the country, according to some reports to UNITA-held territory in Angola.[18]

On the face of it the intervention had been short, sharp and decisive and had succeeded in achieving clear and limited objectives. UNITA was now effectively removed from Congo and the FLEC campaign, denied external bases and supply routes, could be expected to subside once more. There were, however, considerable and enduring political and military costs involved. Reacting immediately to the Angolan incursion from Cabinda, Congo complained to the UN.[19] An emergency meeting of the Security Council was accordingly convened and a resolution passed condemning 'all external interference in the Republic of Congo including the intervention of foreign forces' and called for their immediate withdrawal.[20] The effect was to lessen Luanda's credibility in the interior diplomacy of the UN at a crucial time for the internal peace process. Two months previously, in August 1997, the Security Council was finally provoked by Savimbi's obstruction of the Lusaka process into agreeing sanctions against UNITA. Their implementation, however, had been deferred until the end of October to permit a final chance for compliance.[21] This had been a considerable diplomatic gain for Luanda. But it was now in danger of being tarnished, on the very eve of the imposition of the anti-UNITA measures, by the Congo intervention.

UNITA and its remaining foreign supporters were quick to pick up on this. In the United States, Senator Jesse Helms used his position as chair of the Senate Committee on Foreign Relations to write to Secretary of State Madeleine Albright, to complain of what he saw as the 'tepid US response' to this 'direct violation of the United Nations Charter'. Specifically, he complained of the failure of the Security Council resolution which condemned foreign intervention to name the states involved. He did, however, rather let Savimbi's cat out of its bag by characterizing the intervention, correctly, as 'a strategic assault on UNITA, as the Republic of the Congo had become a key resupply route for UNITA'.[22] Why, it might legitimately be asked, should UNITA require a re-supply route in the midst of a peace process aimed at its disarming and demobilization? However, UNITA, and through it Helms, raised some serious issues about the nature of the MPLA's own commitment to the Lusaka process. UNITA statements also provided an insight, partisan but credible, into the decision-making processes at the centre of the Luanda regime. The intervention in Congo could itself be represented as a breach of the Accords which required that both the Angolan parliament (the National Assembly) and the United Nations Observer Mission be informed of any troop movements. A UNITA statement noted that the 'decision to wage undeclared war ... was taken by the shadowy Government based at Futungo de Belas, the Angolan presidential complex, and not the GURN [the government of national unity and reconciliation established under the Lusaka agreement]'. Nor, the statement continued, had there been any consultation with the National Assembly or the nine UNITA generals now 'integrated' in the FAA.

> The decision to spend millions of dollars to overthrow the democratically elected Lissouba Government was made in Futunga de Belas. The ... expenditure for their aggression against the Republic of Congo did not come from the national treasury. It came from Futungo de Belas, which controls the majority of the country's wealth with no checks and balances.[23]

Whether, as UNITA believed, this decision-making by presidential clique was motivated by a determination to exclude it from participation, whether it emerged simply from a realistic assessment of an already failed Lusaka process, or whether it came merely from the residual 'Stalinist' habits of the 'old' MPLA, it said little for the prospects of a successful outcome for the internal peace process. At all events, American condemnation, restrained in the Security Council in the immediate aftermath of the Angolan incursion, gradually became more robust, and by the end of October Washington's UN ambassador, Bill Richardson, was threatening to suspend US aid to Angola if it did not withdraw from Congo.[24] Forced on the defensive, dos Santos insisted that the Angolan presence was necessary for the maintenance of stability and would be withdrawn when security was restored.[25]

In the event, stability did not return quickly to the Republic of Congo. Sassou Nguessa proved incapable of consolidating his regime, and by the end of 1998 was facing a challenge from Lissouba's former prime minister, Bernard Kolelas. Kolelas, who, of course, had his own 'militia' (the rather unimaginatively named 'Ninjas'), was reportedly in contact with UNITA by early 1999.[26] The Angolans thus found themselves bogged down in an apparently insoluble situation which, uncannily, replicated in miniature many aspects of Angola's own civil war. By mid-1998 Angola officially acknowledged the presence of 2,000 men in Congo (though independent reports put the number at closer to 8,000) and international pressure for their withdrawal continued.[27]

The Intervention in Zaire/Democratic Republic of Congo (Kinshasa)

In the meantime, Angola had intervened in another northern neighbour: the former Zaire, now the Democratic Republic of Congo (DRC). Following the Shaba crises of 1977 and 1978, and under external pressure from Zaire's western patrons, Kinshasa and Luanda had reached agreements designed to prevent the use of their respective territories as bases for attacks against the other.[28] They proved no more meaningful than most such inter-state commitments in Africa. As UNITA cranked up its war against the MPLA regime in the early 1980s, Zaire became ever more important as a rear base and supply channel. At the same time, the Katangan Tiger force of former secessionist gendarmes remained an important component in Angola's security structure. Increasingly, the Angola-Zaire relationship became emblematic of the 'second cold war' in the Third World.

As the Mobutu regime began to disintegrate in 1996 and 1997 various strands around the Angola-Zaire relationship were activated. Luanda organized the air-lift of the Katangan Tigers to Kabila's forces (Kabila himself is a 'Katangan') where they were a crucial component of an otherwise under-trained army. On the other side, Savimbi sent UNITA fighters to support Mobutu's beleaguered national army.[29] The stakes were high for both sides. For Luanda the crisis offered an opportunity finally to pitch UNITA out of its principal foreign base. The end of the Mobutu regime appeared to threaten the economic and logistical basis of

UNITA's war. In recent years some $500 million worth of Angolan diamonds had been traded by UNITA through Zaire, with arms and equipment passing back down to Angola.[30] Angola was among the first to recognise the new regime after the Mobutuists had been driven out of Kinshasa in May 1997. At Kabila's swearing-in ceremony on 30 May dos Santos was effusive, declaring it 'a glorious day for the people of the democratic Republic of Congo, Angola, central Africa and Africa at large'.[31] Maintaining the momentum of its advantage the FAA launched attacks in northern Angola against what it claimed were pro-Mobutu elements dispersed from the DRC.[32] While strictly speaking this may have been accurate, it was substantially misleading, as these were almost certainly UNITA fighters attempting to re-enter Angola after their defeat in the DRC. The confusion surrounding the Zaire/DRC conflict, however, provided hawkish chief of staff of the FAA, General João de Matos (who was himself part of the Futungo de Belas circle) with an opportunity to strike at UNITA outside the constraints of the Lusaka process.

Ultimately, Kabila was to prove a considerable disappointment to many of his friends, both Congolese and foreign, in the first year of his presidency. After months of simmering ethnic and regional tensions, full-scale revolt broke out at the beginning of August 1998. Kabila's former allies to the north, Rwanda and Uganda, were soon implicated in the uprising. Angola too had reason for dissatisfaction with Kabila's performance. The rapid and total exclusion of UNITA from the DRC that Luanda had expected after the fall of the Mobutu regime had not happened. Old Zairean habits continued, with lucrative relationships being established between UNITA and local officials in the south of the country.[33] Angola's military leaders were said to be particularly frustrated at the continued tolerance of UNITA in the DRC.[34] Initially, therefore, Luanda was ambivalent towards the anti-Kabila revolt. If anything, it appeared to be benevolently neutral in favour of the rebels. At the outset Rwanda had informed Angola of its support from the rebellion on the assumption that it would be generally sympathetic. In the early phase of the crisis Angola had permitted the transport of men and arms in Rwandan aircraft across its air-space from their rear base at Goma in the east to Kitona in the west.[35] Luanda reportedly assured the Rwandans that they would do nothing to hinder the rebellion for at least fifteen days.[36] Angolan reluctance to come to Kabila's support was understandable for a number of reasons. A new and less corrupt regime in Kinshasa, particularly one indebted to Luanda, might be more reliable in moving against UNITA. This concern with Kabila's failure to deal with the presence of cross-border guerrilla bases in the DRC was, after all, the main motivation for Rwandan and Ugandan support for the revolt. Also, in August 1998 the Lusaka-brokered cease-fire in Angola was just about holding, but the broader peace process was evidently unravelling, and it was therefore important not to dissipate military resources. This calculation was all the more pressing because, as we have seen, several thousand Angolan troops were still bogged down across the border in the Republic of Congo. And, that intervention had done Angola no diplomatic good in the wider world, particularly in the United States. If the Lusaka process was indeed about to collapse, it was important for Luanda to maintain the maximum possible international 'respectability'.

What then brought the FAA into Zaire in support of the besieged Kabila? The decision appears to have been taken at a meeting in Harare on 18-19 August where the interventionist case was pushed relentlessly by the Zimbabwean president, Robert Mugabe. Even here, Angola's lack of enthusiasm was illustrated by its decision to send only a deputy minister at the head of its delegation. In the event, however, both Angola and, with less obvious reason, Namibia, agreed to join Zimbabwe in a military intervention to rescue Kabila from what at that point looked like impending disaster. There were probably three reasons that moved dos Santos to approve Angolan participation. Firstly, one likely outcome of a rebel success would have been the break-up of the DRC, with the secession at least of the historically separatist Katanga (whence Kabila was reported to have fled as Kinshasa came under rebel pressure). The chaos in the southern regions of the DRC that would accompany this would threaten the security of northern Angola and offer a raft of opportunities to UNITA. Secondly, a close relationship continued between the Katangan Tigers and influential elements in FAPLA/FAA with which they had previously served. Now DRC-based the Tigers were strongly pro-Kabila as a fellow Katangan. Thirdly, the rebels' main advance base at Kitona in the western part of the country was now adjacent to the border with the Cabinda enclave and this was always going to be a major security issue for Luanda on both military and economic grounds. This concern was deepened by a fourth element in the calculation. Reports were beginning to circulate of UNITA involvement with the rebels. These remained unconfirmed, and in the circumstances were probably unconfirmable. When questioned about the role of UNITA in the revolt some time after Angola's intervention, General de Matos was uncharacteristically reticent. There were, he said 'indications' and after due investigation a report would be made to the 'competent authorities'.[37] But even the rumour of UNITA involvement was a potent card in the hands of those, like Mugabe, who were anxious to press Angola into action.

UNITA, for its part, used the closed decision-making around the intervention to point a spotlight at the supposed anti-democratic nature of the Luanda regime as it had done the previous year over the intervention in the Republic of Congo. It also announced, rather gnomically, that 'if MPLA thinks it has interests to defend in (the DRC) UNITA also would like to make it known that it has similar interests'.[38] At no point, though, did UNITA claim or confess to any active involvement in the conflict. Certainly, the UNITA connection had no place in the early announcements of Angola's decision to send forces. The deputy foreign minister who attended the Harare meeting, Jorge Chicote, spoke only of a 'collective decision' to support Kabila militarily. In pursuit of this Angolan forces began to drive back the rebel advance in the west of the country on 20 August. Their main area of operation was around the port of Matadi and the rebel base at Kitona, close to the Cabinda frontier. In the meantime, Zimbabwean troops stiffened the defence of Kinshasa, which was now in serious danger of falling. The intervention reversed the fortunes of the war and saved the Kabila regime from almost certain defeat.

Chicote's statement after the Harare meeting included the first airing of what would become Luanda's standard diplomatic justification for its actions. The intervention was to be represented as a multilateral operation 'authorised' by the Southern African Development Community (SADC). The Harare meeting, which had in fact been called unilaterally by Mugabe with the specific intention of organising a military intervention in support of Kabila, now became a 'SADC summit'. In reality, ten of the fourteen-member community were much less keen on intervention than the three actively involved and the DRC itself, but the organization provided an invaluable source of legitimacy for the interventionist states.[39] This was particularly important, for reasons already explored, in mediating the action to the United States. Admittedly, Washington was probably less uncomfortable with the propping up of Kabila than with the ousting of Lissouba in the Republic of Congo; the DRC intervention could, after all, be represented as a defence of a certain 'status quo'. But Luanda was still concerned to justify its actions in terms of a multilateral mandate. Addressing the House of Representatives International Relations Sub-Committee in mid-September, the Angolan ambassador in Washington, António dos Santos França, put a multiple gloss on the intervention, which was carefully blended to meet American concerns. The stability of the DRC, which had borders with nine states, was crucial for the security of the entire central African region, he argued. For Angola in particular the conflict posed 'a direct threat to Angola's strategic national assets, our on-going peace process, the security of our extensive border with (DRC), and our relations with many of our neighbours'. Therefore, 'at the specific request of President Kabila my government sent forces to the (DRC) as part of larger Southern African Development Community ... operations ... I want to stress that our troops are stationed in the (DRC) as part of the SADC operation, which is a direct response to President Kabila's request for assistance from that organization'. Then, switching back to 'legitimate' national interests, he justified the action 'in order to pre-empt UNITA from utilizing instability in the (DRC) to further stall the Angolan peace process and from exploiting the situation to circumvent UN sanctions, specifically regarding the re-supply of military equipment and movement of UNITA personnel across the border'. Significantly, though, there were no accusations of active UNITA involvement on the rebel side. At all events, the Angolan intervention was limited and its forces would be withdrawn 'as quickly as possible (because) we do not consider ourselves the region's policeman'. A negotiated solution and the formation of a government of national unity was Angola's favoured outcome.[40]

This insistence on the limited nature of Angola's aims in DRC was another *leitmotif* in Luanda's self-justification. In a way of course this contradicted the claim that Angola was acting as a good regional citizen on behalf of the SADC and international stability. But, the two explanations were frequently advanced in tandem. On the one hand, Angola was just part of 'a coalition of SADC nations', on the other it was defending its strategic economic interests in Cabinda and preventing UNITA from exploiting a chaotic situation. In October the official position presented by the Washington embassy for local consumption was reiterated in these terms:

> Angola's decision to support the SADC operation stems from its deep concern for regional stability. The unrest in the [DRC], one of Africa's largest nations,

> has the potential to destabilise the entire central/southern African region. In addition, the rebel's western advances directly threatened Angola's key strategic asset: oil production. At the same time, border security with the [DRC] was at risk and the danger existed that those who seek to destroy Angola's peace process would use the upheaval ... for their own militaristic purposes.[41]

Yet, as we have seen, from the beginning dos Santos did not have the same enthusiasm for the project as Mugabe, and this continued to be the case as the intervention dragged on.[42] With the 'Cabinda corridor' secure after the expulsion of the rebels from Matadi and their base at Kitona in the first days of the intervention, Angola's aims had essentially been achieved. Beyond Luanda's concern with American reaction, it had also to worry about that of South Africa. Nelson Mandela had initially opposed external military involvement in favour of regional negotiation, even in the face of Mugabe's bellicosity. Moreover, after the earlier Angolan involvement in both the Republic of Congo and (pre-DRC) Zaire, Pretoria was becoming suspicious of the overall intentions of Angola in the region.[43] There was now an expectation that, having secured its interests in the west, Angola would not extend its involvement to the rebel heartlands in the east.[44] After the initial engagements, particularly at Kitona where losses were reportedly high, Angola does not appear to have suffered the same level of casualties as Zimbabwe.[45] Its main contribution subsequently seems to have been in the air, with Angolan combat aircraft spearheading ground assaults by other contingents and helicopter gun-ships engaging rebel forces directly.

At all costs Luanda had to avoid an extensive and protracted presence in the DRC, in parallel with that in the Republic of Congo. But by November 1998, long after the objectives in the Cabinda corridor had been achieved, it still retained a force estimated at 4,000.[46] Then in December the Lusaka arrangements in Angola itself finally broke down and full-scale conflict resumed. In launching its offensive at this point, UNITA clearly sought to make strategic capital out of the FAA's engagement in two separate foreign fronts. With up to 5,000 of its best troops (three brigades) in the DRC alone, the Luanda regime had obviously become vulnerable at home. In this way the MPLA's exportation of the war abroad had proved disastrously counterproductive. It now faced massive internal pressure which the interventions in the two Congos had been specifically designed to prevent. By March 1999, dos Santos was pressing Kabila, though without evident success, for new political initiatives to end the conflict. Yet whatever its changing military priorities and the private doubts of the leadership around dos Santos about the nature of the DRC conflict, at the public diplomatic level Luanda remained reasonably staunch behind Kabila. While Angola backed 'all the regional initiatives aimed at a peaceful resolution of the conflict', according to its representative to the UN General Assembly, it did so only 'as long as the legitimate Government ... approved them'. And, with regard to the various military interventions, Angola insisted on the differentiation between 'those forces within the country that were invited by the government ... from those whose presence reflected different motivations'. At the same time however, Angola sought greater Security Council engagement and called for a UN-OAU convened conference 'on the peace stability and security of the Great Lakes region ... with the involvement of all the government, regions, and their respective conflicting parties'.[47] Simultaneously, the FAA was being repatriated. By the beginning of March, according to reports, the Angolan force in the DRC consisted of 'a few hundred' around Matadi, the key to the Cabinda corridor.[48]

Angolan Intervention: an Audit

Any assessment of Angola's various foreign interventions since independence must start from a understanding of their motivation. At various times (and with the happy concordance of UNITA) Luanda's military adventures have been regarded by some neighbours as 'imperialist'.[49] To the extent that any projection of military force outside the national territory could be thus defined, then the accusation has some force. But if the term is used (as it customarily is in the African context) to describe the pursuit of external territorial or economic assets, then the claim is problematic. Certainly, Zimbabwe's (or perhaps more correctly, Mugabe's) far from transparent objectives in the DRC might be so described. But the Luanda regime's concern there, as in the Republic of the Congo and even in São Tomé e Príncipe beforehand, was designed primarily to pre-empt the deterioration of its position in the internal Angolan struggle by what might be described as a policy of 'strategic denial'. This is not to argue that the kleptocratic propensities of the MPLA regime (or what UNITA would describe as the 'Futungo de Belas clique') are now any less developed than those of their neighbours. Nor is it unlikely that private economic opportunities have not been pursued on the back of military intervention. The decline of the once idealistic and visionary MPLA into a corrupt, self-enriching elite was pretty well complete within the first decade of Angolan statehood. But even as the civil war degenerated into a contest for control of resources rather than a battle of ideologies, interventions abroad became primarily extensions of that war by other means in other locations rather than the separate pursuit of foreign resources. Control of oil and diamonds (and these, of course, are only the most obvious riches among Angola's superabundance of natural resources) has been a sufficient war aim for the MPLA and UNITA, and a sufficient excuse for extending the conflict over them abroad.

For the Luanda regime, however, intervention abroad has not been an especially successful strategy in pursuit of victory at home. Certainly, the intervention in São Tomé e Príncipe succeeded in its immediate aims at low cost. Only small numbers were involved in a part-policing, part-deterrent role which saw no bodies returned to Luanda. Assuming, though, that there was indeed a threat to the microstate, either direct or covert, hatched either in Pretoria or some Francophone capital, then Angola's intervention was a timely one. A pro-UNITA 'African' regime in such a strategic location could have been a major problem for Luanda as the civil war intensified in the 1980s. The extent - even the existence - of the external threats perceived by the Pinto da Costa regime in the archipelago in 1978 however are (and will most probably remain) unclear. Assessments of the subsequent interventions in the two Congos are less ambiguous.

In the Republic of Congo Angola's hand was forced by events - indeed by events engineered by its protégé there. It would clearly have been in Luanda's interests if the scheduled elections in 1997 had taken place and Sassou Nguessa had returned to the presidency with a popular mandate. The inevitable violence that followed the squaring up between the contenders' military forces ended the electoral process. Angolan support was now only meaningful if it took a military form. Having ensured the immediate success of 'their' man, however, Angola became increasingly drawn into the violence consequent on his failure to consolidate his regime - a failure due at least in part to his lack of democratic legitimacy. The result was exactly the chaos, exploitable and exploited by UNITA, which

Luanda had sought to avoid. By mid-1999 Luanda, now militarily pressed at home, was pressing Sassou Nguessa to seek an accommodation with the forces of Pascal Lissouba and Bernard Kolelas. While such a settlement would be necessary for the FAA to disengage from Congo, it would leave UNITA's position there at least as entrenched as it had been before its arrival.

The situation is not wholly dissimilar in the DRC. Certainly the relatively limited Angolan involvement in Kabila's initial victory over the Mobutu regime was successful in divesting UNITA of a historical diplomatic and strategic asset. But, as we have seen, the new order proved unable or unwilling to expel the diamond-rich organization altogether. Business continued, if not as usual, then with some continuing vigour. By the beginning of 1998, therefore, what should have been a grand strategy to deny UNITA lodgement across both of Angola's northern borders had begun to crumble. The anti-Kabila rebellion of August 1998 faced Luanda with a dilemma. Should it maintain its support for the Kinshasa regime, underpinning it with military intervention, or should it seek to encourage a new, potentially more effective anti-UNITA regime in Kinshasa? This appeared to be a genuine policy predicament for at least the first two weeks of the rebellion. Its resolution seemed to emerge from the coercive pressure of Robert Mugabe and a grudging assessment in Luanda that the anti-UNITA cause would be best served by maintaining a chastened and ever-more dependant Kabila in office. Consequently, Angola's intervention in late August 1998 comprehensively reversed the tide of the conflict. This merely forced the rebels back on their eastern bases and created the conditions for a protracted war of attrition. Again, as in the Republic of Congo, the intervention contributed to just the prolonged 'UNITA-friendly' chaos it was designed to prevent.

The diplomatic consequences of the DRC intervention were not as damaging for Luanda as those over the other Congo at the global (that is, American) level. But regionally Angola's standing has been diminished. Relations with South Africa and with Zambia (with which the MPLA regime has long had intermittent 'difficulties') have been damaged. Moreover, by coming down for Kabila, Luanda put itself in direct opposition to its allies of the anti-Mobutu period: Rwanda and Uganda. Both these states elicit strong international sympathies from those very elements of informed opinion which in the past were generally supportive of the MPLA in the Angolan war. In March 1999 the Rwandan vice-president and defence minister, Paul Kagame, recalled the previous 'alliance' with Angola in the overthrow of the Mobutu regime and denied categorically (and credibly) any Rwandan or rebel co-operation with UNITA. 'Why', he asked, 'would we want to do that ... we remember that UNITA has worked with the *Interahamwe* and the *génocidaires*'.[50] The best perhaps that Luanda could hope for is that any comprehensive peace agreement would include provision for the exclusion of all outside armed groups from the DRC's territory, and that this would include UNITA. Even if concluded, of course, the enforcement of such an arrangement would prove virtually impossible. In the absence of a durable negotiated peace the DRC might succumb to a de facto partition between its eastern and western region with the latter subject to Kabila's (and therefore Luanda's) nominal control. The effectiveness of this 'control', however, would be questionable. The likelihood would be that a continued Angolan presence would be necessary. Even then, the exclusion of UNITA could not be guaranteed. Neither scenario offers more than a scant return for the military and political costs of the intervention.

The lesson of Luanda's foreign interventions then has been that the exportation of the civil war has had very little impact on its course. In reality, UNITA, while happy to exploit the opportunity of lodgement in neighbouring states has not (at least since the 1970s) been dependant on it. Having once established its own semi-permanent bases within Angola's borders, it has been possible for UNITA to use more distant friendly territories as channels for the export of diamonds and the import of arms and supplies. In the early 1990s it successively 'lost' Namibia and South Africa with no discernible weakening of its military effort. Exclusion from the Congos would have been unwelcome, but not catastrophic. Its network of support, particularly among the more conservative Francophone states of west and north Africa (particularly Togo and Morocco), was always a viable substitute. And, as we have seen, the mere supplanting of regimes thought to be sympathetic to UNITA did not in practice lead inevitably to its exclusion from those territories. Political will, local corruption, the barriers of geographical inaccessibility as well as generalised political instability have first to be surmounted. The dogma of UNITA as creature of malign neighbours which was established early in the civil war has combined with the simple fact of abundant military to tempt Luanda into seeking foreign solutions for want of viable internal ones for essentially internal problems.

Notes

1 Marcum, John, A. (1988), 'Regional security in southern Africa: Angola', *Survival* 30 (1), p. 5 and fn.

2 Legum, Colin (1976), 'Foreign intervention in Angola', in Legum, Colin and Hodges, Tony (1976), *The War over Southern Africa,* Rex Collings: London, p. 36.

3 See Guimarães, Fernando Andresen (1998), *The Origins of the Angolan Civil War: Foreign Intervention and Domestic Political Conflict*, Macmillan: London, pp. 109-11.

4 On the South African invasion of Angola in 1975 see Hallet, Robin (1978), 'The South African intervention in Angola, 1975-76', *African Affairs,* 77 (308), pp. 347-86.

5 Bridgland, Fred (1986), *Jonas Savimbi, a Key to Africa,* Mainstream: Edinburgh, p. 146.

6 For different accounts of the Spínola-Mobutu encounter over Angola see Robinson, R.A.H. (1979), *Contemporary Portugal: a History*, George Allen and Unwin: London, p. 213; Ebinger, Charles, K. (1976), 'External intervention in internal war: the politics and diplomacy of the Angolan civil war', *Orbis* 20 (3), pp. 686-7; Marcum, John, A. (1978), *The Angolan Revolution Volume 2*: *Exile Politics and Guerrilla Warfare, 1962-76,* MIT Press: Cambride MA, p. 251.

7 The Colombian novelist Gabriel García Márquez has provided a compelling, if somewhat romanticised, account of the Cuban's arrival in 'The Cuban mission to Angola', *New Left Review* 101-102, 1977, pp. 123-37.

8 On the nature of American support for UNITA at this time see Wright, George (1997), *The Destruction of a Nation: United States' Policy towards Angola since 1945,* Pluto: London, pp. 99-141.

9 Mozambique in particular was concerned that the colonial past should not be permitted to shape the diplomacy of the new states. Surrounded by the Anglophone states of east Africa, Mozambique was anxious to establish an African regional identity rather than maintain an imperial cultural one. It subsequently underlined this approach by joining the Commonwealth, the first non-former British territory to do so.

10 MacQueen, Norrie (1997), *The Decolonization of Portuguese Africa: Metropolitan Revolution and the Dissolution of Empire*, Longman: London, pp. 117-18.

11 *Africa Contemporary Record, 1986-87,* Vol. 19, Rex Collings: London, 1987, p. B222.

12 Quoted in *Africa Contemporary Record, 1977-78,* Vol. 10, Rex Collings: London, 1987, p. B586.

13 Newitt, Malyn and Hodges, Tony (1988), *São Tomé and Príncipe: From*

Plantation Economy to Microstate, Westview: Boulder Co., p. 116.

14 'Africa's Seven Nation War', ReliefWeb (United Nations) briefing paper, 21 May 1999 (http://wwwnotes.reliefweb.int/files/rwdom...be6070e94a5ff8948 52678600526bbf?OpenDocument).

15 The full text of the Lusaka agreement was issued as United Nations Document S/1994/1441, annex, 22 December 1994.

16 *Keesings Record of World Events* 1997, Keesings Worldwide: Cambridge, 1997, p. 41848.

17 *Journal de Notícias* (Lisbon), 21 October 1997.

18 UNITA's Political Commission issued a somewhat ambiguous 'denial' of this: it considered 'the rumour as pure and dangerous speculation that the illegally deposed President Lissouba could be in Angola in areas under our administration'. Issued by *Kwacha-UNITA Press* 31 October 1997 (http://.kwacha.com/17/english/311097.htm).

19 United Nations Document S/1997/791, 13 October 1997.

20 United Nations Document SC/6429, 16 October 1997.

21 United Nations Document S/RES/1127, 28 August 1997. On this stage of the peace process see MacQueen, Norrie (1998), 'Peacekeeping by attrition: the United Nations in Angola', *Journal of Modern Africa Studies,* 36 (3), pp. 415-18.

22 Senator Jesse Helms to Secretary of State Madeleine Albright, 29 October 1997, reproduced in Kwacha-UNITA Press, 31 October 1997 (http://.kwacha.com/17/english/311097.htm).

23 Kwacha-UNITA Press, Latest News, 31 October 1997 (http://.kwacha.com/17/english/311097.htm).

24 *New York Times*, 27 October 1997.

25 *Centre for Democracy in Angola INC News* [UNITA], 28 October 1997.

26 *The Economist*, 10-16 April 1999.

27 BBC African Service, 5 May 1998 (http://news2.thdo.bbc.co.uk/hi/english/world/africa/newsid%5F88000/8821.stm).

28 Ogunbadejo, Oye (1981), 'Angola: ideology and pragmatism in foreign policy', *International Affairs,* 57 (2), p. 261.

29 *Africa Confidential*, 38 (8), 11 April 1997. These UNITA soldiers should, of course, by then have been presented for demobilisation of integration in the FAA by the terms of the Lusaka agreement.

30 *Africa Confidential*, 38(11), 23 May 1997.

31 *O Pensador* (Angolan Embassy, Washington DC), June 1997 (http://www.angola.org/news/pensador/june97/congo.html).

32 *Keesings Record of World Events*, June 1997, p. 41670.

33 'The Congo at War', ReliefWeb briefing paper, 17 November 1998, p. 15 (http://wwwnotes.reliefweb.int/files/rwdom...83815a86bc23c12566c9006a48

f2?OpenDocument).

34 *Expresso* (Lisbon), 5 September 1998.

35 *The Economist*, 5-11 September 1998.

36 *The Congo at War*, p. 15.

37 *Expresso*, 5 September 1998.

38 Communiqué of the Permanent Committee of the Political Commission (UNITA), 25 August 1998, reprinted by Kwacha-UNITA Press (http://www.kwacha.com/en0809981.htm).

39 In addition to the three interventionist states, Angola, Namibia and Zimbabwe and the then recently admitted DRC itself, the SADC consists of Botswana, Lesotho, Malawi, Mauritius, Mozambique, Seychelles, South Africa, Swaziland, Tanzania and Zambia.

40 Angolan Embassy press release, Washington DC, 15 September 1998 (http://www.angola.org/reference/speeches/congo091598.html).

41 *O Pensador*, October 1998 (http://www.angola.org/news/pensador/october98/congo.html).

42 This is not the place for an exploration of Zimbabwe's motivations in the DRC, but the factors cited have been: the apparently lucrative joint enterprises entered into by the Zimbabwean and DCR elites, in particular between the Mugabe and Kabila families themselves; the considerable debts to Zimbabwe which the Kabila regime had run up in its first year in power; Mugabe's use of foreign military involvement as a means of distracting attention from mounting economic and social tensions at home.

43 *The Congo at War*, p. 16.

44 *The Economist*, 29 August-4 September 1998; *Angola Peace Monitor* ReliefWeb, 3 September 1998 (http://wwwnotws.reliefweb.int/files/rwdom ...4927be6998d885256675007f10deOpenDocument). According to UNITA, an assurance to this effect had actually been given by dos Santos to Mandela. Kwacha-UNITA Press, 26 August 1998 (http://www.kwacha.com/en0809981.htm).

45 Following its losses at Kitona subsequent encounters with the rebel forces in the west (for example at the hydro-electric facility at Inga which supplies Kinshasa's power) appear to have been settled by battlefield negotiation.

46 *The Times*, 4 November 1998. Other forces in the DRC fighting on Kabila's side were estimated as: 3,500 Zimbabweans; 1,000 Sudanese; 1,000 Chadians in addition to up to 8,000 Rwandan Hutus. Namibian numbers were so low as to be virtually negligible.

47 United Nations Document GA/9549, 23 March 1999.

48 *Africa Confidential*, 40 (5), 5 March 1999.

49 See, for example, the various assessments of regional positions in *The Congo at War*.

50 *Africa Confidential*, 40 (6), 19 March 1999.

6 Ethiopia and Eritrea: Insecurity and Intervention in the Horn

Christopher Clapham

Introduction

The states of the Horn of Africa have never fully subscribed to the doctrines incorporated into the Charter of the Organisation of African Unity, prohibiting intervention in the internal affairs of other African states, and promising respect for existing national frontiers. Even though those doctrines were themselves set out at the OAU's founding conference in Addis Ababa, in a document drawn up under the aegis of the government of Ethiopia, they reflected the tactical interests of that government in making common cause with other African states, rather than any commitment to the principle of non-intervention itself. Every government in the Horn has been deeply engaged in the affairs of its neighbours, and none (save possibly the microstate of Djibouti, which has lacked the means to do so) has ruled out the use of military force as part of that engagement. The recent history of intervention has thus reflected, not the breakdown of previously respected conventions of state sovereignty, but a continuation of the complex interactions between political forces in the region that reach back decades, indeed centuries, into the past. This chapter will concentrate on the governments which seized power in both Addis Ababa and Asmara in May 1991, bringing about in the process the separation of Eritrea from Ethiopia, and its emergence two years later as a recognised sovereign state. It will be especially be concerned with the war between Eritrea and Ethiopia that broke out in May 1998, and shattered the good relations between the two countries that had at least ostensibly been achieved since 1991, setting in train a new round of regional instability. A preliminary historical survey is nonetheless essential.

The politics of the Horn, domestic as well as international, is most basically concerned with the interactions (and very often the conflicts) between and within a number of major social groupings which are largely defined by altitude and ecology, religion, ethnicity and social structure, and historic traditions of governance.[1] States, in their modern sense, have been only very partially, and often haphazardly, imposed on these relationships; and the state of statehood in the region, constantly in flux, reflects the current state of play in the continuing attempts by each of these groupings to assert their hegemony over, or autonomy from, any of the others. Central to the region both geographically and politically, the Ethiopian empire sought to impose over as much of it as possible a hegemonic control founded on Orthodox Christianity, the hierarchical social structures of the northern Ethiopian plateau, the Amharic language, and deeply entrenched traditions of Ethiopian statehood. By 1962, this process of hegemonic expansion, maintained (despite vicissitudes) over the previous century, had reached its apogee with the full incorporation of the former Italian colony of Eritrea, and from then onwards Ethiopia stood on the defensive. To the west, an analogously contested hegemony was being imposed in Sudan, this time in the name of Arabism and Islam, over the peoples not only of the south but of the eastern and western regions of the country. From the later 1940s, and especially from the independence of the Somali Republic in 1960, Somalis sought in the name of ethnic nationalism to create a single state, covering the entire Somali-inhabited area, and including substantial parts of Ethiopia, Kenya and Djibouti. From the mid-1950s, virtually from the day of Sudanese independence in 1956, government control over southern Sudan was contested by force; and from the early 1960s, violent resistance likewise started against Ethiopian rule in Eritrea. After the outbreak of the Ethiopian revolution in 1974, a variety of other ethnic, regional and ideologically based movements challenged the government in Addis Ababa, by far the most effective of which was the Tigray People's Liberation Front (TPLF).

The 1970s and 1980s were marked, not only by intensifying conflict between the forces of hegemony and resistance in both Ethiopia and Sudan, but by fragmentation within several of the major counter-hegemonic groupings themselves - notably in Somalia, with the collapse of the nationalist project into fighting between different factions, but also in Eritrea, where the resistance launched by the Moslem-dominated Eritrean Liberation Front (ELF) initially fragmented, and was then reconsolidated under the aegis of the Eritrean People's Liberation Front (EPLF). By 1991, even the formal structure of statehood could no longer be maintained. The Somali state collapsed altogether in January, and the region that had previously formed British Somaliland (prior to unification with former Italian Somalia in 1960) declared its separate independence as the Republic of Somaliland. In Eritrea, the victorious EPLF established *de facto* independence in May 1991, to be formally confirmed two years later, while even in the residual part of Ethiopia, the TPLF-dominated Ethiopian Peoples' Revolutionary Democratic Front (EPRDF), which seized power in Addis Ababa at the same time, recognised the right of 'nationalities' (or ethnic groupings) to self-determination, up to and including secession.

Within this kaleidoscope of peoples, states and armies, what is to count as 'intervention', and what as the maintenance of 'sovereignty' and 'territorial integrity', is deeply confused. Essentially, the doctrine of non-intervention rests on the acceptance by neighbouring states of a common 'idea of the state', in Buzan's terms:[2] a recognition by rulers that their states are formed in similar ways and rest on similar justifications, which in turn give each of them a common interest in the mutual recognition of their sovereignty. In most of Africa (outside southern Africa, where until 1994 white minority rule clearly offended against the idea of the African state), states broadly shared the legacy of colonial partition, which each had an interest in maintaining, and which underlay the non-intervention clauses of the OAU Charter and the Cairo resolution on respect for existing frontiers of 1964. Only with the domestic crumbling of states, under the impact of bad government, civil war and economic failure, did this consensus collapse. In the Horn, it never existed. In principle, some compromise was possible between the rival hegemonies of Ethiopia and Sudan, and the frontier between them was broadly accepted; but in practice, each engaged in at least covert support for counter-hegemonic movements directed against the government of the other, in southern Sudan and in Eritrea and Tigray respectively. The Somali nationalist movement (which sought to remove the late-nineteenth century colonial boundaries, in the name of ethnic unity), and the Eritrean nationalist movement (which sought to restore the late-nineteenth century boundaries, in the name of post-colonial territorial statehood), however, directly challenged the territoriality of existing states. The southern Sudanese movement was caught between the alternative goals of separating from Sudan, along the dividing line formed by internal colonial partition and the major cleavage between indigenous ethnic groups, or else recreating Sudan on a very different basis (secular and nationalist, rather than Islamic and Arabist) from that on which it had hitherto rested. For the Ethiopian government, Sudanese support for Eritrean separatism, and Somali government support for self-determination for Ogadeni Somalis, both counted as external intervention in the internal affairs of Ethiopia; for the EPLF and the Ogadeni Western Somali Liberation Front, the illegitimate incorporation of their respective territories into Ethiopia counted as Ethiopian intervention in their own internal affairs. The contradiction was irresoluble, except by force.

Ethiopia: the Imperial and Revolutionary Governments

Up until 1991, as already noted, Ethiopia was essentially a defensive state. With the incorporation of Eritrea from 1952 (initially under a federal arrangement devised by the United Nations), and the restoration in the late 1940s and 1950s of the Somali-inhabited territories that had remained under British administration after the Second World War, it had achieved its maximum practicable territorial extension. It therefore propounded and enthusiastically supported the OAU non-intervention principles that helped to protect it, and correspondingly opposed, at least in principle, any intervention in the affairs of its neighbours. Even so, a measure of external military involvement occurred. One element in this was an exceptionally high level of militarisation. Not only have the states of the Horn 'needed' much larger militaries than in most of Africa, to protect them both against one another and against internal opposition movements; they have also been exceptionally well placed to acquire them, by linking themselves to global military alliances, especially during the Cold War, which sought regional allies adjacent to the Red Sea and Indian Ocean sea lanes, and to the southern fringe of the Middle East. For Ethiopia, this process started in the late 1940s and 1950s, with the establishment of a military relationship with the United States, which in turn encouraged and permitted 'legitimate' forms of intervention through participation in UN peacekeeping missions, notably in the Congo. As part of its highly successful continental diplomacy, Ethiopia also provided military training for liberation movements directed against white minority rule in other parts of Africa, one of the grateful recipients being Nelson Mandela.

Regionally, Ethiopian military intervention at this period was limited to a brief war with Somalia in 1964, in the course of which Ethiopian jets attacked the town of Hargeisa, and tacit involvement in support of the southern Sudanese Anyanya resistance movement during the first Sudanese civil war. There is however no evidence that this involved any commitment of Ethiopian forces beyond its frontiers, and when changes in the diplomatic relationship with Sudan made it politic to do so, it enabled Haile-Selassie to gain the leverage over the southern Sudanese opposition needed for him to play a key role in brokering the Sudanese peace settlement signed in Addis Ababa in 1972. For the most part, Haile-Selassie's own conservatism, and his interests in maintaining the OAU settlement that he had played the major part in establishing, kept Ethiopian military involvement in the affairs of her neighbours at a low level.

The revolution that broke out in 1974, and rapidly resulted in the establishment of a Marxist military government, might have been expected to lead to a massive increase in external military intervention. It did indeed eventually lead to some increase, but to nothing like the extent that might have been anticipated. For one thing, unlike most modern revolutions, the Ethiopian one remained essentially domestic: its causes were perceived as lying in specific features of the Ethiopian state structure (commonly described as 'feudalism'), rather than in the structure of the international system, or in domestic conditions replicated in neighbouring states. The Ethiopian revolutionary regime, though it became from 1977 the leading African client of the Soviet Union, and broadly sympathised with radical causes, felt no urge to export revolution beyond its own frontiers. For another, its enormous military resources (which after 1977 expanded to armed forces of over 300,000, backed by a full range of Soviet weaponry) had more than enough to keep them busy at home. Far more than intervening in other states, Ethiopia at this time was intervened in itself. The Somali invasion of 1977 was defeated in March 1978 with the help of Cuban military forces and even some Yemenis, while as the EPLF gained ground in Eritrea, so the Sudanese government shifted towards more overt sympathy with it, though without committing any troops, of which indeed the EPLF had little need.

For the Dergue as for Haile Selassie, external military involvement was therefore largely reactive: designed to undercut external support for its domestic opponents, by taking the war to their supporters' home soil. This in turn took the form of manipulating factional divisions within Somalia on the one hand, and supporting the Sudan People's Liberation Army (SPLA) on the other. In Somalia, the government of Mengistu Haile-Mariam primarily supported the Somali National Movement (SNM), which primarily represented the Isaaq clans in the former British Somaliland, and the Somali Salvation Democratic Front (SSDF), which was largely drawn from the Majerteen clan and operated into southern Somalia from across the Ogaden frontier. The seizure of two small towns just across the border in 1981, ostensibly by the SSDF, was plausibly ascribed to the Ethiopian army, but direct military intervention was limited. The Ethiopian government maintained close control over its Somali clients, and paradoxically, their capacity to damage the Siad Barre regime in Somalia was greatly increased in 1988, when the two governments agreed to withdraw support from their respective opposition movements. The SNM was forced out of Ethiopia and launched a premature offensive in northern Somalia, which was suppressed with massive casualties but helped to set in train the progressive collapse of the Somali state that culminated in the fall of Siad Barre in January 1991.

Ethiopian intervention in Sudan was also conducted largely by proxy. Although the breakdown of the Addis Ababa agreement in the late 1970s was due overwhelmingly to internal causes, the organisation, leadership and military success of the SPLA owed a great deal to Ethiopia. Its leader, John Garang, was able to establish control over a united southern opposition, very largely because of his ability to control the flow of Ethiopian military assistance. SPLA fighters were trained within Ethiopia, and Garang himself was effectively appointed to the leadership through Ethiopian influence. Symptomatically, when his chief of staff Kerubino Kuanyin Bol attempted a putsch against him in 1987, he did so by appealing to Mengistu to remove him; instead, Mengistu arrested Kerubino, and handed him over to Garang.[3] The Ethiopian alliance also imposed on the SPLA the need to uphold Sudanese national unity (since Mengistu, with the war in Eritrea on his hands, could not conceivably support secession in his neighbour), and at least ostensibly to seek a solution to the conflict by installing a revolutionary socialist regime in Khartoum.

Ethiopia's direct external military role under the Dergue was however restricted to its own immediate security perimeter, and threats by Mengistu to deploy the Ethiopian army in support of liberation in southern Africa were no more than rhetorical. Ethiopia provided aid and training facilities to liberation movements in the remaining white-ruled states of southern Africa, but though highly dependent on the Soviet Union, and benefiting from the involvement of Cubans in its own wars, it never showed any sign of providing Africa's own Cuban-style intervention force.

The Successor Regimes

The EPDRF and EPLF, which overthrew the Mengistu regime in May 1991, and then came to power in Ethiopia and Eritrea respectively, had little reason to respect the OAU norms on non-intervention, which during their own long struggles had served largely to sustain the state against which they were fighting. At the first OAU meeting that he attended as Eritrean head of state in 1993, the EPLF leader Isaias Afewerki described the organisation as 'an utter failure for thirty years'.[4] They had themselves benefited from their ability to use the open frontier with Sudan as a conduit for supplies of all kinds, and as a refuge for civilian populations and on occasion for fighters. It had been critically important, especially during the great famine of 1984/85, for the import of relief food through channels independent of the Ethiopian government. In the immediate aftermath of victory, it at first appeared that the new governments in both Ethiopia and Eritrea would concentrate on forming and protecting their own new domestic political orders, for which they needed at least a respite from engagement in regional conflicts. Both governments in particular regularised their relations with Sudan, and the EPRDF expelled SPLA fighters from western Ethiopia. Before very long, however, it became apparent that domestic state-building was too closely associated with regional politics for the two to be kept apart, and – though in somewhat altered form – familiar patterns of external involvement reasserted themselves.

The new politics of intervention reflected the new politics of state-formation. The EPRDF's introduction of a remarkable system of ethnic federalism, loosely based on that of the soon-to-be defunct Soviet Union, at least in principle softened the previously rigid centralism of Ethiopian government. Each of the country's 'nations, nationalities and peoples' was accorded, under the constitution of the new Federal Democratic Republic of Ethiopia introduced in1995, the right of self-determination 'up to and including secession'. How genuinely federal and democratic this new system actually was soon became a matter for intense debate. The EPRDF retained the TPLF at its core, with associated parties 'representing' other ethnicities, the status of which was deeply contested. Four core ethnic regions emerged, encompassing the sedentary populations of central Ethiopia, the secession of any of which was scarcely compatible with the continued existence of an Ethiopian state. The status of Tigray in the north was scarcely at issue: it dominated the central government, and the whole structure of ethnic federalism had been evolved to suit it, and corresponded to what could well be regarded as a peculiarly Tigrayan conception of Ethiopian statehood.[5] The historically dominant Amhara region, however great the resentment at a Tigrayan assumption of power at the centre, was so strongly associated with Ethiopian centralism that it could scarcely provide the basis for any viable separatist movement; Amhara opposition to the regime was divided between the yearning to re-create a monolithic Ethiopian state, and the need to promote a distinctive Amhara identity within the new political dispensation. The Southern Ethiopian Peoples' Administrative Region (SEPAR) grouped a large number of ethnicities, whose complex relations with one another, historical subordination to the Ethiopian state, and fear of Oromo hegemony made them relatively easily manageable from the centre. That left the Oromo as by far the most significant challenge to the new political order: as the largest single nationality in Ethiopia, which despite important internal divisions was able to articulate an ideology of Oromo nationalism, and which occupied much of central and southern Ethiopia including the principal zones of export production, it both gained from the federal system and presented a considerable threat to it. Controlling the Oromo became the major political concern of the EPRDF regime.

But this internal reorganisation of the Ethiopian state necessarily affected its external relations, especially because it raised the question of the relationships between peripheral peoples and the central state on the one hand, and groups across state frontiers on the other. At one level, federalism represented a retreat from the previous assertion of imperial (or highland Christian) hegemony, and opened space for the re-establishment of cross-border linkages which had been denied by the claims of territorial sovereignty. Somalis living within Ethiopia, to take the most obvious case, now formally had the right to secede from Ethiopia and unite with fellow Somalis in the Somali Republic, or indeed in Djibouti or the secessionist Republic of Somaliland. Afars within Ethiopia, so far as the Ethiopian government was concerned, could associate themselves with those in Djibouti and Eritrea. The peoples of the western borderlands could look towards Sudan. At another level, however, this softening of the frontiers provided openings for the Ethiopian state to engage in cross-border politics, by promoting a model that might well seem preferable, either to the imposition of centralised statehood by the governments in Asmara and Khartoum, or to the shambles resulting from the collapse of the Somali state.

The Somali case was initially the most urgent, since the EPRDF's accession to power occurred shortly after the fall of the Siad Barre regime, and Ethiopia was necessarily involved – given its long and uncontrollable borders with Somalia – in the politics of state breakdown. Politics within the Somali ethnic region in the new federal system inevitably turned on clan alliances, which were associated with politics across the border. During the US-led and UN-mandated intervention in Somalia in 1992/95, the Ethiopian government broadly had an interest in a settlement that would help to stabilise the area under US or UN control; it also had a good relationship with the United States, which it was happy to help in Somalia. Ethiopia therefore hosted three Somali reconciliation conferences in 1993, though these were effectively preordained to fail, as a result of the contradictions built into the intervention.[6] With the US withdrawal in 1994, followed by that of the remaining UN force in 1995, Ethiopia assumed a more active role. Any pretence of neutrality became impossible to sustain, and Ethiopia supported the opposition to the faction led by Mohamed Farah Aideed (and subsequently his son, Hussein Aideed), and to the Islamist organisation, Al-Ittihad.[7] This support extended to major incursions across Ethiopia's southern frontier with Somalia (i.e. into former Italian Somalia, rather than Somaliland) from 1996 onwards, and the provision of arms to a variety of factions opposed to Hussein Aideed. With the outbreak of the Ethiopia-Eritrea war, which was followed by Eritrean support (in the form of training and arms, rather than direct intervention) for pro-Aideed groups and for the Oromo Liberation Front (OLF) opposition to the EPRDF, Ethiopian intervention was correspondingly stepped up. Whether these interventions had (from the Ethiopian viewpoint) any positive effect, and indeed whether Ethiopia had any continued interest in a settlement in Somalia at all, remained at best uncertain.

Analogously, though less intensively, the politics of the Gambela and Benishangul-Gumuz regions of western Ethiopia were associated with Ethiopia's relations with Sudan, as well as with the containment of the OLF threat.[8] This area has for centuries been a borderland between Ethiopia and Sudan, and many of the people in it have positioned themselves on one side of the border or the other, in response to the current political situation.[9] After 1991, the fragmented local political party system resulting from the introduction of the new politics of ethnic federalism was subjected to the external pressures imposed by the conflict between the Sudanese Islamist regime and the SPLA/NDA on one side of the border, and that between the

EPRDF government in Ethiopia and the OLF on the other. Between 1995 (when Ethiopia broke relations with Sudan after the attempted assassination in Addis Ababa of Egyptian president Mubarak), and 1998 (when relations were restored after the outbreak of the Ethio-Eritrean war), Ethiopian forces masquerading as the NDA occupied towns on the Sudanese side of the border.

Nowhere, however, were the external implications of Ethiopian federalism more problematic than in relations with Eritrea, despite the alliance between the EPLF and the EPRDF that had defeated the Dergue, and the ostensibly good relations between the two governments after the recognition by Ethiopia of Eritrean independence. The fact that the new governments in each state were based on fundamentally different constituent principles was a constant irritant – not least when Ethiopian officials lectured the Eritreans on the need to treat their own 'nationalities' in the same way that Ethiopia had done. One particularly sensitive area was that inhabited by the Afar, who had previously been split two ways between Ethiopia and Djibouti, and were now split three ways, with the separation of the Eritrean strip along the Red Sea that included the port of Assab; joining an internally self-governing Afar region within Ethiopia could well seem more attractive to Eritrean Afars than subjection to a rigidly centralising government in Asmara. At the very opposite end of the long Ethio-Eritrean frontier, close to Sudan in the west, the Kunama people had sided with the Ethiopians during the long war for Eritrean independence, and many of them drifted across into Ethiopian territory after 1991; this was to become the most intensely disputed area during the Ethio-Eritrean war.

The new Eritrean state's insistence on territoriality rather than ethnicity as the basis for statehood might well have been expected to promote good, or at least peaceful, relations with its neighbours. The EPLF regime[10] promoted an intensified form of the territorial nationalism that had characterised other post-colonial African states in the immediate aftermath of independence; it clung rigidly to the frontiers established by Italian colonialism, and sought to create – on the base formed by the long, bitter and extremely costly war for independence – a single composite Eritrean identity. That things turned out in practice very differently indeed was at least in part the result of the ideas of the state promoted by Eritrea's two principal neighbours, Ethiopia and Sudan. Of these, moreover, Sudan – despite its long if tacit support for the EPLF during the independence war – proved the more immediately threatening. The regime dominated by the

National Islamic Front (NIF), which had seized power in 1989, promoted an explicitly Islamist agenda which it sought to extend into both Ethiopia and Eritrea. In Eritrea, whose population was almost equally divided between Christians and Moslems, this agenda was especially dangerous. If even remotely successful, it would have split the newly independent state down the middle, shattering the carefully fostered myth of an unshakeable national unity forged during the 'struggle', and destroying the moral basis for Eritrean independence. The threat was all the more dangerous for having some elements of plausibility: the EPLF had established its supremacy during the 1970s at the expense of the rival ELF, which (though not Islamist) was most strongly established among the Moslem peoples of western Eritrea, while Moslem Eritreans in refugee camps in Sudan provided an obvious target for proselytisation by the Sudanese regime, and infiltration (as members of the Eritrean Islamic Jihad) back into Eritrea. It was not surprising that the Eritrean government reacted vehemently, including a level of public support for the Sudanese opposition that went well beyond the conventions of normal diplomacy – conventions for which, in any event, the EPLF had little use. Though the demands of the war against Ethiopia were to impose on Eritrea (as on Ethiopia) the need for a tactical accommodation with Sudan, this was very evidently no more than a tactical response to a still greater crisis elsewhere. Though relations with Ethiopia were, until 1998, less immediately threatening, the redrawing of internal administrative boundaries in both countries provided the clearest indication of their opposing conceptions of statehood. In Ethiopia, as already noted, these boundaries were changed to as to bring (so far as possible) people of the same 'nationality' under a single jurisdiction; in Eritrea, on the other hand, they were redrawn in such a way as to incorporate people of different ethnicities within the same regions, even where this had not been the case before. While cast in terms of an ideology of national unity, this could also be interpreted as indicating the discriminatory nature of Eritrean nationalism, in that the new boundaries incorporated within all of the new regions (apart from the Afar region, which was too distant to make this practicable) highland Christian populations, with which the EPLF regime was particularly associated. Other sensitive issues such as land tenure were likewise resolved in ways which favoured highland agriculturalists, at the expense of the mixed or pastoralist forms of subsistence characteristic of the lowland (and Moslem) zones.[11]

Other features of the EPLF regime also helped to prompt the disastrous 1998 war. One was that, while formally clinging to the principle that the inherited colonial frontiers defined the territoriality of the Eritrean state, it adopted an ambitious and unilateralist idea of where these frontiers lay, which it was quite ready to go to war in order to defend. This led first to an attack late in 1995 on the Yemeni-administered Hanish islands in the Red Sea; French mediation resulted in the two states accepting binding arbitration, and by the time that this resolved the dispute unequivocally in favour of Yemen, Eritrea was engaged in its vastly more serious border war with Ethiopia. In 1996, Eritrea claimed Djibouti-administered territory which would have brought the Eritrean frontier significantly closer to the strategic Bab-al-Mandab.

Beyond this, however, the new Eritrean government was suffused with the intense and understandable pride and sensitivity that derived from its thirty-year struggle for independence – qualities which, in the eyes of others, readily assumed the character of arrogance. On the one hand, these led to a conviction that there was nothing that Eritrea could not achieve, and to an assumption that the heavily militarised and hierarchically directed system that had proved so effective in the struggle could be used to achieve such goals as national unity and economic development. On the other, the constant perception of threat led Eritrea – like other states formed in rather similar circumstances, such as Israel and post-1994 Rwanda – to seek to control its own security perimeter, and in the process to external intervention. Eritrea's intense sensitivity to its own sovereign rights was thus unaccompanied by any reciprocal recognition of the rights of others.

One issue that brought this out was the question of citizenship. As a new state, carved out of an existing one, Eritrea had to determine who were its citizens and who were not. Ethnicity was of little help, for a territory derived from colonial demarcation, all of whose principal peoples extended across its frontiers into Ethiopia or Sudan, while as a 'diasporic' state,[12] whose population had been widely scattered as a result of war, place of residence was of little help either. The solution adopted was to recognise as Eritrean anyone descended, through either parent, from ancestors born within Eritrean territory, and in the process to incorporate many individuals of mixed descent. These inevitably included many people living in Ethiopia, who drew attention to themselves by voting in the Eritreans-only referendum on independence in April 1993, which was conducted in Ethiopia as in other parts of the diaspora. At the same time, non-Eritrean Ethiopians were expelled from Eritrea after May 1991, many of them conspicuously accumulating as homeless people on the streets of Addis Ababa. More insidiously though less verifiably, the impression gained currency among Ethiopians that Eritrea continued to exercise undue influence within their own state: that Eritrean military forces were stationed in Ethiopia, that Eritrea gained disproportionate economic benefits from its continued use of the Ethiopian birr as currency, and that national policy was subordinated to Eritrean interests.[13]

The Ethio-Eritrean War

The war that broke out between Ethiopia and Eritrea in May 1998 brought these issues to a head, and in the process exposed the intimate connections between external intervention and domestic state-building in both countries. Despite the intense and partisan rhetoric on each side, there is actually very little question about the sources of the conflict.[14] The frontier between Ethiopia and Eritrea defined by colonial treaty (the precise demarcation of which was itself open to dispute) differed in places from the boundary between the administrations on the ground, in a way that led to areas that apparently fell within Eritrea being actually administered from the Tigray region of Ethiopia. There is some evidence that these discrepancies – which, given the origins of African state frontiers, are by no means exceptional in the continent – date back not just to the period between 1962 and 1974, when the boundary was merely a domestic one between different regions of Ethiopia, but to the period before 1935. After 1991, these discrepancies were acknowledged, but left to later resolution between governments that were in any case closely allied, and had more important issues on their hands. The issue was exacerbated, as relations between the two countries in any event cooled, by regional cadres in Tigray – the heartland of the Ethiopian regime – who particularly resented what they saw as EPLF arrogance, and issued a map of the region for use in schools which incorporated the Ethiopian-administered areas within Tigray.[15] The immediate precipitant of conflict occurred in April 1998, when an armed Eritrean patrol, within what it regarded as Eritrean territory, was fired on and several of its members killed by Tigrayan forces.

The outraged Eritrean reaction was to send its army to occupy in force the whole disputed area. Insofar as there was any element of calculation in this move, and there may not have been much, it appears to have rested first on a conviction – born of the independence struggle – of the Eritrean army's complete invincibility, and second on the assumption that an ethnically fragmented Ethiopia would be unable to provide effective resistance. The invasion by a state of some three million people of territory administered by a neighbour twenty times as large could otherwise only be explained as a rush of blood to the head. In any event, both calculations, if calculations they were, proved to be mistaken. A sense of territoriality is deeply entrenched in the cultures of highland Ethiopia and Eritrea alike, and the immediate popular reaction in Ethiopia was to cement support for their own government against Eritrean 'aggression', in the process bringing out latent anti-Eritrean feelings which the Ethiopian government had until then sought to control. Eritrean military confidence was likewise badly damaged when in March 1999 the Ethiopians, at considerable cost, succeeded in retaking most of the contested area. Later attempts both by the Ethiopians to capture the remaining disputed zones, and by the Eritreans to recapture what they had lost, were repulsed with heavy losses. Unlike most African wars, but in a manner all too reminiscent of the war in Eritrea up to 1991, much of the fighting consisted in infantry attacks on fixed and heavily defended positions, with appalling loss of life; total casualties by October 1999, roughly evenly distributed between the two sides, were estimated at over a hundred thousand men.[16]

The outcome was to leave Eritrea locked in a long and damaging war against an enemy much larger than itself, and on which its own economy heavily depended – a disastrous outcome for any prospect of political stability and economic development. After the failure of an initial mediation by the United States and Rwanda, when Eritrea rejected a proposed settlement that after its subsequent defeat it would have been happy to have accepted, subsequent attempts at diplomatic resolution of the dispute, in which the territory at issue was negligible in both value and extent, dragged on for the next two years. The respective bargaining positions of the two sides reflected a clear assessment of their strengths and weaknesses: Ethiopia stuck to the principle of 'non-aggression', and insisted that Eritrea withdraw all its forces from territory that it had occupied during the dispute, before any demarcation of the boundary; Eritrea conversely struck to the principle of territorial demarcation, and correspondingly refused to withdraw from any territory from which it had not been expelled by force. At the time of writing in March 2000, there had been little major fighting for some nine months, but no settlement had been achieved.

There is no plausible reason to suppose that either side deliberately embarked on the conflict in order to consolidate its domestic political position, though in the event, this is what occurred. Meles Zenawi's government in Addis Ababa was clearly completely taken aback by the turn of events, not least by the upsurge of popular Ethiopian nationalism that followed the Eritrean attack. The TPLF, from which it was heavily drawn, had regarded Ethiopian nationalism with suspicion, and the division of the country into separate ethnic jurisdictions reflected its own conception of Ethiopia as a grouping of different 'nationalities'. After the initial shock, it was able to reinvent itself as the defender of Ethiopian territorial integrity, and to emerge rather stronger in domestic political terms than it had been before, but there is nothing to suggest that it entered into the war with this in mind. On the Eritrean side, too, the war could be seen as helping to revive the spirit of Eritrean nationalism that had prevailed during the struggle, and to consolidate support for the regime of Isaias Afewerki, which had proved to be arrogant and hierarchical, and insensitive to any expression of opinion from civil society or the grassroots. But it appears to have been every bit as surprised by the outcome of events as the Ethiopian government, and whatever short-term advantages it had gained were heavily outweighed by the longer term consequences for Eritrean development.

The most important outcome of the conflict may well prove to be the entrenchment of the separate identities of Ethiopia and Eritrea. The long Eritrean war had been fought, from the Ethiopian side, in the conviction that Eritrea was indeed part of the motherland, and its eventual secession was greeted with sorrow and regret. Even though, by 1991, Eritrean independence was a *fait accompli*, and its recognition by the new Ethiopian government was the only possible basis on which peace could be restored, many Ethiopians continued to blame the Meles Zenawi regime for dismembering the country. In May 1998, however, Eritrea became the 'other', against which Ethiopian nationalism and territory were defined, and large numbers of 'Eritreans' were expelled from Ethiopia as enemy aliens. There were certainly Eritreans with close EPLF connections working in sensitive positions in Ethiopia, who could plausibly be regarded as threats to national security. Equally, resentments remained at the expulsion of Ethiopians from Eritrea in 1991, which was not at that time reciprocated by Ethiopia, and at the apparent flaunting of their Eritrean identity by those who voted in Ethiopia in the independence referendum of 1993. The expulsions nonetheless extended to large numbers of people with only the most distant connections to Eritrea, many of whom had been born in Ethiopia and spoke no Eritrean language. Their expulsion, counterproductive as it was in developmental terms (since immigrants of Eritrean origin occupied many skilled positions, not least as motor mechanics), reflected a redefinition of Ethiopia from which former co-nationals were now excluded. On the Eritrean side, the redefinition of an Eritrean identity as excluding Ethiopia had already taken place, in the period leading up to the independence war and during it, but any idea of an association between the two states, which Isaias Afewerki himself had previously raised, was definitively buried.

Conclusion

In a post-Cold War world, in which external support for the maintenance of African states has been dramatically curtailed, Ethiopia and Eritrea have – like other states in the continent – had to look to their own resources in the struggle to assure their survival. The upheavals in their external environment, which have been particularly important in the one region of sub-Saharan Africa to be deeply embroiled in Cold War alliances, have coincided with even greater changes in their own domestic state structures, as Eritrea has emerged as a recognised sovereign state from the long war for independence; and as Ethiopia, shorn of its northern province and of direct access to the sea, has disowned the previous commitment to a centralised and unitary state based on the hegemony of the Christian highland zone, and sought to reinvent itself as a confederation of ethnic republics. Unlike neighbouring Somalia, and to some extent Sudan, neither Ethiopia nor Eritrea have tumbled into state collapse. Both of them retain organisational capacities and reservoirs of national loyalty that are most strikingly illustrated by their ability to engage in a costly war against one another which – unlike the great majority of wars in Africa – falls straightforwardly into the category of state-against-state conflict.

The 'interventionist' activities in which both of them have engaged in turn derive very largely from the in-built weaknesses of their own processes of state-formation, and have been exacerbated by the attempts of each to exploit the weaknesses of the other in the course of their present war. In the Ethiopian case, this has led to direct military intervention in Somalia, as well as to a complex and changing involvement in the affairs of Sudan; steadfast Ethiopian support for the government of Djibouti, which with the loss of the Eritrean ports has resumed its earlier status as by far Ethiopia's main access to the sea, might itself be regarded as a tacit intervention. Eritrea, driven by the sensitivities and military self-confidence derived from the victory of the EPLF in the long independence war, has been more overtly interventionist than its much larger southern neighbour. It has sent its forces into Djibouti and Yemeni territory, given very public support to the Sudanese opposition, and – in an astonishing display of self-confidence that may yet prove its undoing – claimed and occupied territory administered by an adversary twenty times its size.

But although both Ethiopia and Eritrea can thus be classified, in the title of this volume, as 'African interventionist states', any hegemonic ambitions on their part are deeply subverted by poverty, insecurity and internal division. Both states, despite some recovery since 1991, remain among the poorest in the world, in each case facing major problems even in feeding their populations. Their domestic political systems, however different in their formal structure, are in each case responses to a recognition that their statehood is imposed on potentially highly fissile social bases. The region of the world in which they are located remains highly unstable – partly, of course, though by no means entirely, became of the contribution to that instability that they have made themselves. Neither Ethiopia nor Eritrea retains any plausible prospects of realising its hegemonic ambitions, and each will be fortunate – especially in the light of their foolish descent into war against one another – to cope with its own internal centrifugal forces.

Notes

1 See Clapham (1995), 'The Horn of Africa: a conflict zone', in Furley, Oliver (ed), *Conflict in Africa,* I.B. Tauris: London.

2 See Buzan, Barry (1983), *People, States and Fear: the national security problem in international relations,* Wheatsheaf: Brighton; I have sought to apply this concept to the relations between African states in Clapham (1996), *Africa and the International System: the politics of state surviva,l* Cambridge University Press, pp. 44-56.

3 Johnson, Douglas (1998), 'The Sudan People's Liberation Army', in Clapham, C. (ed), *African Guerrillas,* James Currey: Oxford, p. 60.

4 *Keesings Record of World Events*, 1993, p. 39500.

5 I have explored this argument in Clapham (1996), 'Eritrean Independence and the Collapse of Ethiopian Centralism: Causes, Consequences and Implications', *Geopolitics and International Boundaries*, Vol. 1 No. 2, pp. 115-129.

6 See Clapham (1998), 'Being Peacekept', in Furley, Oliver and May, Roy (eds), *Peacekeeping in Africa*, Ashgate: Aldershot, pp. 303-319.

7 The most detailed account of this involvement of which I am aware is in an unpublished report by Patrick Gilkes to the Save the Children Fund, *Somalia/Somaliland: is there a way forward?*, August 1999; for the knock-on effects on Somalia of the Ethiopia-Eritrea war, see Patrick Gilkes and Martin Plaut (1999), *War in the Horn: the conflict between Eritrea and Ethiopia*, RIIA: London, Discussion Paper No. 82.

8 See Young, John (1999), 'Along Ethiopia's western frontier: Gambella and Benishangul in transition', *The Journal of Modern African Studies*, Vol. 37 No. 2, pp. 321-346.

9 See James, Wendy (2000), 'In the Ethiopian orbit: flag-waving on the western border', in James et al. (eds), *Regional Ethiopia* (forthcoming 2000).

10 After independence, the EPLF was cumbersomely renamed the People's Front for Democracy and Justice (PFDJ), but the familiar acronym is used here for the period both before and after independence.

11 See notably Joireman, Sandra (1996), 'The minefield of land reform: comments on the Eritrean Land Proclamation', *African Affairs*, Vol. 95, No. 379, pp. 269-285; Tronvoll, Kjetil (1998), 'The process of nation-building in post-war Eritrea: created from below or directed from above?', *Journal of Modern African Studies*, Vol. 36 No. 3, pp. 461-482.

12 This very useful term has been coined by Ruth Iyob, 'The Ethiopian-Eritrean Conflict: diasporic vs. hegemonic states in the Horn of Africa, 1991-2000', *Journal of Modern African Studies*, forthcoming, to draw attention to similarities between Eritrea and other states, such as Israel and RPF Rwanda, which have likewise sought to gather in their scattered citizens from distant parts of the world.

13 Though every aspect of the Ethio-Eritrean relationship has become clouded in bitter controversy since 1998, my concern here is with perceptions from the Ethiopian side. For an example, see Medhane Tadesse (1999), *The Eritrean-Ethiopian War: Retrospect and Prospects*, Addis Ababa, pp. 112-162 *passim*.

14 For partisan commentaries from either side, see Medhane Tadesse, *The Eritrean-Ethiopian War*; and *Eritrean Studies Review*, Vol. 3 No. 2, 1999. For appraisals by external observers, see Abbink, Jon (1998), 'The Eritrean-Ethiopian border dispute', *African Affairs*, Vol. 97 No. 389, October; and Patrick Gilkes and Martin Plaut (1999), *War in the Horn: The Conflict between Eritrea and Ethiopia* RIIA: London, Discussion Paper 82.

15 There is no truth in the common allegation that the new Ethiopian banknotes, issued after the introduction of a separate Eritrean currency in January 1997, incorporated these 'new' boundaries: I have examined all of the notes concerned, which show the conventional frontier between the two states.

16 'Battling for Badme', *Africa Confidential*, Vol. 40 No. 22, 5 November 1999, p. 2.

7 Sudan

Peter Woodward

Introduction

In retrospect, it seems almost inevitable that Sudan would be listed as an interventionist state, whether by accident or design. Sudan is the largest country territorially in Africa and has borders with nine other states: Egypt, Libya, Chad, Central African Republic, Democratic Republic of Congo (DRC – formerly Zaire), Uganda, Kenya, Ethiopia and Eritrea (since 1993). In addition, it has an extremely heterogeneous population and a weak state, a combination which has contributed to the fact that for the large majority of the years since independence in 1956 Sudan has experienced civil war – mainly, but not exclusively, in the south of the country. It has been that instability above all that has been central to Sudan's attempts to play an interventionist role.

The most spectacular dimension of intervention has been ideologically driven, and associated mainly with the period since 1989 when a coup d'état brought to power a military regime which has been closely linked with the National Islamic Front (NIF), the political party of the Muslim Brotherhood. However though this coup did introduce the most prolonged period of ideologically-driven intervention, it was not the first such development.

Sudan's unstable domestic politics have thrown up a variety of regimes down the years, but on the whole foreign policy has been fairly conservative, and neither particularly active, nor interventionist, especially in the early years, of which Howell and Hamid wrote in 1969, 'For most of Sudan's independence the main feature of its foreign policy has been the lack of one'.[1] However the overthrow of General Abboud's regime (1958-64) was followed by a short-lived interim government which experienced 'a brief fit of radicalism'. Thus in 1964-65, Sudan saw itself as linked to support for rebel movements in a number of neighbouring states, especially anti-Western movements. One of these was in Eritrea where the US Kagnew communications base outside Asmara symbolised all that the new Sudanese regime regarded itself as opposed to. The Eritrean Liberation

Front (ELF) had begun operating in 1962 and had been exploiting the Sudan border, but it was only in 1964-65 that it found encouragement in government circles in Sudan. Revolt was also once more underway in Congo (Zaire), with the Simba movement in the north resurrecting the Lumumbist tradition. To the west civil war was also beginning in northern Chad which claimed to be linked to radical Arabism, still just about in its heyday.

However these Sudanese interventionist tendencies were soon checked as the country was swiftly made aware of the price of such activities. CIA agents blew the lid on support to the Simba, much to the Sudan government's embarrassment; but more seriously Hailie Selassie in particular made it clear that encouragement for the ELF would be met by Ethiopian support for the Anya Anya guerrillas, who had begun civil war in the southern Sudan at almost the same time as the ELF first appeared inside Eritrea. Sudan was being reminded of just how fragile it is, and a return to an elected government produced a more diplomatic and less interventionist approach to foreign policy under the premiership of Mohammed Ahmed Mahjoub.

There was a further brief period of radical rule following Ga'afar Nimeiri's seizure of power in 1969, but it looked north towards union with Egypt and the apparently similar new regime in Libya under Colonel Gaddafi, rather than towards Sudan's African neighbours. In any case Nasser's death and the failed attempt at a communist backed-coup in Sudan in 1971, led to Nimeiri's shift to the West and a quieter foreign policy. The major exception was with regard to Ethiopia following the latter's revolution which began in 1974. As Ethiopia moved in the direction of the Soviet Union and Marxist-Leninist policies, so it stepped up its attempts to crush opposition forces in Eritrea and Tigre. In response the latter made growing use of Sudan in their struggle, thus contributing to the deterioration in relations between the two countries. When civil war re-opened in southern Sudan in 1983, it was not surprising that the southern Sudan People's Liberation Army (SPLA), turned immediately to Ethiopia for support (and behind it the USSR and Cuba).

Sudan had also been connected to developments in Uganda, especially with regard to the Amin regime, a fact that was not to be forgotten in the latter country.[2]

Islamic Militants and External Intervention

The Islamists who seized power through a coup in 1989 did not have a clearly defined foreign policy, but in the succeeding years they soon formulated one. In particular the leading figure, both ideologically and organisationally, Dr Hassan al-Turabi, soon came out with his vision of Sudan's external relations, and actively trumpeted it around the world.

His vision was essentially Islamist in character. He argued that Muslims should be linked at a number of different levels. At base Muslims belonged together in households, but also in wider communities, right up to the Commonwealth of Muslims: *dar al-Islam*, and the *Umma* (the community of Muslims). This was not to be regarded as a single monolithic structure, so much as an inspiration towards which all Muslims were obliged to strive. Non-Muslims could find their place in *dar al-Islam*, as they had always done in the past. European imperialism had destroyed the last great pan-Islamic achievement, the Ottoman Empire, but there was a long tradition of seeking such an ambition. Writers since Jamal al-Din al-Afghani in the nineteenth century had called for such an aim, and the revolt of Mohamed Ahmed al-Mahdi in Sudan had sought (unsuccessfully) to take his message of purifying Islam far beyond Sudan's borders.

After the crushing experience of European imperialism had come nationalism and other ideologies, but all had failed, and with them the nation-state had been a 'resounding failure'.[3] Though the Muslim countries had established the Organisation of the Islamic Conference (OIC), it was led by pro-Western states which were dependent and manipulated (as shown in the Gulf War), and was therefore politically impotent and totally unrepresentative of the 'true spirit of the community that animates the Muslim people'. Instead, 'as Muslims tend towards their common ideals, they would perforce move towards closer unity; and that would undermine the moral foundation and the positive structures of the present nation state...However, once a single fully-fledged Islamic state is established, the model would radiate throughout the Muslim world' becoming in time 'a focus of pan-Islamic attention and affection'. It was his view that Sudan after 1989 was in the process of becoming just such a beacon. 'Muslims would forever aspire to the ultimate ideal of the caliphate restored, of one central authority that holds the Muslim world together', though 'countries may remain as areas of self-management for the full enrichment of Islam in the particular environment'.

However Turabi did not envisage that the *dar al-Islam* had to be achieved by confrontation and force, 'the present trend towards unity derives more from the inside revival of Islam, as spirituality for society, rather than the excitation of Islam as the battle cry ... It is the common enemy that draws Muslims together'.[4] It would prove less a threat, than a 'positive contribution to the human community in general'.

In order to give expression to his views, in 1991 Turabi was the leading light in the establishment in Khartoum of the Popular Islamic and Arabic Conference (PIAC). Representatives of the pan-Islamic movement were invited from a number of countries, and Turabi was elected as Secretary-General of PIAC, in which capacity he travelled widely seeking support for it. The PIAC endorsed the leading role of Sudan as a beacon for other Muslims to follow.

i) *Intervention in Africa*

As indicated, there had been Sudanese involvement in the internal affairs of a number of its African neighbours in the past, and there was an obvious carry-over from the pre- to the post-1989 position, especially with regard to the Eritrean People's Liberation Front (EPLF), and the Tigrean People's Liberation Front (TPLF), later to become the Ethiopian People's Revolutionary Democratic Front (EPRDF). Sudanese security had actively assisted these groups, especially in the latter stages of their confrontations with the Dergue and their sweep into power in 1991. Sudan clearly felt that they owed it a debt, and it expected good relations with the two new governments.[5]

However in the following years, it became clear that there were very different agendas at work. The leaders of the new governments in Ethiopia and Eritrea made it known that they did not regard themselves as in any way behoven to those countries which had assisted them on their paths to power. Moreover they were themselves secularist in outlook, and determined to build (in the case of Eritrea) and re-build (in Ethiopia) viable and independent states. This outlook appeared in time at odds with the pan-Islamic movement being hatched in Sudan. Indeed, at its first conference the PIAC committed itself to aiding Oromiyyah Islamiyyah amongst the predominantly Muslim community of the Oromo in Ethiopia (the largest sub-national grouping in the country), as well as Jihad Eritrea among the mainly Muslim peoples of lowland western Eritrea. Issayas Aferworki of Eritrea was characteristically outspoken in denouncing Sudan, and the latter tried to respond in a placatory manner by expelling Jihad Eritrea, which retreated to Saudi Arabia. However relations soon deteriorated once more with new Eritrean complaints to the UN in 1994, after which diplomatic relations between the two countries were broken off. Sudan's embassy in Asmara was later handed over by Eritrea to the Sudanese opposition National Democratic Alliance (NDA) as its headquarters, and Issayas called openly for the overthrow of the government in Khartoum.

For a while, relations with Ethiopia were less strained. In particular the Sudan army was allowed access to western Ethiopia which assisted attacks against the SPLA, seen initially by the new government in Addis Ababa as an ally of the former dictator, Mengistu Haile Mariam. However relations began to deteriorate, though not as publicly as with Eritrea, until in 1995, Ethiopian accused Sudan of being involved in the attempted assassination of President Mubarak of Egypt in Addis Ababa.

Sudan's support for Islamists in the Horn of Africa was not confined to its immediate neighbours. The chaotic situation in Somalia – before, during and after the US-led UN intervention of 1994-95 – provided opportunities for both Sudan and Iran to encourage local Islamists. However such endeavours proved of only limited success, for the deep divisions along clan and sub-clan lines proved stronger than efforts to forge unity around Islamic calls. While there were contacts with faction leaders, the latter were far from willing to submit themselves to undue outside influences, as they pursued their own interests and rivalries.

Eritrea, Ethiopia and Somalia all had substantial Muslim communities to which the Sudanese Islamists could endeavour to provide encouragement. To the south in Uganda the Muslim community was far more of a minority and viewed by government there with a degree of suspicion. There were memories that Idi Amin's notorious regime from 1970-79 had claimed an identity with Islam and received support from certain Arab states. Many of Amin's followers had left with his overthrow, and remaining Muslims were inclined to be quiescent, while the government from 1986 was keen to encourage the return of the Asian community, some of whom were Muslims.

Instead of a projection of Sudanese power through linkage with Muslims, somewhat bizarrely Sudan found itself supporting a movement which claimed for itself a Christian background, albeit a most unorthodox one: the Lord's Resistance Army (LRA). The origins of this had less to do with the outward extension of Sudan's Islamist regime, and more with the continuing war in the southern Sudan.

The overthrow of Mengistu in Ethiopia in 1991 had been a major blow to the Sudan Peoples Liberation Army (SPLA). Ejected from Ethiopia, Uganda became even more important to it as a source of support and a conduit for supplies from various sources. From Uganda's standpoint there was an old friendship and natural sympathy between President Yoweri Museveni and SPLA leader John Garang. Moreover Uganda referred to the perceived threat of Islamism promoted by Khartoum in southern Sudan, if not directly in Uganda itself. The Sudan Government had hoped that without Ethiopian support the SPLA could be defeated in the south, but though it suffered setbacks the southern movement was able to stage something of a recovery by the mid-1990s. It was then that Allah, in the form of the Sudanese Islamists, teamed up with the Lord as proclaimed by the LRA leader William Kony.

Resistance to Museveni's government in northern Uganda combined a weird spirituality with ethnic marginalisation. The new mainly southern- and western-back government in Uganda from 1986 signalled the marginalisation of the north and attempts to avenge the loss of power after the years of successive northern rulers; Obote (twice), Amin and finally Okello. Among the Acholi, initial resistance took the form of support for Alice Lakwena and the Holy Spirit Movement (HSM).

> However weird it may seem to European eyes, the HSM was a political manifestation of an Acholi society driven into a corner after Museveni's assumption of national power. Acholi proved eager to follow prophetic or charismatic leaders to win a war that was virtually lost, as conventional means had proved inadequate.[6]

Lakwena led an extraordinary march from the north towards Kampala, and was stopped only after a battle at Jinja in 1987.

However, Alice Lakwena's defeat and departure for Kenya was not to the end of religious resistance amongst the Acholi. A man claiming to be her cousin by the name of Joseph Kony, once apparently a catechist of the Roman Catholic church, emerged as leader of the LRA and sought to re-open the conflict in the north. At first it seemed that there might be a negotiated peace between the government and the LRA, but by the end of 1994 this hope had faded and the relationship between Sudan and the LRA was growing.

From Sudan's point of view it was simply that the obvious response to Uganda's support for the SPLA was to assist the LRA, another of the many proxies both the government and the SPLA armed in the course of the long civil war.[7] Sudan provided the LRA with weapons and fairly secure bases on Sudanese territory. In addition to the destabilising north-east Uganda, the LRA was to harass Sudanese refugees in that region, apparently because of possible support for the SPLA: and where possible to attack the

SPLA within southern Sudan. But it was in Uganda that they caused most trouble, with large displacement of population in Gulu and Kitgum districts.[8]

The LRA may have been the most bizarre projection of force against Uganda by Sudan, but it was not the only one. Sudan also encouraged the West Nile Bank Front (WBNF) led by former Amin minister Juma Oris; while Uganda also blamed Sudan for supporting opposition forces attacking western Uganda from Zaire/Democratic Republic of Congo (DRC), which became the justification given for sending Ugandan troops across that border.[9]

In contrast to Uganda, Kenya was less directly involved with Sudan. This was partly due to Kenya's traditionally low-key foreign policy, and partly to the fact that religion has not been the factor in Kenyan politics that it has in Uganda. Nevertheless Kenya was aware of possible Islamism, and blocked an attempt to create a Muslim political party. The Islamic Party of Kenya was banned and described as 'Arab fundamentalists', while in 1993 its leader Sheikh Khalid Balala, was arrested for incitement for threatening to call for a *jihad*.[10] Awareness of an Islamic threat was also kept alive by the 1998 bombing of the United States' embassy in Nairobi (and simultaneously the US embassy in Dar-es-Salaam); though Sudan went out of its way to disclaim any connection with the terrorists.

Sudan's attitude to Zaire/DRC has long been essentially connected with the war in the south. With the long-running hostility to Uganda, it was unsurprising that Sudan has supported the power-holder of the moment in Kinshasa opposed to alleged ambitions of Uganda across the latter's western border. First it had been Mobutu and then Kabila (once Museveni and Kagame had turned against him), with repeated allegations from Uganda that Sudanese troops operated inside Zaire/DRC.

The Central African Republic (CAR) was perhaps the least significant of Sudan's many neighbours. Strategically it bordered an area of less importance for either side in Sudan's civil war that other areas of the south. Moreover CAR was in the French sphere of influence in Africa, and Sudan sought not to antagonise France. The Islamists in particular have made an exception of France. Turabi is partly French-educated, and certainly has found France less hostile to Sudan since 1989 than other Western powers: partly perhaps in an attempt to extend its sphere of influence at the expense of the 'Anglo-Saxons', while at least partially allaying France's 'Fashoda complex'.[11]

In contrast Chad has been a former French colony with which Sudan has been more actively involved. The problem in Chad has had less to do with either Sudan's civil war or the promotion of Islamism, than the long instability in Sudan's large western neighbour. Ever since the early 1980s Sudan has been an important factor in developments in Chad. When the northern Chadian factions fought for power following the downfall of Malloum in 1979, Sudan backed Habré who took refuge in the western Sudanese region of Darfur as he prepared for his successful attack ousting Libyan-backed Goukouni Oueddi. (Sudan was backed in this anti-Libyan move by the United States and Egypt; while France late became a supporter of Habré as well.) However, after the overthrow of President Nimeiri in Sudan in 1985, relations between Sudan and Libya improved. After Idriss Deby unsuccessfully challenged Habré in 1989, he too went to Darfur where with Sudanese and Libyan help, he prepared to overthrow Habré the following year. Sudan's support for Deby owed less to any religious dimension than to ethnic ties: he was of the Zaghawa peoples who straddle the Sudan-Chad border and were influential in the new government in Khartoum. Though Sudan sometimes uses Islamic rhetoric with regard to relations with Chad, its main concern is to retain links with those in power in N'djamena, a strategically important state at the centre of the Sahara.

ii) *Intervention in the Middle East*

While the focus of the book is on Africa, it would be unrealistic to limit Sudan's projection of Islamism to Africa alone. Its activities there were part and parcel of the wider agenda, and thus its activities in the Middle East must be reviewed as well.

While in its African perspectives Sudan was seen as encouraging guerrilla groups with an Islamist character, as in the cases of Jihad Eritrea and Oromiyyah Islamiyyah, with regard to the Middle East, it was essentially a case of supporting terrorist movements, some of which were more 'Islamic' than others. There was both a pull and a push factor as far as groups in the Middle East were concerned.

The pull factor was the welcome accorded to many groups that turned up in Khartoum, with the justification that Sudan was offering a refuge to 'brothers in Islam'. In addition to welcoming them and providing a base for the continuation of their operations, it was also widely alleged that the newcomers were called on to help the training of Sudanese forces, including the new militia, the People's Defence Forces (PDF), and that some even participated in the civil war in the south, which the government proclaimed as a *jihad*.

The push factor was the changing situation in the Middle East, partly due to the end of the Cold War, which was making life less comfortable for various groups associated with the use of terrorism. The end of the war with the Soviet Union in the Middle East had left a number of trained, rootless, Afghan veterans from around the Muslim world – referred to simply as the 'Afghans' – for whom Sudan offered one of the few refuges available. Syria's growing respectability internationally was making some groups seek a new home, as were developments in Lebanon and Palestine. Militant Iranians were also said to be amongst the 'refugees' as Sudan also sometimes referred to them. In addition there was the growing confrontation of state and Islamists in north Africa, notably Algeria and Egypt, and to a lesser extent Tunisia. As a result it was claimed that various groups including Hizbollah, HAMAS, the PLO and Islamic Jihad were amongst those finding shelter in Sudan. The groups included a number of leading figures, including Osama bin Leiden. Formerly linked to the 'Afghans' (many of whom had been trained in Pakistan by the CIA), bin Leiden had found sanctuary in Sudan after being expelled from his country of origin, Saudi Arabia. In Sudan he was involved in business circles as well as in terrorism.[12] In 1993 the United States put Sudan on its select list of states supporting terrorism (together with Cuba, Iran, Iraq, North Korea and Syria).

The Middle Eastern country most directly affected by Sudanese-based terrorists was Egypt. Sudan has always had a particularly complex relationship with Egypt, a former imperial power in the nineteenth century which felt that Sudan's independence in 1956 was contrary to Egypt's continuing claim of sovereignty over the country. Moreover in spite of Sudan's independence, Egypt had continued thereafter to be an important factor in the complex and confusing machinations of Sudanese domestic politics. More particularly the Sudanese Muslim Brotherhood, of which the NIF was an extension, was itself an offshoot of the Egyptian movement. It was thus natural for the NIF to be interested in the growing confrontation in Egypt in the early 1990s, and given its record elsewhere, unsurprising that it offered a home to Egyptian Islamists. It was equally understandable that Egypt should seize on this to blame Sudan for acts of terrorism in Egypt, even though the roots of such actions lay firmly within its domestic politics. Most dramatically the actions with which Sudan was alleged to be connected included: harbouring Omer Abd al-Rahman, later jailed in 1996 for his part in organising the bombing of the World Trade Centre in New York; and involvement in the attempted assassination of President Mubarak in 1995, after which Sudan's failure to hand over three Egyptian suspects who sought refuge led to international sanctions being imposed. While Egypt was the most obvious case of alleged Sudanese support for terrorism in the Middle East, Algeria and Tunisia also made similar accusations from time to time.

Rowing Back

With the passing of UN sanctions against Sudan following the attack on Mubarak in Addis Ababa there could be little doubt in the Sudan government of the degree of isolation that the country was experiencing internationally. Through its interventionist policies, it had clearly made itself a host of enemies: the majority of its neighbouring states; the world's single superpower; and many European countries as well. Isolation was accompanied by a sharp drop in foreign aid, and worsening relations with international financial institutions, contributing to the accelerated decline of Sudan's economy.

At the same time it had few if any compensating friends. From 1988, it had been close to Iraq and this relationship survived the change of regime in the following year. The links were less ideological than military and political: with the ending of the Iran-Iraq war, Iraq was in a position to supply Sudan with arms which were much needed in the civil war; while Saddam Hussein was keen to promote his importance in the Arab world. In the Gulf War of 1990-91, Sudan was one of Iraq's few supporters, with Turabi feverishly denouncing Western violation of the Muslim world. But Iraq's military humiliation put an end to the main value of the relationship from Sudan's point of view (though there were continuing stories of links in the area of alleged chemical weapons development in Sudan).

In its place Sudan pursued Iraq's former enemy, Iran. In spite of Iran being an Islamic theocracy, Turabi and his fellow ideologues had had their differences with it. However there was a fresh need for arms in Sudan; while Iranian ministers were keen to seize an opportunity to be active in promoting Islam internationally. Iran had weapons to spare; it also financed sales from China; and sent experienced instructors who helped reorganise Sudan's armed forces and police on Iranian lines. But by 1994 there was a waning of Iranian enthusiasm for Sudan's performance; while Iran itself began to develop a more 'conventional' foreign policy involving a reduced commitment to Islamic militancy internationally.

The continuing accumulation of enemies, and loss of friends, was reaching the point by 1997 when the situation was in danger of closing in on the Sudan Government. Supported ever more openly by its enemies, the Sudanese opposition was uniting. Together with the SPLA, various northern Sudanese parties and groups formed the National Democratic Alliance (NDA) with its headquarters in Asmara. At the beginning of 1997 the NDA was in a position to open new fronts in eastern Sudan, to supplement the continuing conflict in the southern Sudan. There were repeated accusations from Sudan that the United States in particular was supporting this stepping up of the civil war, especially when at the end of 1997, Secretary of State Madeleine Albright appeared to call for the downfall of the Sudan government while on a visit to Uganda. America's attitude was further demonstrated by the missile attack on a pharmaceutical factory in Khartoum North in August 1998, which it claimed on the basis of little or no evidence was linked to the production of chemical weapons.

Realising its growing danger the Sudan Government had already started to retreat from its radical international posture, and begun a targeted 'charm offensive'.[13] With the United States appearing obdurate, some European powers looked more promising. France in particular seemed a likely candidate for further improved relations. Apart from Turabi's personal warmth towards France, it was suggested that Sudan might prove helpful in the continuing moves by France to seek to intervene in the worsening crisis in Algeria. In addition in 1994 Sudan had 'discovered' that the wanted international terrorist 'Carlos the Jackal' was living in Khartoum and he was shipped to France for trial and imprisonment.[14] It all paid off as commercial and political ties strengthened, and France called for a softening of the international community's treatment of Sudan. It was a message echoed in some quarters in Germany.

In the Arab world the crucial attitude was that of Egypt. The attack on Mubarak in 1995 had raised understandable wrath, but there was too concern for developments in Sudan, especially the possible separation of north and south which in Egyptian eyes would complicate the vital issue of the Nile waters. In consequence Egypt tried to woo all sections of the NDA on the one hand, while encouraging divisions in the Sudan Government which might distance Turabi and the ideologues on the one hand from President Omer al-Beshir and the armed forces on the other. But it was a somewhat speculative policy, and one which made Egypt seem all things to all men, apart from Turabi and his followers. Nevertheless Sudan was eager to be seen to respond to Egypt's growing efforts to be involved in peacemaking. Egypt was joined in this in the Arab world by Libya, keen to rehabilitate itself internationally and be seen to be an influential force in Africa – albeit mainly by the power of the purse.

There was also an attempt by Sudan to try and improve relations with African neighbours. This was particularly important since they (and Sudan) were grouped together in the Inter-Governmental Authority for Development (IGAD) which from 1994 had taken over as the forum for repeated rounds of Sudan peace talks. IGAD was increasingly supported by European and North American 'Friends' – later 'Partners' of IGAD. Kenya played a leading part in IGAD talks, a move welcomed by Sudan which had always seen Kenya as less threatening than other African neighbours. In particular Kenya's rivalry with Uganda meant that the mutual hostility of Uganda and Sudan could be at least partly discontinued within IGAD. It was therefore unsurprising that a Kenyan diplomat based in Nairobi was chosen to head a Permanent Secretariat to facilitate IGAD's Sudan peace efforts in 1999.

However on the Eastern border the Sudan Government had a stroke of good fortune of which it could hardly have dreamed. In 1998 Eritrea and Ethiopia went to war over an arid strip of land across which their mutual border was disputed. Thus two of Sudan's most important enemies and active supporters of the NDA were turning on each other; and Sudan was soon doing its utmost to capitalise on the situation by posing as a potential friend to both. Neither Eritrea nor Ethiopia went as far as ejecting the NDA, but both were pre-occupied with their own conflict, and both made some response to Sudan's overtures.

By 1999 Sudan may have won few strong friends, but it had moved some distance in breaking out of its earlier isolation, and putting some of its enemies, most notably the United States and Uganda, somewhat on the back foot.

Conclusion

Sudan appears to have come full circle between 1989 and 1999. Having embarked on grandiose plans to do away with the failed nation state and work instead for the Islamist cause in north-east Africa, while serving as a beacon for the whole Muslim world, Sudan has learnt the hard way that people in glass houses shouldn't throw stones.

In the course of those ten years Sudan's retreat towards more conventional international relations, especially since 1995, has not though been accompanied by a renewal of trust with its neighbours. Sudan's unsuccessful efforts at regional destabilisation will not be forgotten, at least while the present Islamist regime remains in power. Indeed, as a result of its efforts, Sudan found itself on the receiving end of destabilisation efforts by some of its neighbours. Eritrea may have been the most vocal of those neighbours in calling for the overthrow of the Sudan Government, but others were also supporting the opposition in such efforts, especially Ethiopia and Uganda. It was the conflict between Eritrea and Ethiopia, rather than any change of heart by those two countries, that has at least partially helped Sudan off the hook.

Indeed, far from spreading its Islamist message, the Sudan Government was even forced towards compromises domestically. With its army unable to win the civil war in the south, and with the northern and southern opposition uniting in the National Democratic Alliance, the government was forced into compromises in its effort to survive. Potentially the most dramatic of these was made in IGAD talks in Nairobi in 1998 when it was agreed in principle with the SPLA that there could be self-determination for the Southern Sudan, albeit with significant differences between the two sides over practicalities. It may yet result in the division of the country, and the contraction of the Sudanese state rather than the Islamist outreach proclaimed in 1989.

Yet even if contained, Sudan's past efforts at becoming an interventionist state may still have an important effect. While mutual distrust reigns in north-east Africa, the important goal of greater co-operation is harder to attain: yet it remains a vital necessity. There can never be full internal political stability while suspicious, if not hostile, neighbour-relations continue, because the majority of the states are too fragile internally and too vulnerable externally. At the same time the issues of regional environmental security will grow with rising populations and limited resources. Co-operation could improve resources, especially the Nile river system, but without co-operation, it will prove increasingly inadequate, especially for Egypt and Sudan. There will need to be further constructive developments between the states of the region if the growing problems faced by all are to be addressed in the new millennium.

Notes

1 Howell, John and Hamid, Mohammed Beshir (1969) 'Sudan and the outside world, 1954-1968, *African Affairs*, 68, p. 299.

2 Woodward, Peter (1988), 'Uganda and southern Sudan: peripheral politics and neighbour relations', in Hansen, H. Bernt and Twaddle, M. (eds), *Uganda Now: Between Development and Decay*, James Currey: London. Also Woodward, Peter (1991), 'Uganda and southern Sudan 1986-89: new regimes

and peripheral politics', in Hansen, H. Bernt and Twaddle, M. (eds), *Changing Uganda*, James Currey: London.

3 The quotations are from the printed version of Dr Turabi's address to the Royal Society of Arts, London, 27 April 1992. For more on his ideology, see: Hassan al-Turabi (1989), *The Islamic Movement in Sudan*, IRRS: Khartoum, in Arabic; Abdelwahab El-Affendi (1991), *Turabi's Revolution: Islam and Power in Sudan*, Grey Seal: London; Niblock, Tim (1991), 'Islamic Islamic Movements and Sudan's Political Coherence', in Bleuchot, H., Delmet, C. and Hopwood, D. (eds) *Sudan: History, Identity and Ideology*, Ithaca Press: Reading.

4 Ibid.

5 Woodward, Peter (1996), *The Horn of Africa: state politics and international relations*, IB Tauris: London, chapter six, *passim*.

6 Doom, R. and Vlassenroot. K. (1999), 'Kony's message: a new *koine*? The Lord's Resistance Army in Northern Uganda', *African Affairs*, 98, No. 390, p. 30.

7 On the SPLA, see Johnson, D. H. (1998), 'The Sudan People's Liberation Army and the problem of factionalism', in Clapham, C. (ed), *African Guerrillas*, James Currey: Oxford.

8 Amnesty International (1997), *Uganda: Breaking God's Commands: the destruction of childhood by the Lord's Resistance Army,* Amnesty: London.

9 Interview with H. E. Dr Ruhakana-Ruganda, Uganda, July 1999.

10 *Africa: South of the Sahara*, 1995, Europa Publications: London, p. 490.

11 For a discussion of the attitudes of France towards the 'Anglo-Saxons', see Prunier, Gerald (1995), *The Rwanda Crisis, 1959-1994: The History of a Genocide*, Hurst: London, pp. 104-6.

12 *Africa Confidential,* 39, 28 August 1998.

13 As a small example of the charm offensive, I was myself officially invited to visit Sudan in 1997, having been declared *persona non grata* in 1991.

14 An informed French source, Gerard Prunier, simply says that 'Carlos the Jackal', aliases for Illich Ramirez Sanchez, 'was sold by the Sudanese government to the French Interior Minister Charles Pasqua', Prunier, *op cit,* p. 219n.

8 SADC's Intervention into Lesotho: an Illegal Defence of Democracy?

Roger Southall

The armed intervention into Lesotho by the South African National Defence Force (SANDF) and the Botswana Defence Force (BDF) in September 1998 following the repudiation by opposition parties of a recent election result provoked a massive controversy. Formally, it was conducted to preserve democracy and prevent a military coup, yet most informed observers deem it to have been conducted in contravention of international law. Worse, even if the intervening parties could claim a strong moral and political case for their action, the incursion was widely perceived as a diplomatic-cum-military bungle which precipitated an orgy of looting, arson and violence which left the main street of Maseru, Lesotho's capital, a burnt out shell, with mayhem having also affected other towns. Furthermore, as well as raising far-reaching questions concerning the necessity for the intervention, it brought into focus other issues concerning the operational efficiency of the SANDF and South African intelligence, the credibility and consistency of South Africa's foreign policy, and the role and status of the Southern African Development Community (SADC). Finally, the intervention provoked unusually intense international interest in the parochial political battles of Lesotho and gave impetus to the perpetual debate about the viability of that country's status and its relation to South Africa. However, that Lesotho's latest election was about to trigger such a tumult was far from evident when its voters went to the polls on 23 May 1998.

Part One: The Course of Events[1]

The Background to the Intervention

Back in 1993, the Basutoland Congress Party (BCP), the historical vehicle of anti-colonial nationalism, had won an overwhelming victory in an election in Lesotho brought about by pressures upon the then military government to withdraw to the barracks. Under the plurality electoral system inherited from Britain, the BCP won 75 per cent of the popular vote and 65 seats compared to a 20 per cent vote and no seats won by the Basotho National Party (BNP), which had ruled the country since independence until displaced by the military in 1986. But internal divisions saw the ruling party split in 1997. When the aged and ailing Ntsu Mokhehle, the founder and leader of the BCP, lost control of the latter's machinery as potential successors wrestled for power, he formed a new party - the Lesotho Congress of Democrats (LCD) - and took with him a majority of the country's elected MPs. Unorthodox, yet not actually unconstitutional. But in consequence, the key questions about the 1998 election were: given the plurality electoral system, how would the vote split between the LCD and the BCP? If it split down the middle, would this allow the BNP to increase its number of seats? Would Mokhehle still be able to carry the popular vote, or would the BCP be able to claim the legitimacy of history?

Following initial threats of boycott, the opposition parties participated in an election which some 150 international and 400 Basotho electoral monitors subsequently declared more or less free and fair. This judgement was particularly striking because of the nature of the result, for the LCD was reported as having won 60 per cent of the popular vote and 78 out of the 79 seats contested on election day. (It also won a further seat in a constituency where voting had been delayed). As in 1993, the mechanics of the plurality system had worked to deliver one party a virtual clean sweep.

Even if the electoral process had been fair, the result left 40 per cent of the voters unrepresented in the lower house of parliament. This would have been problematic in its own terms, but it became even more of an issue because, despite the validation of the election by the electoral monitors, the principal opposition parties cried foul. The BNP and BCP, hitherto sworn enemies, forged an alliance of convenience, with the insignificant but noisy Royalist Marematlou Freedom Party (MFP) joining in. Together, they proclaimed that the election had been rigged and that the government was illegitimate. Their supporters were then mobilised to demonstrate in Maseru, and the opposition alliance openly called for the King, Letsie II, to exercise powers he does not constitutionally possess to dismiss the government. Meanwhile, the opposition case was taken up by sections of the South African and international media, all of which contributed to a growing sense of crisis.

Mokhehle had led his party into the election, but as prearranged, he was immediately succeeded as party leader and Prime Minister by Paseka Mosisili, a former academic. However, with the forces of opposition beginning to take control of the streets in Maseru, Mosisili proved indecisive, failing dismally to make a vocal response to the Opposition allegations, even though rumours were circulating that the government was contemplating banishing the King and declaring a state of emergency. Underlying his uncertainty was Mosisili's realisation that his government was unable to rely upon the security forces.

During the years of its rule, the BNP had stuffed the army (formed in the early 1980s out of a paramilitary police unit) with its supporters. The relationship between the army and that party had been fractured by the South African backed coup which displaced the BNP in 1986, yet the dominant faction of the BNP led by its present leader, Evaristus Sekhonyana, had retained its close connections. When the BCP had assumed office in 1993, it was therefore faced by a largely hostile military. This hostility had been confirmed when the army backed a brief dismissal of the BCP government by King Letsie in August 1994. This episode had only ended when, acting on behalf of SADC, the newly elected ANC-led government in South Africa acted in concert with Botswana and Zimbabwe to insist that democracy be restored. This pressure subsequently resulted in the return of the BCP to office in mid-September 1994.

It was this previous involvement by SADC in Lesotho's internal affairs which now paved the way for a further engagement. This reflected growing regional and South African concern at rising tensions in the kingdom, as from 11 August, hundreds of opposition supporters began to congregate outside the King's palace in Maseru to protest against the alleged rigging of the election. In advance of the march on the palace, the police commissioner had ordered that protestors should be turned back from whence they had come, but his instructions were not carried out. Opposition youths made for the palace, where they received food and other sustenance. When army chief Lieutenant-Colonel Makhula Mosakeng ordered the crowds to disperse and they refused, teargas was used against them by soldiers following orders, but a second contingent of troops aimed their weapons at their colleagues, who then backed off.

Such incidents spoke of mounting tensions within the military. Some observers construed this as a possible divide between fractions loyal to the government and to the opposition respectively - yet this was to overlook more complex internal divisions which, inter alia, had seen the break out of hostilities between soldiers from the Rajamotse and the Makaonyane barracks leading up to the King's coup of 1994. Whatever the fault-lines, there was clear warning that the sustained opposition protest might work to inflame divisions within the army and precipitate a more general crisis.

Given its increasingly tenuous control of events, the LCD government proved to be in no position to gainsay SADC's proposal, driven by South African Vice-President Thabo Mbeki, that the best way to resolve the crisis was via the appointment of a Commission to examine the conduct of the recent election and to adjudicate upon its validity. The resultant SADC Commission began work in the second week of August and was headed by Judge Pius Langa of South Africa. It then proceeded to its work speedily and efficiently, but the announcements of its findings were to be delayed by what was referred to as the need to report to SADC leaders when they were meeting at a summit in Mauritius. In the event, the report, dated 9 September, was destined not to be made public until 17 September - a delay which allowed accusations to fly that its allegedly 'explosive' findings were being doctored in favour of the LCD. Consequently, its judgement - that although there had been administrative deficiencies, there was insufficient evidence to indicate that the election result was invalid - was rejected by the opposition alliance, which issued demands for fresh elections and the formation of a government of national unity.

In the meantime, the internal dynamics of the situation had been transformed by an army revolt, which saw junior officers round up Mosakeng and other senior officers on 11 September. The officers were reported as saying that they were merely trying to create a non-partisan defence force by ridding the army of a top structure loyal to the LCD. However, another interpretation suggests that the senior officers' commitment to upholding the government was itself extremely uncertain, and that any reluctance on their part to intervene politically was largely shaped by SADC warnings that an opposition-supporting coup would not be tolerated. In contrast, the junior officers were more reckless.

Whatever the case, Mosakeng went on Radio Lesotho that night to announce his own resignation and those of 28 senior colleagues. Rumours of a coup were countered by government announcements that it was still in office, yet it was increasingly evident that it was losing its grip on power, as reports indicated that the BNP, the soldiery and the police were working together to paralyse the functioning of government.

SADC diplomatic efforts continued under South African Safety and Security Minister Sydney Mufumadi, but on 20 September the LCD refused to attend all-party talks called to resolve the crisis citing a lack of security for its delegates. Mufumadi subsequently reported that the attempt to mediate collapsed when the opposition parties declined to meet with the LCD at a neutral venue in Pretoria. On the same day (21 September), Deputy Prime Minister Kelebone Maope revealed that the LCD government had appealed to SADC for assistance. The very next day, the SANDF marched across the border.

SADC's South African-led Intervention

In the early hours of Tuesday, 22 September, 600 troops of the 43rd Mechanised Brigade of the SANDF crossed into Lesotho via the Maseru border post with the objectives of neutralising the 2,000-strong Lesotho Defence Force (LDF), and securing Radio Lesotho, High Commissions and Embassies, the Royal Palace, the airport and other infrastructure (notably the Katse Dam in which South Africa had a major interest), and thereby providing an enabling environment for negotiations to take place between the political parties. They were followed in the evening by a further 200 troops of the BDF, whose particular task was defined as guarding Maseru. The apparent supposition was that the intervention force would meet limited resistance. Events proved any such expectation dismally wrong.

Matters went wrong from the beginning. One arm of the intervention force reportedly made for the Hilton Hotel on the understanding that it was the palace. When these troops did eventually arrive at the palace - on the other side of town - they entered through the front gate, ignorant of the fact that there were two other entrances to the rear, from which armed opposition youth made a hasty exit. The latter made for the town centre, where they launched an immediate orgy of destruction, with anything that was associated with South Africa becoming their target. Shopwindows were smashed, looters made off with whatever they could lay their hands on, hundreds of cars were hi-jacked, and shops were deliberately fired. By the next morning, practically every commercial building along the capital's main street had gone up in smoke, as meanwhile the opposition (mainly BNP youth) had fanned out to Lesotho's smaller towns such as Maputsoe, Mohales' Hoek and Mafeteng and wreaked their vengeance there.

Maseru was raped because it was left unprotected. Whilst the SANDF troops despatched to the palace were provocatively raising a South African flag, their colleagues were moving in on three main targets: Makoanyane and Rajamotse barracks close to Maseru, and a small guardpost established to protect Katse Dam. Resistance was heavy at both the barracks. In the event, as at the palace, the majority of those opposing the SANDF escaped by the rear, so that although, for instance, fighting was over at the Makoanyane base by the 24 September, only 149 prisoners had been taken. However, those who escaped were armed. Colonel Robbie Hartslief, officer commanding the SADC force, reported on the 24 September that his troops had secured all military bases around Maseru and were in control of the military situation, but he conceded that the SANDF would encounter problems flushing the rebels out of the hills and that the large number of armed youths remained a major security threat.

Meanwhile, a controversial encounter had taken place at the Katse Dam. The SANDF had arrived in four helicopters. Reports indicate that the LDF soldiers holding the base were initially approached by Sergeant Jerome Sax, who informed them that the SANDF was taking over. However, rather than laying down their arms, the LDF contingent killed him. A medical officer, Dr. Johan Nel, who moved forward to assist Sax was also shot. In the battle that ensued, a further South African soldier was injured, and the helicopters took off and strafed the base, killing all the 16 RLDF soldiers present.

Whilst all this was happening, mobs were rampaging through the streets of the capital. However, once the BDF arrived, on the 23 September, minimum initial effort was made to re-impose order. Numerous press reports testified to SADC soldiers passively standing by whilst looters pillaged shops, forcing some businessmen to mount their own armed guard. It was only by about the second evening (the 23 September) that SADC troops were ordered to adopt a more active stance towards the gangs of looters. A dusk-to-dawn curfew imposed upon the capital only took effect by the third night.

By the 23 September, Mangosutho Buthelezi (who was Acting as South African President in the absence of both President Mandela and Vice-President Thabo Mbeki), declared that the situation in Lesotho had been stabilised. But newspaper reports suggested that this had been at the cost of some 58 LDF and 8 SANDF soldiers killed (although it subsequently emerged that the figure for the LDF was an overestimate). There may also have been up to 100 civilian casualties (deaths and injuries), whilst the victims of the violence also included many expatriates who had been extricated by their national authorities and in excess of some 2,000 Basotho refugees (mainly members of the LCD) who had fled across the border to neighbouring South African towns.

By the first weekend after the intervention, a further 1,000 LDF soldiers had surrendered to the SANDF - and had been released and instructed to report back with their weapons. But BNP leader Sekhonyana raised the prospect that the remaining rebels still at large might stage hit-and-run missions against refugees across the border. Press analysis suggested the threat of civil war. The SANDF moved to contain such threats by increasing the number of its troops to 3,500 in early October.

The Political Aftermath

The intervention drew furious criticism from many quarters in South Africa. The opposition parties called for an emergency debate in parliament, variously accusing the operation of having been hastily conceived, haphazardly executed and of doubtful international legality. Their concerns were echoed by their counterparts in Botswana, and by various human rights organisations such as the Black Sash and church organisations which argued that South Africa had failed to explore all avenues for a peaceful resolution of the crisis. Although editorials varied, press comment was overwhelmingly critical.

In contrast, the operation drew support from a variety of organisations (for instance, the South African National Civics Organisation, the National Council of Trade Unions and the South African Communist Party). However, such was the vigour of criticism that SADC was forced into an increasingly vocal defence of its actions. President Mugabe quelled speculation that he was at odds with the intervention, and Buthelezi stressed the collective nature of the decision-making that had preceded the intervention. But South Africa and SADC moved to defray further criticism by calling upon the main political actors in Lesotho to normalise the situation by resuming negotiations. However, whereas the opposition alliance demanded that the government should resign and be replaced by a government of national unity to run the country prior to new elections, the LCD stated that its precondition for even entering talks was that it would consider neither new elections nor resigning in favour of a government of national unity.

Following considerable arm-twisting, an all-party meeting with a SADC mediating team culminated in a statement made by Thabo Mbeki on the evening of 2 October that a political solution had been found centred around agreements that the LCD would stay in power, that new elections conducted by a reconstituted Independent Electoral Commission (IEC) would be held within 15-18 months; that a 'security presence' would remain in Lesotho until the country's own security forces were able to perform their constitutional role; and that the opposition parties had given an undertaking to cease mobilising resistance to the government on the basis that the elections of May 1998 were flawed. Reports spoke of the LCD having conceded early elections under a transformed electoral system that would provide for increased representation for losing parties.

Mbeki's announcement was subsequently denounced by the opposition, which insisted that there had only been tentative agreement on some issues. However, following further negotiations, the SADC mediating team managed to secure a compromise which would provide for a) the LCD to remain in government but b) for a multi-party committee to debate all activities relating to the election. This would include responsibility for all electoral matters and the appointment of a new IEC.

Following further pressure, the opposition finally accepted the restoration of the LCD to office alongside the creation in November of a 24 person Independent Political Authority (IPA), composed of two members drawn from all political parties which had participated in the disputed May elections, which was charged with preparing for new elections within fifteen to eighteen months.

Part Two: The Objectives, Legality and Conduct of SADC's Military Intervention

The Political Objectives and their Realisation

According to Buthelezi, the intervention by SADC was launched at the explicit request of a legitimate government to pre-empt a military coup. SANDF soldiers who had died had laid down their lives for 'the region's collective security, democracy and stability'.[2] Mandela later stressed that although Mbeki had worked very hard to achieve a political settlement, the LDF had worked very hard to take over the government. This had resulted in a 'virtual coup'. A statement from Zimbabwean President Robert Mugabe similarly declared: 'Any military attack to undermine a sovereign government is viewed by all of us in the SADC and the OAU as rebellious and therefore as a matter of great concern wherever it occurs'.[3]

This then was the official line. SADC had intervened to arrest a coup designed to overthrow a democratically elected government, and to re-impose order upon a rapidly deteriorating situation which threatened to spread disorder beyond Lesotho itself. Furthermore, the military operation itself was conducted in a humane manner with minimum loss of life. The forces of disorder in Lesotho were then to be compelled to resolve their differences with the government in a constitutional and peaceful manner.

The strength of SADC's position is that orderly government *had* broken down in Lesotho, and that a government which had recently won a sweeping victory at the polls was being challenged by an opposition alliance whose leading element, the BNP, had a history of extremely dubious democratic credentials. Furthermore, it would seem that whilst the opposition was talking negotiations with the SADC mediators before the intervention occurred, the BNP was simultaneously organising the 'virtual coup' by mobilising its youth militia, recklessly urging the LDF to intervene, backing the dismissal of the senior officers, and urging the King to take unconstitutional action. From this perspective, therefore, the SADC intervention *did succeed* in preventing a coup, and it *did succeed* in backing a democratically elected government.

This writer was one of the few commentators in South Africa who argued that the SADC intervention was politically justified (even if the actual conduct of the intervention was bungled).[4] However, in retrospect this judgement needs to be qualified in that it is not completely clear that, at the time the decision to launch the intervention was made, SADC was wholly convinced that the LCD had not rigged the election.

Careful dissection of the election results and of the Langa Report, indicates that the complaints of the Opposition about the election were largely baseless. There were undoubtedly many administrative flaws in the electoral process, and there may even have been an attempt from within the IEC to introduce a number of ghost voters. However, not only did the Langa Report reject eight out of the Opposition's ten major complaints, but post hoc analysis indicates that even if every single 'ghost voter' had voted in favour of the LCD, the Opposition would only have won a grand total of 4 seats.[5] As in 1993, the real problem lay with the manner in which the demographic spread of government and opposition supporters around the different constituencies interacted with the plurality electoral system to deny appropriate representation for minority interests. As in 1993, the peculiarly inequitable outcome of the election indicated the urgent need for a reform of the electoral system towards proportional representation. However, the awkward fact remains that the Langa Report was a remarkably limp document, whose detailed findings rejected the opposition case, but whose major conclusion was merely that it could not 'state that the invalidity of the elections (had) been conclusively established', nor could it 'postulate that the result does not reflect the will of the Lesotho electorate'(Langa Report, 1998, para.7.7).

It has been proposed elsewhere[6] that the lukewarm finding of the Langa Report may have been a product not just of the indecisiveness of the commissioners, but of an assumption within the office of Vice-President Mbeki before the Commission was established that the LCD had indeed rigged the election - a belief which would seem to go back to the de facto alliance which was forged between the ANC and the BNP during the late 1970s and early 1980s when the latter, as the government of the day, was making Lesotho available to the former as a sanctuary for refugees and a base for operations. In short, if after the delivery of the Langa Report, the South African government shifted its position to endorsing the LCD as the victor in the elections, it seems to have done so with a lack of conviction. In consequence, two other factors are likely to have been more persuasive.

First, the key SADC actors in this particular drama were the troika of Zimbabwe and Botswana as well as South Africa. As the parties which had worked together to reverse the 'King's coup' in 1994, they were particularly alarmed by the junior officers' rebellion and convinced that it was a precursor to a military intervention. In a region where, post-apartheid, all three governments had good reason for wanting explicit commitment by SADC states to the norms of civil rule and democracy, they were not prepared to stand back and see that commitment breached by the weakest member state within the regional organisation.

Second, Pretoria was almost certainly motivated by the urge to restore political order, as it feared the spill-over effects (via a mass exodus of refugees and the exportation into its own territory of Lesotho's internal crisis) which might follow from a coup. In contrast, although South Africa's own Department of Defence and those opposed to the intervention were to cite South Africa as acting to protect its material interests in Lesotho (notably its massive investment in the Lesotho Highlands Water Project, which will redirect water to the country's thirsty industrial heartland in Gauteng), such reasoning was probably low down the scale, for the simple reason that a coup would not directly have threatened these. South African commerce and industry had never directly suffered in previous coups, and it would scarcely have been in an incoming military government's interests to compromise the Water Project, which is set up to become a major revenue earner for the impoverished, landlocked country. Indeed, as the SANDF's action to secure the Katse Dam demonstrated, South African investments were far more likely to be threatened by an adverse popular and military reaction to an intervention than they were by South Africa remaining on the sidelines.

The fact that SADC underestimated the danger posed to physical plant by the opposition supporters and that South Africa did have to move quickly to absorb a couple of thousand refugees serves only to underline the dismal ineptitude of South African intelligence.

Having said all this, it does not follow that SADC's aim of providing a framework for the different parties in Lesotho to resolve their differences was easily realised. As discussed above, the very fact of the intervention and the bitter anti-South African sentiments which it fostered was to render attempts to bring about an inter-party agreement extremely difficult. None the less, the record indicates that by late November SADC had brought the different parties to a genuine compromise which embodied *second-best* solutions for both sides to the conflict. The LCD government remained in power, but was forced to concede an early election and the establishment of the IPA as a forum for mediation about a long-term electoral and political solution; and the Opposition were compelled to concede their demands for a government of national unity in favour of guarantees of an early election and the establishment of the IPA.

How we allocate responsibility for the subsequent failure of the conflicting parties in Lesotho to maximise this opportunity for creating a more consensual politics is more controversial. To cut a long story short, the IPA was less than successful as a forum for resolving conflict. On the one hand, the LCD resented its existence and in the months that followed its establishment, effectively undermined the IPA by failing to provide it with accommodation and the resources required for it to function. Worse, during its early months especially, the LCD's delegates simply failed to attend its meetings. Meanwhile, the efforts of the majority of opposition delegates - drawn from parties which represented only a tiny fraction of the population - were devoted less to forging a compromise than devising an electoral system which would maximise their personal chances of election to the next parliament. The inevitable result was a stalemate and a failure to agree. In this circumstance, it is arguable that more should have been done by South Africa to facilitate mediation of differences - but against that, the South African government may have felt that with its neutrality under attack from the opposition, Lesotho's politicians should be left alone to resolve their problems. South Africa knew there was a device in the post-intervention agreement which, in the event of the failure of the IPA to agree upon arrangements for a new election within a given time span, provided for matters under continuing dispute to go to binding arbitration.

This is what eventually occurred, and in November 1999, a South African Judge appointed as the arbitrator ruled that Lesotho should adopt a mixed electoral system whereby 50 members of parliament should be elected by first past the post, and 50 by proportional representation, but with the important proviso that for the election of 2000 (now foreseen as taking place in around

September of that year), 80 MPs would be elected by FPTP, and 50 by PR. Although clearly favouring the LCD, this arrangement will provide for incorporation of leading Opposition politicians into the next parliament, and is regarded as pointing the way out of the present crisis with some prospect of allowing for a longer term settlement.[7]

The Operational Efficiency of the SADC Intervention

The SADC forces were mandated to establish control over the South African-Lesotho border, to protect South African assets and to stabilise Maseru in order to create a safe environment for Lesotho's political parties to negotiate.[8] These objectives were located within the political context of preventing a military coup.

Neethling, who works for the SANDF's Military Academy, notes that in its post-mortem, the SANDF claimed that the South African government had not made it clear that its 'Operation Boleas' was a peace enforcement, rather than a peace support, operation.[9] None the less, he argues that the SANDF's immediate objectives were clear, and that the operation was in no way hampered by political uncertainty. He also notes that, although the cost of the operation (24 million Rands between 22 September and 2 November) strained the SANDF's smaller, post-apartheid budget, there was no indication that the operation was hampered by financial constraints. He therefore concludes that 'a lack of resources and inadequate logistic support cannot be seriously considered as an impeding factor in conducting the intervention operation in Lesotho'. Furthermore, as far as the SANDF was concerned, 'the forces had been correctly composed in the light of intelligence reports and the operational appreciation of the level of resistance expected' and that they had been committed to the doctrine of using minimum force.

Whatever the official positions, it is manifest that the important aspects of the intervention were severely flawed.

The extent of the military bungle is obvious. The harm done to the economy by the looting and arson was very considerable. 1,045 businesses reported damage, with estimated damage to premises amounting to M96,944,000 and stock losses amounting to M163,850,000. Almost all Maseru branches of South African chain stores were attacked and gutted, and the offices above them destroyed, but it was probably small (248) and very small businesses (266) employing just a few people which were most badly affected. Virtually all of the latter were uninsured. The damage was clearly discriminatory: the Taiwanese business community was particularly badly hit, but businesses known to be owned by supporters of the BNP were left undamaged. Overall, it was reckoned that there would be an immediate loss of 1,506 jobs in an employment scarce economy, whilst the long term effect upon investor confidence was incalculable.[10]

Those who completely disagree with 'Operation Boleas' query whether all the possibilities of peaceful persuasion had been thoroughly exhausted before the decision to intervene was made. Apartheid South Africa had precipitated the military coup in 1986 by imposing a virtual blockade from outside; and democratic South Africa, Botswana and Zimbabwe had cajoled a reversal of the King's coup of 1994 by a mixture of arm-twisting and negotiation. Critics remain unconvinced that all such avenues had been explored on the latest occasion. In any case, they say, even if the military had intervened, how long would SADC have allowed such a government to have lasted?

The more immediate critique focuses upon the inadequacy of despatching a force of 600 SANDF troops to confront a 2,000 strong RLDF, a failure to deploy the most suitable units (some soldiers had no previous combat experience), the failure to co-ordinate a simultaneous entry by the BDF, and the dismal lack of intelligence. There were particular criticisms that Maseru need not have been left so dismally unprotected from the rioting. Even once the BDF arrived, minimal initial effort was seemingly made to re-impose order. BDF soldiers were reportedly discouraged by the hostile reception that they encountered; and numerous media reports testified to SADC soldiers passively standing by whilst looters pillaged whatever was left in the shops. It was only by about the second evening (the 23 September) after the intervention, as small-arms fire continued to punctuate the smoke and as snipers took potshots at the SADC troops, that the latter were ordered to adopt a more active and aggressive stance. A dusk-to-dawn curfew imposed upon the capital only took effect by the third night. Other critics pointed out the inadvisability of the intervention having been led by Colonel Robbie Hartslief. Although he himself came out of the imbroglio rather well, it was argued that a SANDF contingent led by an Afrikaner who was unable to speak Sesotho was always likely to be construed as an invasion force. In contrast, had the SANDF awaited the BDF, the operation would have appeared more like a genuinely SADC operation, rather than a South African one with a SADC fig-leaf.

Most embarrassing for the South African government was the fact that many such criticisms were made explicitly by senior elements within the military. According to Colonel Hartslief, the 'fog of war' rather than inadequate intelligence or strategic planning was responsible for the difficulties which the SANDF encountered. But other officers were less tactful. Speaking at a symposium just after the operation, there were complaints that the army had been sent into Lesotho 'blindfolded', and Chief of Special Forces Brigadier-General Borries Bornman complained that the 'wrong people' had been despatched to Lesotho on the basis of inadequate planning, preparation and information.[11] It was also subsequently admitted that the degree of armed resistance which the SANDF had met had been unexpected, and that there had been significant loss of intelligence collection in Lesotho following the withdrawal of a South African military attache in April 1998 (just before the election!). There were inadequate aerial photographs, and intelligence liaison with the BDF was minimal. For all that SANDF chief General Sipho Nyanda subsequently deplored the leaking of such criticisms, it is difficult to avoid the conclusion that those who approved the military logistics for this operation gifted their critics with sufficient ammunition to query their competence. Furthermore, if subsequently there had been any degree of humility about the way matters had gone wrong, or if leading politicians (notably Mandela, Mbeki and Buthelezi) had hinted at their having been in some way at fault, then criticism might have been more forgiving. As it was, remarks by Mandela that South Africa could not assume financial responsibility for the disaster, because the damage had been wreaked by the Basotho themselves, provoked outrage from sections of the South African media, which alleged that their new government was acting no better than its apartheid predecessor. Finally, whatever the excuses that were made, the Lesotho operation manifestly asked major questions about the command structure of the newly integrated SANDF.

The Legality of the Intervention and its Regional Implications

The consensus of opinion is very much that the intervention was *not* founded upon sound international legal ground. SA and SADC cannot be faulted for coming to the help of a legitimate government, recently elected, which requested assistance. However, this appears not to have been sufficient to validate a *military* intervention. SADC argued that the intervention was carried out in terms of a) the guarantee of Lesotho's stability forged by South Africa, Botswana and Zimbabwe which terminated the King's coup of 1994; and b) SADC's own state security agreements, particularly Article 5 of the protocol on politics, defence and security agreed at the organisation's Gaberone summit in 1996. This latter provides for intervention where there is large scale violence between sections of the population, or between armed or paramilitary forces and sections of the population, if there is a threat to the legitimate authority of the government, or if there is any crisis that could threaten the peace and security of other member states. However, neither of these instruments had been formally ratified by the member states. That is why, according to Seiler, Pretoria subsequently referred to the intervention as justified by 'customary international law'.[12]

Commentators also argue that the intervention was not legal in terms of UN procedures. Chapter VIII of the UN Charter provides for the use of regional bodies, such as SADC, for peace enforcement purposes, but only with the prior authorisation of the Security Council. Yet SADC had not sought such authorisation, and could not claim the UN's endorsement. Indeed, for all that there are good grounds for arguing that current UN procedures are too cumbersome for the proper conduct of intervention operations in Africa, there is little doubt that peacekeeping is essentially a UN responsibility, that it should be endorsed by the world body, and conducted in accordance with the internationalist ethos of the UN Charter. Whilst the UN now seems prepared to form partnerships with regional organisations in Africa for the effective management of conflict in Africa, the specifics about such arrangements have yet to be clarified and formalised. In these circumstances, the intervention in Lesotho was always going to be portrayed by its critics as illegitimate and partial to the LCD.[13]

Even if the intervention flowed from noble motivations, its imperfect legality was always likely to undermine its success by providing a moral basis to the LDF and the Opposition for resistance. All this points to the urgent need for SADC to conclude a defence pact amongst its membership, and to secure the necessary authority for future interventions from the UN. As it was, the intervention indicated not only that SADC's institutional framework but also that South Africa's foreign policy appeared to be in considerable disarray.

The Implications for South Africa's Foreign Policy

The immediate problem for South Africa posed by the intervention was that it invited criticism that the Mandela government was acting little better than its predecessor. There was already growing resentment throughout the region at what was increasingly perceived to be South Africa's new hegemony. Hitherto, discontent had focussed upon the massive outward movement of South African capital into Africa, the extension of trade inequalities, and an alleged arrogance which goes with it. But the dubious legality of the intervention and Lesotho's de facto status as an encircled and powerless dependency inevitably encouraged perceptions of South Africa as a bully.

Second, the handling of the intervention was taken as evidence of inconsistency in South Africa's post-apartheid Africa policy. This latter was touted as based upon principle rather than pragmatism, and as one which placed an emphasis upon human rights and peace-making and building. Consequently, the decision which preceded the intervention into Lesotho, which saw South Africa setting its face against SADC countries extending military support to the dubiously democratic regime of President Kabila in the Democratic Republic of Congo (DRC) to counter armed rebels, earned high praise from most commentators on both moral and logistical grounds. In contrast, the shift from an insistence upon the need for a negotiated settlement in the case of the DRC, and the attempted armed imposition of a political solution in Lesotho, inevitably aroused concern.

All in all, for all that its foreign policy was proclaimed as being based upon enlightened principles, South Africa's intervention suggested that in practice it was based upon *ad hocery* and that it had not yet attained the right blend of strategies and practices to implement its proclaimed role as regional leader, mediator and peacemaker.[14]

The Intervention in Perspective

How SADC's intervention into Lesotho will come to be viewed in the long term will depend upon at least four major factors.

First, whereas it is unlikely that the operational conduct of the intervention will be remembered positively, SADC's involvement may eventually be judged according to whether it has laid the basis for non-violent resolution of political conflict within Lesotho. Lesotho's post-independence politics have been peculiarly antagonistic, and the environment for consolidating democratic practice is less than favourable. Against this, there are some reasonable grounds for hoping that the intervention may have paved the way towards a less fractious politics. The most immediate marker will be how the country's politics progress towards the forthcoming election. Given the failure of the IPA to agree around a new electoral system, and given the fact that the 80 + 50 formula for the 2000 election has, essentially, been imposed by SADC arbitration, it is almost inevitable that the terms of the settlement will be hotly debated by the LCD and its opponents, and indeed, that the election campaign will involve a re-run of debates about the justice of the 1998 election and of the intervention. However, the prospect that the result of the 2000 election will be accepted by the losers (however reluctantly) will be greatly enhanced by the facts that the arbitration provides for Commonwealth supervision of the process. But more importantly, the new electoral system, however imperfect, will provide for the inclusion of opposition leaderships within the next parliament; and furthermore, there will be no lack of appreciation that SADC will not tolerate any physical challenge to the result. The successful conduct of the next election will then hopefully provide for the holding of more representative, 50 + 50 contests thereafter.

The second criterion upon which the success of the intervention will come to be judged amplifies the first. It relates in particular to the extent to which SADC's involvement may lead to the civilianisation of politics in Lesotho. The outcome of Lesotho's democratising election of 1993 was always likely to be compromised by the LDF's historical connection to the BNP. Following the intervention, the LCD has been insistent upon prosecuting those personnel alleged to have been principally involved in rebelliously overthrowing their senior officers; and the SANDF has been involved in a major restructuring initiative intended to bring about a more efficient, less politicised army. The smooth progress of this exercise allowed for the departure of from the country of the main body of SADC troops in May 1999. Again, this has all been highly controversial. Nonetheless, it is arguable that a more civilianised politics in Lesotho could only have been made possible by a breaking of the intimate link between the LDF and the BNP, and by attempting to render a reformed army subject to civilian authority (as opposed to its becoming re-oriented to underpinning the LCD). Only time will reveal the extent to which this restructuring will have been successful - but of the necessity of weaning the army away from political involvement there can be no doubt.

Third, and controversially, I argue that Lesotho should forge a closer relationship with South Africa which recognises the peculiar limits of its existence. Whether the events of September 1998 were an 'invasion' (as propagated by the Opposition) or an 'intervention' (as maintained by SADC), the post-apartheid reality would seem to be that South Africa has become increasingly drawn into Lesotho's politics as an external guarantor of democracy. South Africa was invited to into the country to defend a democratically elected government in 1994, and yet again, in even more dramatic circumstances, in 1998. If the current post-intervention negotiation process fails to forge a more stable and formally democratic order, a repeat performance is more than likely. In short, it is in the interests of both countries that a proper defence agreement be drawn up, with SADC's imprint, which would provide an unambiguous legal framework and procedures under which any further intervention might be launched. Such an outcome would represent an acceptance of unequal power relations by Basotho politicians which would be realism writ large. But in the longer term 'a diminished sovereignty' for

Lesotho could be a 'protected sovereignty, and more importantly, a foundation for peace, democracy and development'.[15]

Finally, the enormous controversy which surrounded the intervention will probably come to be seen as one of the factors which has contributed to current moves towards SADC creating an institutional framework for forging a common defence and security policy. As noted by Dludu, it was easy enough for the SADC member states to agree on strategies when there was a clear enemy in Pretoria.[16] But where the enemy is disputed, as in the contemporary DRC and Angola, the evolution of a rules-based system for resolving regional conflicts is becoming increasingly urgent.

Notes

1 The account that follows is constructed from media accounts and interviews as also summarised in Southall, R. (1998a), 'Is Lesotho South Africa's tenth province?', in Lambrecht, K. (ed.), *Crisis in Lesotho: The Challenge of Managing Conflict in Southern Africa,* Foundation for Global Dialogue: Braamfontein, pp. 19-15, Southall, R. (1998b), 'Lesotho: Democracy at Gunpoint? South Africa Intervenes', *Southern African Report*, Vol. 14, No. 1, pp. 12-17, and Southall, R. and Fox, R. (1999), 'Lesotho's general election of 1998: rigged or de rigeur?', *The Journal of Modern African Studies,* Vol. 37, No. 4.

2 *Eastern Province Herald,* 24 September 1998.

3 *Mail and Guardian,* 25 September – 1 October 1999.

4 Southall, R. (1998c) 'Big mistake in Maseru was miscalculating the strength of resistance', *Sunday Independent*, 27 September.

5 Southall, R. and Fox, R. (1999), op.cit.

6 Southall, R. and Fox, R., op.cit.

7 Constitution of Lesotho (Amendment) Bill, 1999.

8 Sutton-Pryce, T., Baudin, C. and Allie, N. (1998), 'Baptism of Fire for SANDF', *Salut*, November, p. 26.

9 Neethling, T. (1999), 'Intervention in Lesotho: Reflections on the SANDF's Participation in Operation Boleas', Paper to the Congress of the South African Political Science Association, 29 June – 2 July.

10 LCCI et al. (Lesotho Chamber of Commerce and Industry, Association of Lesotho Employers and Sechaba Consultants) (1998), *Lesotho 1998: Assessment of Damages to Business and Loss of Employment.*

11 *The Star*, 1 November 1998.

12 Seiler, J. (1998), 'Learning from Lesotho', unpublished manuscript.

13 de Coning (1998), 'Conditions for Intervention: DRC and Lesotho', *Conflict*

Trends, Vol. 1, pp. 20-23.

14 Van Nieuwkerk, A. (1998), 'The Lesotho crisis: implications for South African foreign policy', in Lambrecht, K. (ed.), *The Crisis in Lesotho: The Challenge of Managing Confflict in Southern Africa,* Foundation for Global Dialogue: Braamfontein., p. 15.

15 Southall, R. (1998a), op.cit., p. 25.

16 Dludu, J. (1999), 'No Nato, just an organ for southern Africa', *Business Day,* 2 November.

9 From Intervened to Intervenor: Rwanda and Military Intervention in Zaire/DRC

Mel McNulty

Introduction

Inter-African intervention has emerged since the Cold War as an effective, if blunt, instrument for effecting political transition in a state's strategic sphere. Observers have noted the 'new willingness of African armies to engage in conflicts beyond their borders, which threatens to make armed insurrection, with the help of neighbours, the preferred means of political change on this continent'.[1] Rwanda, like all states and particularly those which have themselves been objects of intervention, does not undertake intervention lightly. Historically, it has not been expansionist, although it has been suggested - by former president Bizimungu among others - that the Treaty of Brussels of 1910, which included the Masisi plains of north Kivu in the then Rwandan kingdom, provides a historic justification for recent Rwandan involvement in Kivu province of eastern Congo-Zaire. However, this justification was not acted upon until 1996, when Rwanda launched its first intervention into the eastern provinces of its giant neighbour, Zaire (now the Democratic Republic of Congo). And despite the initial success of this intervention, it has not sought to intervene directly in any other neighbouring state.

In his chapter on Angola, Norrie McQueen notes that all of that country's interventions 'were essentially external projections of Angola's continuing internal conflict', and that 'perhaps nowhere else in Africa has the fragility of the domestic-external dichotomy in security issues been better illustrated than in Angola – whether in the importation of foreign forces or the exportation of its own'. In reponse to this latter point, it will be argued here that Rwanda's experiences as intervened and subsequently as intervenor, although in dramatically different circumstances, represent a similar tension, although it was the Rwandan *ancien régime* which, from 1990 to 1994, imported foreign forces for the specific purpose of forestalling its overthrow. Rwandan interventions post-1994, on the other hand, revealed the urgency of the post-revolutionary administration's search for external security, domestic stability and latterly, access to resources.

A dramatic sequence of events has meant that Rwanda and Angola, through their readiness to intervene, became involved - initially together but subsequently on opposite sides - with up to seven other African states in wars in Congo-Zaire. Adebayo Adedeji takes this to be key evidence of a trend:

> [T]here is a growing tendency for neighbouring countries to intervene directly in their neighbours' internal conflicts. It is now known that Uganda, Rwanda and Burundi assisted the Laurent Kabila forces in the civil war that overthrew the Mobutu regime ... Two years later when the Rally for Democracy (RCD) spearheaded the rebel movement against the Kabila government, these three countries became engaged on the side of the rebels while Zimbabwe, Angola, Namibia, Central African Republic and Chad joined forces with the DRC government to crush the rebellion. Thus, nine neighbouring countries have been involved in the ongoing civil war in the DRC.[2]

Each of these intervening state's geopolitical, strategic and historical situations is unique, although there are many similarities and indeed overlaps in the intervenors' motives, mechanics and discourse. Each has a political, strategic and/or economic interest in the Zairean-Congolese state which in the declining years of the Mobutu regime (1995-97) offered rear bases, supply routes, resources and often direct support for Rwandan, Ugandan, Burundian and Angolan armed groups. For the governments of those neighbouring states, particularly the fragile post-genocide administration in Kigali, intervention in Zaire was seen as essential to their own security. Since the outbreak of the second Congolese war in August 1998, intervenors in Congo-Zaire have mined a rich seam of resources, literally and metaphorically, to the extent that their interventions have become self-funding or even profit-making.

Rwanda - driven by the successful use of armed intervention by its new leaders - was the leader in advocating and implementing the 1996 and 1998 interventions in Congo-Zaire. Despite the apparent supremacy of a crude profit motive in recent times, in order to understand the Rwandan interventionary impulse it will be necessary to consider Rwanda's recent interventions as a result of a sequence of events. These stem originally from the colonial legacy of division and partition, and the Belgian-sponsored creation in Rwanda of a sectarian, one-party regime which depended for its survival on the exclusion or elimination of its opponents. In order to consider the expansion of the war through intervention into another state, we need to begin by re-examining the sources of conflict in the region. Thereafter, Rwanda's intervention in the affairs of its giant neighbour may only be explained in light of the intervenor's regional and domestic imperatives, and of its history as an object of intervention since 1990.

External Intervention in Rwanda

The first external interventions in the historic kingdom of Rwanda date from the colonial period. From 1919, when Belgium under League of Nations mandate took over the German colonial territory of Ruanda-Urundi, Belgian colonial governors exploited differences in Rwandan society by elevating a minority social group (Tutsis) to administer colonial rule to the detriment of the majority (Hutus). The process of decolonisation from Belgian rule did not protect Rwanda from external intervention, or free it from its colonially-distorted history. In fact, its crippling sectarianism was reinforced by the very nature of the Belgian-inspired - and supervised - 'social revolution' of 1959, a sectarian pogrom which saw the killing or exiling of over half a million Tutsis, abandoned by the Belgians when they displayed evidence of anti-colonial ideas above their station. This reversal of ethnic patronage was assisted by the direct intervention of Belgian military personnel, who armed, trained and commanded the new Rwandan army.[3] The idea that the majority - Hutu - had been oppressed not by Belgium but somehow independently by Tutsi genetically predisposed to dominate was embraced enthusiastically by PARMEHUTU (*Parti pour l'émancipation des Hutu*), led by Grégoire Kayibanda, who would found the Rwandan First Republic and become its president. More precisely, the consolidation of PARMEHUTU and its seizure of power at the Belgians' behest and to the detriment - indeed the physical exclusion - of their Tutsi fellow-citizens, was part of a strategy in Brussels to maintain Belgian influence on the continent - most importantly in the vast Belgian Congo - by passing power to proxies and clients.[4]

Violent expulsions of Tutsi recurred during the 1960s and early 1970s, and the exclusion of those remaining Tutsi from employment, public life, and political, economic or military power created a quasi-apartheid system of discrimination. Ethnic categorisation continued, as in colonial days, to be displayed on a Rwandan's compulsory identity card. The net effect was that inter-ethnic tension became the definer of the country's problems, and sectarian prejudice and exclusion key features of the state because deemed essential to the state's survival. Fearful of betrayal, President Kayibanda had surrounded himself with supporters and family members from southern Rwanda, distributing patronage disproportionately to those he felt he could trust. As a result, erstwhile PARMEHUTU supporters from the north and centre of the country grew isolated from the president and distant from the levers of political and economic power he controlled. Crucially, Kayibanda failed to retain control over the army, allowing his Chief-of-Staff Juvénal Habyarimana to build a power-base for family, friends and allies drawn from the latter's home region in Gisenyi, north-western Rwanda. Habyarimana claimed that President Kayibanda was unable to protect the country against sporadic interventions from neighbouring countries by *inyenzi* ('cockroaches') - small bands of exiles seeking his overthrow, the precursors of the Rwandan Patriotic Front. Neither could he guarantee peace and stability in the climate of sectarian revenge which would follow such attacks. Exploiting this insecurity, Habyarimana seized power in a military coup on 5 July 1973.

It was soon apparent that the new regime would seek to shift blame for civil conflict through the scapegoating of unspecified troublemakers, an enemy within who were to be held responsible for any of the state's shortcomings. However, the exiles problem endured. Habyarimana insisted that 'the glass was full': densely populated, Rwanda, with a population of 8 million in 64,200 square kilometres, was too overcrowed to allow the exiles to return. Over 15 years, the tranquility, indeed introspection of this 'little Switzerland of Africa' concealed the state's gradual hardening as it failed repeatedly to address the basic injustice upon which it was built: the forcible exclusion of up to 600,000 citizens.

In 1986, the Rwandan exile community in Uganda was in the vanguard of the successful campaign by that country's National Resistance Movement/Army (NRM/A) to overthrow President Milton Obote. The Rwandans were of course aware of the precedent for inter-African intervention set in the region by Tanzania's popular 1979 intervention in Uganda which overthrew Idi Amin, and they realised early that their Ugandan experience could usefully be applied to the Habyarimana regime in neighbouring Rwanda. A disproportionate number of the NRA's senior commanders were drawn from Uganda's Rwandans, notably Chief-of-Staff Fred Rwigyema, and Intelligence Chief Paul Kagame. Following the NRM's victory in 1986, the militarily experienced Rwandans became aware of growing resentment of the prominence - perceived as dominance - of Rwandans in the new Uganda's army and administration. Rwigyema and Kagame represented a generation of exiles radicalised by combat and aware that, as Rwandans, they would always be stateless until their 'right to return' was granted or seized. Accordingly, the Rwandan Patriotic Front (RPF) was founded in Kampala in December 1987.

On 1 October 1990, the RPF launched its long-anticipated offensive against the Habyarimana regime, crossing into Rwanda from bases in Uganda. If the war had been left to run its course, the RPF would have triumphed quickly, given their numerical and material advantage. The Rwandan government army (*Forces Armées Rwandaises* - FAR) numbered 5,200 in 1990 against the RPF's estimated 7,000, and were poorly trained and short of munitions. The original, core RPF (termed 'the Ugandans'), on the other hand, were well-trained, well-armed, and highly motivated, with a hunger for land, nationality and reparations typical of dispossessed peoples. They also benefited from the material support of a neighbouring state, Uganda. Indeed, the provenance of these well-armed troops reinforced Rwandan government claims of a 'Ugandan invasion' although this was primarily an intervention by its own exiled co-nationals. Facing imminent overthrow, Habyarimana swiftly requested a counter-intervention from his principal foreign backer, France. His request was met swiftly with an intervention, codenamed *Opération Noroît,* whereby 300 French troops from bases in the Central African Republic, along with front line Zairean forces of President Mobutu's presidential guard, halted the RPF offensive.

It is important to note here that Zaire intervened in Rwanda some six years before Rwanda (under the RPF) intervened in Zaire. Indeed, the 1990s inter-involvement of these countries in each other's political and military affairs was not entirely new. Zaire and its diminutive eastern neighbours had long had cross-border interests due to migrations of population. Shally Gachuruzi notes that:

> With the independence of Zaire [Congo] in 1960, Rwandese and Burundians who were in Zaire became Zaireans. For five years, until 1965, Zaire adopted and preached a policy of non-interference in the internal affairs of Rwanda and Burundi, but that did not last. When President Mobutu came to power in November 1965, Zaire's position of noninterference in the internal affairs of other countries changed.[5]

The role in 1990 of the Zairean troops was key to the Habyarimana government's survival, in that unlike the French, they were sent to the front line as dispensible cannon fodder. Their repulsing with French support of the RPF's first, conventional offensive, changed the nature of the conflict into a protracted guerrilla war. Moreover, their involvement at this crucial early stage was to create a lasting resentment among RPF leaders for Mobutu's Zaire, and sow the seeds for the subsequent, post-genocide Rwandan interventions there. However following this initial success, the Zaireans' subsequent looting and terrorising of the Rwandan civilian population meant that Habyarimana was forced to demand their withdrawal.

Nonetheless, Zaire would remain an indispensible supply route for weapons up to, including and subsequent to the Rwandan state's recourse to genocide in 1994. The significance of Mobutu's Zaire as a source of regional instability, comparable by some accounts to that of apartheid South Africa for the southern continent, explains the subsequent imperative for post-genocide Rwanda and other threatened states to co-operate in its destruction in 1997.[6]

France meanwhile claimed its 1990 intervention was designed to protect French citizens, a claim lent weight by a simultaneous intervention by Belgium. However, Belgium withdrew its troops after a month when the immediate threat subsided. French troops were to remain for three years; their numbers never dropped below 250, and at one point - following the subsequent RPF offensive in February 1993 which was also halted with French assistance - French military personnel officially numbered 680. Following the genocide and in an effort to forestall an RPF victory, France's re-intervention in Rwanda from June to August 1994, *Opération Turquoise*, covered the retreat of the defeated FAR and the genocidal *interahamwe* militias, along with a massive human shield of some two million refugees, into eastern Zaire. From 1994 to late 1996, the ex-FAR/Interahamwe regrouped and rearmed, often with external assistance, and used the massive refugee mini-states at Goma and Bukavu as rear bases from which to launch attacks into Rwanda, notably against genocide survivors who might have given evidence against them in the Rwandan courts or at the International Criminal Tribunal for Rwanda at Arusha, Tanzania. By December 1996, Rwanda's new military leaders decided to take the war to their opponents, and intervene directly in Zaire to break up the camps, separate refugees from *génocidaires* and destroy the latter.

Rwanda as Intervenor 1: Zaire 1997

Although destruction by the Rwandan patriotic Army (RPA) of the refugee camps of Kivu province was Rwanda's short-term goal, it is now apparent that it sought a bigger prize of overthrowing Mobutu and helping install a friendly leader in Kinshasa who would be susceptible to Rwandan influence and would remove permanently the ex-FAR/Interahamwe's capacity to attack Rwanda. This wider aim was made possible by linking Rwanda's security imperatives to the long-term goals of Congolese nationalism and its campaign against Mobutu, dating back to 1965. Shouldering these forces and allying itself with Uganda and Angola, Rwanda helped created the broad anti-Mobutu coalition led by Laurent Kabila, which became the Alliance of Democratic Forces for the Liberation of Congo (AFDL).

Faced with this unprecedented challenge, Mobutu tried to hold power by his usual means: playing the card of ethnic divide and rule which had brought such devastation to the Congo in the 1960s and on several occasions since. His target this time was the Rwandophone population of Kivu province - first generation Banyarwanda and Congolese Tutsis or Banyamulenge - whom he stripped of their Zairean nationality and declared non-citizens. However, for the first time the tactic backfired; the victimised and suddenly denaturalised Rwandophone peoples of eastern Zaire fought back, having been armed and trained by neighbouring states with administrations now hostile to Zaire, and also urgently seeking the security which only the destruction of the Mobutist state could bring. Added to this was the application of twice-tested Ugandan model of African *maquisard* warfare by one of its architects, Paul Kagame, successfully transposed from the narrower confines of Ugandan bush war and Rwandan guerrilla campaign to the vastness of Zaire.

This was not to be a purely Rwandan operation, although it was clearly Rwandan-led. It is now a matter of record that the RPF Army, spearheaded the AFDL campaign. Rwandan officers planned and directed military operations, and mid-level commanders led AFDL forces throughout the swift, seven-month march on Kinshasa. Rwandan troops participated in the capture of at least four cities (Lubumbashi, Kisangani, Kenge and Kinshasa), and Rwanda had provided arms and training for those forces even before the rebellion began.[7] The RPA's well-tried tactics were particularly effective against a demoralised and disintegrating regular army. With little fighting, it was often sufficient to surround a town, announce its fall, and leave a corridor for the demoralised and unpaid *Forces armées zairoises* (FAZ) to loot and flee.

It is also important to note that of anti-Mobutu – and subsequently anti-Kabila – forces, Rwanda has had greatest flexibility to intervene. The interventionary capacity of Rwanda's fellow intervenor (and occasional co-belligerent) Uganda is limited, in theory at least, by a separation of political power. Oliver Furley notes in his chapter on Uganda that: 'Parliament has criticised [the UPDF's] intervention in the Congo war… where suspicions have been raised that army officers have been intent on securing business deals in the mineral-rich areas far away from Uganda's borders'.[8] However in Rwanda, decision-making and control over military deployment – ironically on the French fifth republic model - is concentrated in the hands of the presidency in a highly centralised polity. There has been little public debate in Rwanda over the cause and effect of its interventions.

The absence of an external counter-intervention was crucial to the AFDL campaign's success. When the Banyamulenge rebellion broke out in Kivu province in late 1996, former colonial power, Belgium, had already long-distanced itself from the embarrassing and 'unfrequentable' Mobutu. The US swiftly decided to pull the plug on its former Cold War client. Only France persisted with the line that Mobutu alone could save Zaireans from themselves and the inevitable ethnic bloodbath that would follow. However, when in November 1996 the RPA broke up the refugee camps and nearly a million refugees returned to Rwanda, this new Rwandan regional military assertiveness (albeit crudely violent) pulled the carpet from under French demands for a 'humanitarian intervention' to freeze the conflict and force the AFDL into a power-sharing compromise with Mobutu.

The RPA-backed AFDL was also effective in its propaganda and careful media management. Crucial for the campaign's unimpeded progress was the absence of foreign camera crews. No images were recorded of the destruction of the refugee/fugitive camps or the killing of ex-FAR and Interahamwe personnel, as well as many of the refugees among whom they were sheltering; most accounts indicate that the RPA/AFDL killed 200,000 people at this time. This has been denied by Rwanda. However; expressing his wish to relieve the pressure of international censure on the new AFDL administration, Kagame admitted in July 1997 that his forces had indeed led the offensive against Zaire, and that the killing of *génocidaires* and refugees in Kivu province was an inter-Rwandan affair.[9]

In sum, the initial establishment by the AFDL and RPA of a buffer-zone along Rwanda's western border served a dual purpose: the break-up of the refugee camps there, which had been used as secure bases for the ex-FAR/Interahamwe to launch attacks against Rwanda, and from which by late 1996 an reinvasion was presumed imminent; and the subsequent destruction of those forces - whether separate from or sheltering amongst the refugees they had forced to retreat with them deeper into Zaire. International expressions of horror at the bloodshed this policy entailed took little account of the failure of the international community to bring those forces to justice, and this failure's contribution to the irresistible pressure on the Rwandan government to act when faced with urgent popular demands for security and retribution. This ruthlessly efficient application of victor's justice, to a problem which had proved insoluble to the international community, should have come as no surprise. Declarations from leading figures in Kigali throughout 1996, as attacks on genocide survivors and witnesses within Rwanda increased, made clear that the Rwandan government would stop at little to ensure its survival. Colette Braeckman noted at the time that Kagame had made plain since 1995 his determination to sort out the security problem himself if the international community was unable to do so.[10]

Essential for the achievement of both goals was to make a clear distinction between them, that is, between Rwanda's immediate security need on the one hand, and the larger issue of the governance of Zaire. By December 1996, when a Canadian-led international intervention had been agreed, the RPA had destroyed the eastern Zaire camps, and up to a million refugees began to return to Rwanda. The argument from Kigali was that there was little for the intervention to do; Paul Kagame tells how: 'When the Canadians came here we told them off. We said there were two issues: the problem of refugees, and that of a rebellion aimed at changing the situation in Zaire. Let us handle the situations separately.'[11]

The claim of intervention in self-defence (i.e. to protect the intervening state's nationals in the intervened state), although only technically justified in international law, is widely accepted as a derogation from the non-intervention norm enshrined in the UN Charter's Article 2(4). Invoked by France and Belgium in 1990, the same claim would be one of those used by the RPF-led government to justify this first intervention by its forces in Zaire, namely to protect the denaturalised Banyarwanda and Banyamulenge population of Kivu province. Those Western powers which had failed so spectacularly in 1994 to fulfil their obligations under the 1948 UN

Genocide Convention could scarcely criticise this claimed forestalling of the extension of the Rwandan genocide to eastern Zaire as a pretext for intervention. In terms of protecting vulnerable populations, including their co-nationals, Rwanda could in fact claim the same justification under international law - protection of 'nationals' - as France and other extra-African intervenors had done so frequently since 1960. Unfortunately for the entire region and particularly the Congolese people, however, one intervention did not prove enough to achieve Rwanda's goals of security for itself and vulnerable Rwandophones in Kivu nor, some now argued, to satisfy its ambition for regional hegemony.

Rwanda as Intervenor II: DRC 1998 to Present

The first anniversary of Mobutu's overthrow was marked by growing criticism of the AFDL regime on two fronts. Kabila's human rights performance showed little improvement on Mobutu's, and the Democratic Republic of Congo was soon trapped in a vicious circle apparent at its rebirth: Mobutu's overthrow had been facilitated by the intervention of assertive regional powers responding to their own security imperatives, responses which often paid scant regard to Western models of human rights. International finance and diplomacy initially sought to isolate the DRC for its failure to observe these models, and effort focused on gaining access for the UN Human Rights inquiry team established in September 1996. However Kabila's government conspired to stop the Special Rapporteur carrying out investigations into killings during the AFDL campaign, in a welter of megaphone diplomacy over the composition of the team and the terms of its mandate. After months of fruitless effort the Secretary General announced the misson's withdrawal. The team's June 1998 report concluded that the AFDL, with Rwandan support, had committed violations of international humanitarian law, human rights law and crimes against humanity from October 1996 to May 1997 in eastern Zaire. The report acknowledged that the team was unable to confirm or disprove most of the allegations of these violations and was unable to pinpoint responsibility among the AFDL, the Rwandan military and other armed groups including ex-FAR/Interahamwe, the retreating FAZ, and locally-recruited Mai-Mai rebels, which operated in the area at the time. These conclusions were refuted by both the DRC and Rwandan governments, who alleged that the team was biased, its witnesses partial and its report incomplete.

In the face of Kabila's non-co-operation and apparent complicity in massive human rights abuses, the financial assistance essential to rebuild the DRC and meet its population's expectations of the new regime was not forthcoming. At the same time, the new Congo's regional allies had grown deeply disillusioned with the leader, Laurent Kabila, whom they had assisted to power. Initially elated at his lightning success, Kabila's regional patrons, and indeed the Congolese people, soon grew impatient with a lethargic administration and an unglamorous leader who failed to meet the exacting standards of what had been hailed the 'New African Political Order'. Most importantly, the security problems in eastern DRC which had driven Kabila's original sponsors were not solved. Those sponsors now found themselves confronted with a paradox which should have been apparent at the start: Kabila had no army of his own with which he could even begin to impose order and security across the DRC's vast territory. He had been swept to power through military intervention by his patrons, without whom he had few forces to command, but whose continued presence was undermining his popularity. The defeated former Zairean army could scarcely provide the embryo of a new national army; it was corrupt, demoralised and would need to be rebuilt from scratch before it could offer even the flimsiest guarantee of Congolese security.

Kabila's textbook reaction was to seek to scapegoat foreigners. The crux came in July 1998, with Kabila's populist declaration that all foreign forces should leave the DRC, notably the Rwandans who had, by all accounts, overstayed their welcome in Kinshasa. This demand was ill-received in Kigali and Kampala, where political and military leaders now realised that their empowerment of Kabila had been a serious strategic error, and they expressed in no uncertain terms their disapproval of Kabila's new assertiveness. However, Kabila retaliated - much as Mobutu might have done - by encouraging hostility towards 'Tutsis', Rwandans and eastern Congolese in general. These populations were targeted and killed in towns and cities across the DRC.

Just over a year after the fall of Mobutu, the wheel seemed to have come full circle as Rwanda and Uganda began planning further interventions in DRC. Following a new insurgency in Kivu province, Rwanda and Uganda were instrumental in the creation of the *Rassemblement congolais pour la démocratie* (RCD) in August 1998. This was to be, to all appearances, the AFDL Mark II. Its initial leadership included representatives from a spectrum of Congolese opposition groups, and its military forces consisted of mutinous soldiers from Kabila's newly-formed army, reinforced by Rwandan and later Ugandan forces.

The second DRC war was swiftly underway, again spearheaded by the region's most experienced army, the RPA. As the campaign began, there were reports of serious human rights abuses, including massacres, against the local civilian population in eastern DRC, with some commentators concluding that the Rwandan civil war of 1990-94 has simply been relocated to Congolese territory, with the Congolese civilian population as pawns or innocent victims of more powerful outside forces. To make matters worse, this second Congolese war expanded exponentially as, to resist a Rwandan and Ugandan attempt to seize Kinshasa with airlifted forces, Kabila called on other states to come to his assistance as the legitimate (or at least de facto) president of a Southern African Development Community (SADC) state which had been invaded. Lured by the promise of access to the DRC's abundant resources, Kabila successfully achieved a counter-intervention by Zimbabwe, Namibia, Angola and (briefly) Chad (see the following chapter).

With the intervenors' initial attempts to recreate their 1997 success thwarted, the conflict settled down into a pattern of attrition. The intervention by Rwanda and Uganda (in support of DRC rebels) soon became a quasi-occupation, and it was apparent by late 1998 that neither side could inflict a decisive defeat on the other. With Kabila's rule under attack from his former patrons and their Congolese allies, the Kinshasa government now sought international support for allegations of human rights abuse in eastern DRC by its new opponents. It invited the Special Rapporteur to visit the country and recognise that massacres were committed against refugees and internally displaced persons in 1996 and 1997. Kabila's hand was greatly strengthened by the coming-to-blows of Rwandan and Ugandan forces at Kisangani, in a dispute apparently driven by little more than competition for loot, on three occasions in 1999 and 2000. In the May 2000 confrontation, Rwandans and Ugandans shelled the city and killed over 200 Congolese civilians.

All parties to the conflict in eastern DRC have been responsible for massive violations of human rights, but the large presence of Rwandan troops greatly exacerbates the situation. Its forces – and those Congolese groups which depend on their support – are profoundly unpopular with the majority of the people in the territory they occupy, although their precipitate withdrawal would leave Rwanda's Congolese allies, especially the Rwandophone population of north and south Kivu, extremely vulnerable. Although the pervasive control and security mechanisms which characterise Rwanda and Burundi have not been recreated in eastern DRC, there is a framework of administration in urban areas under the control of rebel forces and/or their regional backers.

However, the externally-backed rebel alliance soon proved fragile as it became apparent there would be no lightning victory for pro-Rwandan forces this time. In May 1999 the RCD split into two factions: RCD (Kisangani), headed by a well-known left-wing academic, Professor Ernest Wamba dia Wamba; and RCD (Goma), headed by Dr Emile Ilunga. The split reflected the division between the RCD's backers which was demonstrated so graphically at Kinsangani: Uganda backed RCD(K) in north-eastern DRC, while RCD(G), dominant in the Kivus and parts of south and central DRC, is to all intents and purposes an extension of the RPA.

Following a further split in RCD(K), the *Mouvement de libération congolais* (MLC) emerged in October 1998 and opened a second front against Kabila in the Equateur region of northern DRC. It is headed by an entrepreneurial businessman, Jean-Pierre Bemba, the son of a Congolese millionaire who has served in the governments of both Mobutu and Kabila. The MLC has achieved significant military success north of the Congo river, with considerable logistical and tactical support from the Ugandan army. The two RCD groups and the MLC have held talks to develop a common political and military strategy, but many attempts by their external backers to unify the rebels have failed.

However, all three rebel groups and their regional sponsors have sought throughout to remove Kabila, and to this end they are signatories of the August 1999 Lusaka Ceasefire Agreement which offers them a place in a National Dialogue (which seeks to establish a consensual, inclusive Congolese government), and a role for their forces in a newly constituted Congolese army. The rebels claim that Kabila has wasted the country's wealth, failed to bring peace, stability and security to the DRC, divided the army and repressed democracy. However for most Congolese, the RCD factions are seen as Ugandan and Rwanda puppets, and neither has created an identity as a legitimate Congolese political movement. The MLC in contrast emphasises its Congolese nationalist credentials, and has at times appeared most likely to topple Kabila. Bemba has popular support in Equateur province and potential to be a credible presidential candidate, especially if he could extend his appeal to other parts of the country. However, he remains heavily dependent on Uganda for military support.

Rwandan troops are likely to remain in DRC as long as the ex-FAR/Interahamwe continue to operate there. Since the outbreak of the second Congolese war, these 'negative forces' have been re-armed and re-trained by several external powers, including Zimbabwe. They were not included in the August 1999 Lusaka ceasefire agreement; except insofar as Rwanda insisted that their forcible disarmament and demobilisation was essential to a solution of the DRC war. Since 1999, however, senior ex-FAR officers, and many Interahamwe militia members sought by the Rwandan and international courts for genocide crimes, have been incorporated into Kabila's *Forces armées congolaises* (FAC). Their aim remains to topple the current, post-genocide administration in Rwanda.

It is hard to imagine circumstances in which the disarmament of armed groups foreseen by Lusaka could happen. The danger remains that in the absence of such disarmament, the RPA will retain a permanent, though hugely unpopular, presence in the DRC. However in four years of almost unlimited access to eastern DRC, the RPA - the most formidable army in the region - has been unable to defeat the coalition of 'negative forces' which, in the supreme paradox of its intervention, the Rwandans' very presence helps hold together. Throughout 2000, the Rwandans were tied down in the Kivus by the FAC, Interahamwe and locally-recruited Mai-Mai operating together.

At the same time, Kabila's monopoly of power in the third of Congolese territory still controlled by Kinshasa in late 2000 was made possible by the existence of an external threat, used to explain away the administration's failings and undermine opposition. Under the terms of the Lusaka ceasefire agreement, Rwanda should withdraw its forces from DRC, although this is dependent on the unlikely eventuality that a sufficient UN force could be mustered to fill the security vacuum.

By late 2000 it had become apparent that Rwanda might never withdraw fully from DRC. Despite the failure of its intervention to topple Kabila, it had achieved one of its principal objectives: the distancing of the direct military threat to Rwandan territory from forces of the Rwandan ancien régime. However in the time it has taken for this objective to be achieved, a new and more prosaic motive has emerged: the prolonged intervention and de facto control of much of eastern DRC has made the intervention self-financing and even profitable for many of those involved. In these circumstances, some means of financial reward may have to be found for returning troops for fear that they could present a threat to their own government. It is not insignificant that Rwanda may be exploring the possibility of volunteering troops withdrawn from DRC for UN peacekeeping duty.

Conclusion: a Permanent Intervention?

What then could be the exit strategy for Rwanda's intervention in DRC? From the Rwandan perspective, enduring Rwandan control, albeit at one remove, over the Kivus, is clearly the best option and would in fact be a realisation of the pre-colonial Greater Rwanda concept. This would ensure the protection of the Rwandophone population of the region, and would of course give Rwanda a continued monopoly of the region's resouces and markets.

On the other hand, according to Rwanda's official discourse which at its insistence was included in the 1999 Lusaka ceasefire agreement, Rwanda will withdraw within its own borders when its armed opponents have been disarmed – 'tracked, disarmed, cantonised and documented'.[12] Chapter 20 of the OAU-commissioned report on Rwanda of the International Panel of Eminent Persons (IPEP), published in July 2000, offers a number of important conclusions in this regard, notably re Lusaka Annex A chapter 9 [Disarmament of Armed Groups]. The IPEP stated that:

> Until disarmed... these 'non-state actors' have an interest in the continuation of the war and a capacity to act as spoilers of the entire agreement, much as Rwanda's Hutu Power leaders undermined the [1993] Arusha accords... [D]isarming these rebel groups is obviously the key to the future.[13]

Nonetheless, the security threat to Rwanda, the original justification for its Congolese interventions, no longer seems paramount. Moreover, there is evidence that President Kagame could demonstrate sufficient pragmatism to negotiate with génocidaires if necessary, and that space could be created within the Lusaka process for such a development. His meeting with Kabila at Eldoret, Kenya in June 2000 indicates that accommodation between sworn enemies is possible. Following the hypothetical completion of withdrawal by Uganda - long weary of its Congolese involvement - Rwandan withdrawal might be the only way to allow room for the national dialogue and a decision among Congolese about their county's future to take place. It would also remove the only declared justification for the continued Zimbabwean presence. Although Kabila could easily find other reasons not to co-operate, it removes his principal excuse for intransigence. Similarly, if Rwanda has withdrawn, Kabila will have no further need for his de facto alliance with the ex-FAR/Interahamwe/Mai-Mai and others, unless, that is, he wished to pursue a purely inter-Congolese civil war which in the absence of external support he would be unlikely to win.

Rwanda has been militarily overstretched in eastern DRC, and its leaders know it is embroiled in a war it cannot win on its own terms. Its offer in August 2000 to withdraw 200km from its previous positions in Kasai, although publicly intended to demonstrate a commitment to the Lusaka process, indicates a desire to consolidate its forces in a quasi-permanent buffer zone in the Kivus. Although any redrawing of borders to acknowledge the de facto annexation of parts of Congolese territory would be anathema both to Africa and to the wider international community, a mechanism may be found to allow Rwanda a droit de regard (although not a droit d'ingérence) in the provinces of DRC which it borders. In the meantime, it is clear that an end to conflict in eastern DRC necessitates a withdrawal of foreign armies in general, and a formal commitment to nonintervention by Rwanda in particular.

Notes

1 'Rebels Backed by Angola, Take Brazzaville and Oilport', *New York Times*, October 16, 1997, ref. in Austin, Kathi (1999), 'Light Weapons and Conflict in the Great Lakes Region of Africa', in Boutwell, Jeffrey and Klare, Michael T. (eds), *Light Weapons and Civil Conflict*, Rowman & Littlefield: Oxford, p. 45, note 24.

2 Adedeji, Adebayo (1999), 'Comprehending African Conflicts' in Adedeji, Adebayo (ed), *Comprehending and Mastering African Conflicts*, Zed Books: London, and Ijebu-Ode: African Centre for Development & Strategic Studies, p. 3.

3 Crucial here was the role of Colonel Guy Logiest, whose shaping of events he describes in his own account, *Mission au Rwanda: Un Blanc dans la bagarre Tutsi-Hutu*, Didier Hatier: Brussels, 1988.

4 Prunier notes that: '[T]his was a very strange "revolution" indeed. The break between the Belgian authorities and their long-coddled Tutsi elite had come about only because the colonial administrators felt betrayed by their erstwhile protégés. They now considered them as a mixture of backward traditionalists and revolutionary communists, and unlikely combination which was not dissimilar from the way the British then regarded the Mau Mau movement in

neighbouring Kenya. What would later be touted as a "social revolution" resembled more an ethnic transfer of power. (...) "The revolution is over," declared Colonel Logiest in October 1960. This was an appropriate declaration, for inasmuch as the "revolution" had been a Belgian-sponsored administratively-controlled phenomenon, its end could be administratively proclaimed just as its beginning had been administratively made unavoidable.' Prunier, Gérard (1995) *The Rwanda Crisis: History of a Genocide*, Hurst: London, pp. 50, 52.

5 Gachuruzi, Shally B. (1999), 'The Role of Zaire in the Rwandese Conflict', in Adelman, Howard and Suhrke, Astri (eds), *The Path of a Genocide: The Rwanda Crisis from Uganda to Zaire*, Nordiska Afrikainstitutet: Uppsala, p. 51.

6 See McNulty, Mel (1999), 'The collapse of Zaire: implosion, revolution or external sabotage?', *The Journal of Modern African Studies*, 37:1, March.

7 *The Washington Post*, 9 July 1997, 'Defense Minister Says Arms, Troops Supplied For Anti-Mobutu Drive', by John Pomfret.

8 Oliver Furley's chapter, p. 13, of manuscript, to be published in the *Journal of Commonwealth and Comparative Politics*, Vol. 38, No. 3.

9 Interviewed in *The Washington Post*, 9 July 1997.

10 Braeckman, Colette, *Le Soir*, Brussels, 21 August 1997.

11 Major-General Paul Kagame in an interview with Mahmood Mamdani, 11 July 1997, distributed on list <rwandanet@msstate.edu>.

12 Lusaka ceasefire agreement August 1999, Annex A, 9.1.

13 OAU report on Rwanda of the International Panel of Eminent Persons (IPEP), July 2000.

Part Three
Victims of Intervention

10 DRC: Africa's Scramble for Africa

Gerry Cleaver and Simon Massey

The intervention of Rwanda in the Congo, which is discussed in the previous chapter, was followed by the intervention of a number of other states, making the war a unique type of struggle not previously experienced in Africa since independence. It is not a world war, or a continental war, but it has been called with some legitimacy a 'scramble'. Not all of Congo's neighbours have intervened. Tanzania, with a long border with the DRC, has suffered severely in economic and environmental terms by the war, as hundreds of thousands of Congolese refugees poured over the border, but the government has notably kept out of the war itself. Zambia also has refrained from any serious involvement, as have two other neighbouring states, Congo Brazzaville and the Central African Republic. Uganda has a lengthy and very disturbed border with Congo and so has felt obliged to intervene for strategic and defence considerations, as the government claims, but some of the other intervenors have borders surprisingly far distant from the DRC yet they have also opted for intervention. The motives and the scale of their interventions will be discussed in this chapter.

The Background

The war in the Democratic Republic of Congo is a great tragedy affecting the bulk of central and southern Africa. The complex entanglements of this war have weakened the participants and made them more vulnerable internally and externally.

The war is in reality a continuation of the 1996-97 rebellion against Mobutu, which in turn was directly linked to the genocide in Rwanda in 1994 and its consequences. However it would not be too difficult to trace the roots of the current conflict back even further. In several respects the current fighting in the DRC represents the linking together of a number of civil wars from neighbouring states e.g. Rwanda, Uganda, Angola and

Sudan. The DRC has ceased to exist as a state in empirical terms and is in danger of becoming a huge governmental void in the heart of Africa, delineated only by the borders of its neighbours. Thirty two years of Mobutu's rule, following the depredations of colonialism and the immediate post-colonial anarchy, have wrecked the Congo. Mobutu's kleptocratic regime ruined first the mineral and then the diamond industries and reduced the infrastructure, both physical and human, to a shambles. Congo was and still is, in no position to resist foreign incursion on its own. It is dependent on external assistance and is prey to those of its neighbours who cast covetous eyes upon its undoubted natural wealth.

Laurent Kabila came to power in the DRC in May 1997 backed by Rwanda, Uganda and Angola. In very short order he proved to be no better than his predecessor. He proved to be inept economically; he alienated potential Congolese political allies and was stigmatised as a Rwandan puppet. In an attempt to reinforce his credibility as a Congolese nationalist, he ordered all foreign troops out of the DRC on 27 July 1998. The Rwandans in particular had been frustrated by Kabila's inability to deal with the ex-FAR and Interahamwe forces in DRC and had been seeking a political alternative to their would-be protégé for some time. On 2 August 1998 an army rebellion broke out in eastern DRC; it rapidly spread to the west of the country and only intervention by the forces of Angola and Zimbabwe prevented Kabila's fall. An offensive in the west secured this part of the DRC for Kabila but his forces and those of his allies were unable to make serious inroads into the rebel gains in the east. A stalemate set in and the DRC was de facto partitioned. The rebels have made steady progress toward their goal of capturing the mineral rich area around Mbuji Mayi.

This war is being fought in some of the most inhospitable forests in the world and conducting any sort of military operations in this kind of terrain is very difficult. There are no clearly defined front lines and areas of control are vague; communications are poor, the roads are dreadful and air transport is paramount. So this cannot be a high tech conflict. These circumstances better suit the soldiers of Uganda and Rwanda with their experience of guerrilla warfare rather than the troops of Kabila's allies, Angola, Zimbabwe, Namibia and Chad, whose forces are designed for use in more open terrain. This war is linked directly and indirectly to conflicts in a number of neighbouring states, namely Angola, Uganda, Rwanda, Congo Brazzaville, Central African Republic, Sudan and Burundi. It is this that makes finding a solution so difficult.

The Rebels

The rebels are a mixture of ex-Kabila allies in the Alliance of Democratic Forces for Liberation (ADFL), frustrated politicians, disgruntled soldiers, Banyamulenge Tutsis (that is the long-established Tutsi population in south-eastern Congo) and entrepreneurs on the make. The RCD (Congolese Rally for Democracy), formed on 1 August 1998, has now split into two factions supported by Uganda and Rwanda respectively. There is also a new rebel faction, the MLC (Congolese Liberation Movement), supported by Uganda and formed in response to the RCD's failure to popularise the rebellion amongst ordinary Congolese. The Uganda and Rwanda armies have failed to form a united command and have recently been fighting each other in Kisangani, ostensibly in support of their respective factions of the RCD, but, more likely, over access to the diamond trade.

Kabila may not be very popular himself but he has succeeded, amongst the Congolese at least, in portraying the rebellion as a foreign invasion. He has played the ethnic card in stirring up hatred for the Congolese Tutsis, the Banyamulenge. They in turn consider that the war has in fact failed to address their security concerns and this has led to tensions in their relationship with Rwanda.

Uganda

Uganda has become involved in the DRC because of concerns over the security of its western borders. In the case of Uganda, this threat came from the Allied Democratic Forces, West Nile Bank Front and the Lord's Resistance Army, all rebel groups within Uganda. It supported Kabila's efforts in this field once he had seized power. In April 1998 there were reports of WNBF and Sudanese troops using Garamba National Park in the north-east of the DRC as a base for operations against Uganda, and Uganda's involvement in the current conflict has failed to provide it with the security it desires. The ADF continues to launch attacks within Uganda and the abduction of and murder of tourists in Bwindi National Park in March 1999 shows how vulnerable her western border remains.

Uganda's occupation of the north-eastern portion of the DRC has provided a safe area for the Sudanese People's Liberation Army in its war with the regime in Khartoum. As a consequence, the Sudanese government has supported Kabila with planes and men. On 4 August 1999 Sudanese planes bombed Makanza and Bogbanga, rebel-held villages north east of Kinshasa and killed over 500 civilians.

The war has also exposed corruption within the Ugandan military and government elites. Many officers seem principally concerned with exploiting the mineral wealth they control. The recent purchase of broken down tanks from the Ukraine and unfit rations from South Africa has caused a scandal for President Museveni and dented the international image of the Uganda government. The Ugandan military had also to act in the autumn of 2000 in support of the leadership of its wing of the rebel movement, against internal opposition. As with all other combatants the war in the DRC is proving very costly for the Ugandans and they have had to increase their military expenditure. In November 1999, for example, they purchased 7 MiG21 jet fighters from Poland. In addition there have been spectacular 'fallings out' with Rwanda, most notably in June 2000 in Kisangani when the rival armies battled each other for a number of days. Two other clashes between them took place. Ostensibly about control of diamond extraction in the area, the conflict also revealed deeper tensions over local dominance in the sub-region.

Zimbabwe

The official justifications put forward by Zimbabwe, together with its coalition allies Angola and Namibia, for intervention in DRC had no basis in international law. The initial explanation was that the combined operation was based on a decision of SADC's Organ for Politics, Defence and Security. First proposed at a meeting of SADC foreign ministers in January 1998, the Organ soon fell victim to rivalry between Zimbabwe and South Africa. The potential for intervention in conflicts was frequently discussed and Mugabe was elected the Organ's first chair. However, a definitive agreement on the scope of the Organ was neither framed, nor ratified. Thus, Mugabe was in no position to speak or act on behalf of a security structure still in formation.

Likewise an alternative justification that the intervention was authorised by a decision of the regional Inter-State Defence and Security Committee (ISDSC) had no basis in law. The ISDSC, founded in 1975, had grown to encompass all members of SADC. The Committee, more of a talking shop for regional security issues, had always been informal, without a headquarters or secretariat. An ad hoc meeting in Harare on 18 August supported intervention. However, beyond the fact that the ISDSC had never claimed a mandate for mutual defence intervention, only four of its fourteen members were present, undermining its authority as potential legitimising body.[1]

The regime of Robert Mugabe has suffered considerable damage due to its involvement in the DRC. This widened an existing split with South Africa, particularly the personality clash with Nelson Mandela. It has put an enormous strain on an already weakened economy, and the war costs at least £1 million per day. The Zimbabwe government has claimed that the DRC is meeting these costs as well as claiming that it is receiving assistance from France, Libya and Angola and arms from China. However the main financial beneficiaries of Zimbabwe's involvement in the Congo appear to be close associates of Mugabe and by inference Mugabe himself. The rights to market Congolese cobalt have been given to a company – Ridgepoint, which is owned by Wheels of Africa, a conglomerate run by a Zimbabwean, Billy Rautenbach, who is a close associate of Mugabe. Ridgepoint now also have the concession to the Kababankola cobalt mine and in November 1998 Rautenbach was made Chief Executive of the Congolese state mining corporation, Gecamines. Many contracts in support of Zimbabwean forces in the DRC have gone to ZANU-PF members. The transport contract has gone to a company owned by General Zvinavashe, head of the Zimbabwe air force and commander of the pro-Kabila allied forces in the DRC. The upshot of all this is that many in Zimbabwe believe that the war is being prosecuted for the benefit of the political elite, and combined with the economic problems of Zimbabwe, this has led to growing political instability.

Militarily Zimbabwe has committed most of its frontline strength to the DRC, with approximately 13,000 men. The terrain is alien to them; reportedly they do not know why they are there and what they are fighting for. Morale is low and desertion rife; casualties have been high, with 700-1,000 killed. The army suffered a bad defeat near Kabinda in late May of 2000. Material losses have also been high: at least six jet fighters and two helicopters as well as numerous military vehicles have been lost. These will be costly to replace for Zimbabwe though there are reports of a purchase of twelve Mi35P helicopter gunships.

In January 1999, there were reports of a coup plot and arrests of officers; journalists reporting the story were arrested and tortured apparently with the approval of Mugabe. The war continues to be costly and unpopular and it is undoubtedly a contributory factor in the general atmosphere of political instability in the country. Economically the adventure has been expensive. In November 2000, the Zimbabwean finance minister announced a reduction in the allocation of defence expenditure for operations from Z$3.3 billion to Z$2.2 billion (US$40 million). This was rather optimistically in anticipation of a successful implementation of the Lusaka accords, the shaky peace agreement signed in July/August 1999. So far the war has cost approximately US$200 million, which Zimbabwe cannot afford. It still has about 11,000 troops in DRC; many have not been paid recently and now receive their allowances in DRC scrip rather than currency. Zimbabwe has spent considerable sums on weaponry including three MiG23 fighters from Libya, where 400 Zimbabwean personnel are undergoing training.

By the end of November 2000 there were signs that the mercurial leadership of both Mugabe and Kabila was rapidly destroying the relative credibility of these 'African dinosaurs'. Growing debt and civil unrest at home left Mugabe's position barely tenable. Moreover, Mugabe was dismayed that Rautenbach had been replaced at Gecamines by George Forrest, a Belgian magnate, despite reports that Mugabe had interceded with Kabila on his behalf.[2] Mugabe's statement that the coalition was looking for a 'middle ground' might indicate a realisation that for Zimbabwe further involvement in DRC was not worth the candle.

Chad

In September 1998 the Chadian press began publishing sightings of heavy transport aircraft flying south from N'Djaména.[3] As rumour spread Chad's president, Idriss Deby, was forced to admit that Chadian troops had been deployed to DRC under conditions of secrecy and without a report to, or debate by, the National Assembly. The number of troops involved has been estimated at between 1,000 and 1,500.

The intervention was justified on the grounds of regional security and defence of the principals of territorial integrity and the inviolability of borders. Sekimbaye Bessane, Chadian minister of communications and government spokesman, defended the deployment on this basis, tinged with an element of self-preservation – 'Chad is in the subregion, and if a neighbouring country is destabilised our turn may not be far away ... this is why we do not want to wait for a surprise'.[4]

Chad shares common membership of the Communauté Economique des Etats d'Afrique Centrale (CEEAC) with DRC, although the organisation has no common defence protocol. The two countries have no contiguous borders. Moreover, although Chad has known threats to its territorial integrity, its recent history has not been one that demanded such a dramatic and principled stand. The long running dispute between Chad and Libya over ownership of a tranche of land separating the two countries, known as the Aouzou Strip, was settled by a decision of the International Court at The Hague in 1994, following which Libya withdrew its garrison. Chad has also had a series of minor confrontations with Nigeria over disputed islands in Lake Chad. Moreover, despite its history of factionalism and almost constant internal strife, the aim of the warring parties has rarely been the dismemberment of the existing state.

Justifications for Deby's action lie elsewhere. The rapprochement with Libya following the Aouzou Strip settlement is key. N'Djaména has scant control over the majority of its own territory and, despite sizeable battle-hardened armed forces, is unable to project force beyond the occasional border skirmish with neighbouring states. Tripoli has shown a renewed and vigorous interest in sub-Saharan affairs. As the Economist Intelligence Unit points out, 'one tactic that Libya has employed to good effect in the region is to "buy" favour with neighbouring states through favourable business deals and even outright grants'.[5] Chad has benefited from these overtures. Colonel Gaddafi has offered to underwrite the planned oil extraction project in southern Chad if the existing international consortium pulls out of the deal.

Tripoli's realignment of policy interest away from Greater Arabia and toward sub-Saharan Africa coincides, and is reliant on, the lifting of Libya's current pariah status in much of the West. The release of the Libyan security agents accused of involvement in the bombing of the Pan-Am airliner over Lockerbie in 1988 is part of the strategy. Direct involvement by Libyan troops on the ground would undermine the portrayal of Libya as a force for peace. Thus, when Chadian troops deployed to DRC many opposition voices were quick to accuse Deby of being in Gaddafi's pocket. Acheikh Ibn Oumar of the exiled *Conseil Démocratique Révolutionnaire* (CDR) described Chad as acquiring the reputation of 'international bounty hunter'.[6] The independent journal *N'Djaména Hebdo* saw Chadian involvement as prefiguring, if not frequent continent-wide excursions on Gaddafi's behalf, at least Chad becoming Libya's 'armed wing in the sub-region'.[7] Whilst the basis for the finance and logistics of transporting and maintaining the Chadian contingent in DRC remains imprecise - Gabon and Angola have been said to have contributed - Chadian government spokesmen have pointedly refused to deny that Libya stood the bulk of the costs.[8]

A further parallel advantage is that deployment in DRC did not exacerbate the ever-fragile triangular relationship between Chad, Libya and the former colonial power, France. The Deby era has seen a diplomatic dance between the three capitals as Paris and Tripoli took it in turn to vie for favouritism from, or issue veiled threats to, N'Djaména. Yet, in the case of the war in DRC, both countries were behind Kabila. The volte-face that saw Kabila reject Rwanda and Uganda - together perceived in Paris as the front for an 'anglo-saxon' conspiracy - allowed France to readdress its policy in the region. In the light of the diplomatic and military disaster that was the last French intervention in Rwanda, *Opération Epervier*, a large measure of caution and well stated neutrality needed to be observed. Nonetheless, the fact that intervention from the pro-Kabila African alliance averted a pro-American Rwandan/Ugandan ascendancy in DRC was the cause of satisfaction at the *Quai d'Orsay*.

For Deby, direct intervention in DRC also gave an opportunity to the long-standing concern that southern Sudan might act as a base for insurrectional supporters of former president Habré. Prior to the ousting of Habré the Sudanese People's Liberation Army led by John Garang, a southern Sudanese rebel movement fighting the Islamic government in Khartoum, received logistical aid and telecommunications equipment from N'Djaména. Uganda supported the SPLA as a bulwark against rebel groups operating out of Sudan. Deby feared that a victory for the anti-Kabila alliance would allow Uganda to devote more military energy to securing a permanent SPLA bastion in southern Sudan that might act as a springboard for a rebel invasion of Chad. For his part Deby had reason to thank the government of Omar al-Bashir. Deby came to power on the back of a coup d'etat launched from Sudan. A significant number of his *Mouvement patriotique du salut* (MPS) were Sudanese who shared a common ethnicity with the Zaghawa fighters from Chad.

By intervening in Chad, Deby was playing for high stakes. For many years the most conflict-prone country in Africa, Chad remained tense with sporadic bouts of violence interlarding a lengthy and complex transition to democracy under Deby. A weakening of security within the country could provide the opportunity for a disaffected faction to move against the government. The Chadian armed forces themselves remained factionalised. The experience of elements of the army fighting as a unit in the DRC – the possibility of morale-sapping casualties and the occasion for intrigue far away from N'Djaména – must have been a further worry for Deby.

The gamble was lost. The Chadian troops, though reasonably well trained and battle-hardened, were not jungle fighters. Moreover, their officers had little conception of the political context in which they were to act. The consequence was a high attrition rate amongst the Chadian contingent. In late November the government announced that a Chadian reconnaissance patrol had been involved in a major engagement with rebel forces at Yakiti-Bouta in Equateur province. As a result a dozen Chadian soldiers had been hospitalised of which two had died.[9] Disquieting rumours spread that the figure was much higher. An Ugandan officer gave the figure as nearer 200 as having been killed and others taken prisoner.[10] This figure was confirmed to the authors during an interview with Ugandan army commander Major-General Abubaker Jeje Odongo.[11] These figures tally with the stories told by troops involved in the battle evacuated to hospital in N'Djaména.[12] More worrying still was the reason that these evacuated soldiers gave for taking such heavy casualties. Since their arrival relations between the foreign contingents and the Forces Armées Congolaises (FAC) had been fragile. Chadian troops, deemed better trained and equipped, had been ordered into front-line positions ahead of the Congolese troops. This minimised the opportunity for looting on the part of the FAC. When the Chadian reconnaissance unit encountered the rebel ambush they found themselves caught in crossfire as an FAC unit acting as rearguard simultaneously opened fire from behind.[13]

It should be mentioned that the bulk of the troops used in the DRC were former rebels from southern Chad, the *Forces armées pour la république fédérale* (FARF) that had recently reconciled with the government. Whilst FARF fighters had been incorporated in the army, there was no guarantee that events in the future might see them return to fighting the government. The annihilation of this body of men, although ostensibly a military disaster for Chad, had some potential benefits for Deby's own domestic security. Even so, with the benefits of intervention essentially notional and the nightmare turn of events on the ground very real, Deby was the first leader of the pro-Kabila alliance to withdraw. Public opinion was resolutely against the operation. The independent press published articles describing the intervention as 'a major humiliation' and describing deployment of Chadian troops as 'slave trafficking'.[14] Opposition parties in the normally quiescent National Assembly began to question the continuing secrecy over the conduct of the operation. Most significantly, a rebellion surfaced in the northern prefecture of Tibesti. Although small, the fact that it was led by a former Defence Minister, Yussouf Togoimi, was enough for Deby to realise that dispatching front line elements of his army at a time of rebellion was a luxury he could not afford.

The outbreak of rebellion had further implications for Deby's survival. The rugged northern prefectures of Biltine, Ennedi and Tibesti, known collectively as BET, had been a main source of rebellion since Chad's independence. Libya was the ubiquitous associate of rebellion during this period. Intelligence that another former president, Goukouni Oueddei, a sometime friend of Gaddafi, supported the rebellion, suggested that this uprising might have the real potential to succeed. Despite official denial from both Chad and Libya, the ever-changing relationship between the two countries was once more under reappraisal. Moreover, there were reports that after the initial injection of logistical support, Libyan funds for the deployment had diminished leaving the Chadian troops in DRC short of rations and living on the land.

In late May 1999, Deby attended the Libyan-sponsored peace summit in Sirte. On his return to N'Djaména Deby announced the withdrawal of Chadian troops from DRC.

Namibia

As with Chad, Namibia deployed its forces in DRC under conditions of secrecy, without recourse to parliament and with a media embargo. Despite daily reports on the BBC World Service that there were credible sightings of Namibian troops fighting alongside government forces in DRC, Windhoek continued to deny giving any support to Kabila.[15] Even after admitting Namibian involvement, the government restricted information to the press. By December the Ministry of Defence had stopped briefing the country's most influential newspaper, *The Namibian*, citing inaccuracies and distortion in its reports. Limitation on freedom of the press to access information has been one of several contingent socio-economic reverses precipitated by Namibia's involvement in DRC.

Namibia does not share a border with DRC. Namibian troops entered DRC at the same time as their counterparts Angola on 21 August 1998. The size of the force was estimated at around a few hundred at the start of the intervention, but increased to approximately 2,000 as the fighting became entrenched.

Namibia's president, Sam Nujoma, justified intervention as necessary to preserve 'peace and stability in the region'.[16] Reiterating support for the Kabila government in November 2000, Namibian Finance Minister Nangolo Mbumba asserted that 'the world, including many African states, stood with Namibia during its difficult times … our presence in the DRC is in recognition of that contribution ... Namibia should not be selfish when it comes to rendering solidarity'.[17] However, more distinct motives concern Namibia's strategic orientation within an increasingly polarised SADC and the Nujoma family's personal investment portfolio in DRC.

During its protracted war of independence Nujoma's South West Africa People's Organisation (SWAPO) forged strong links with the ruling parties in Angola and Zimbabwe. However, since the 1994 South African elections relations between Windhoek and Pretoria have become very close. South Africa's belated support for the intervention was pointedly not affirmed by military involvement, whilst Mandela and Mbeki have been essentially concerned with maintaining the integrity of SADC. Given that the primary animus within SADC is between Zimbabwe and South Africa, and that Namibia is the junior partner in the interventionist coalition, Nujoma seems to believe that continued involvement in DRC will not fundamentally undermine relations with Pretoria.

Would Nujoma risk South African disapproval purely to reassert old fraternal ties? Aside from the growing costs in both human and material terms, one reason for the increased press restrictions is the involvement of the Nujoma family in diamond operations in DRC. Aaron Mushimba, Nujoma's brother-in-law, has been given a stake in the Miba diamond mine.[18]

In April 2000 Gwen Lister made the point that Namibia's intervention in DRC was 'taking its toll, not necessarily in terms of huge losses of human lives to Namibia (at least, not yet), but most certainly in the socio-economic sense'.[19] The casualty toll remains imprecise, but clearly exceeds government figures.

The DRC operation coincided with an enforced increase in troop numbers in a Namibian army that supported around 6,000 personnel in 1998 (the maximum authorised army size is 10,000). Around 9,500 unemployed former combatants from SWAPO's People's Liberation Army of Namibia (PLAN) have campaigned vigorously for pensions or employment. The incorporation of these former fighters into the armed forces has facilitated the currently dynamic foreign policy. The army has also been bolstered by investment in weaponry. A deal with India to buy four Allouette helicopters and four MiG25 fighters will add an armed component to the previously unarmed 'air wing'.

According to the Economist Intelligence Unit, the influx of PLAN veterans in the Namibian army will 'further add to the already crippling cost of Namibia's public-sector wage bill'.[20] Defence spending for 1999/2000 amounted to N$732m over N$443m for 1998/1999, an increase of almost two-thirds. This also amounts to a rise from 6.4 per cent to 10.3 per cent of total government expenditure.[21]

The enhancement of Namibia's defence capacity and the growing rapport between Namibia and Angola in DRC has helped to create a wider battleground environment for the offensive against the Angolan rebel movement União Nacional para Independência Total de Angola (UNITA). Namibians (and Zimbabweans) have taken the battle to UNITA on Angolan territory, whilst Angolans have fought UNITA units in Namibia. Increased insecurity for civilians living along the Namibia/Angola border has ensued. Whilst most of the casualties have been caused by UNITA rebels there have also been instances of poorly-paid Angolan government troops looting Namibian villages.

Namibia's role in the DRC conflict has been an instance of a country punching above its regional weight. As costs and domestic criticism increase Nujoma is likely to look for an exit strategy. Much will depend on Angola's lead.

Sudan

Khartoum's involvement in DRC is essentially based on the extent to which the conflict can dilute the military pressure exerted on Sudan by anti-Sudanese states in the region. The al-Bashir government has been even less forthcoming about its involvement than the other intervening states. Kabila met al-Bashir in Khartoum in mid-October after the initial rebel assault on Kinshasa had been repulsed. Whilst the Sudanese government implied support for Kabila, questions concerning troops in DRC, bombing raids by the Sudanese airforce on rebel positions, the transport of supplies to the Congolese government and support for pro-Kabila non-state actors in the conflict were diplomatically stonewalled. Sudan's presence in DRC remains assumed rather than officially acknowledged, hence no government justifications for intervention have been made.

Conflict in DRC has been beneficial to Sudan in several ways. Throughout the 1990s Sudan has accused Uganda, with justification, of giving support to Garang's SPLA. Uganda sees the SPLA as a bulwark against insurrectionary groups, notably the Lord's Resistance Army (LRA) operating from Sudanese territory and with presumed Sudanese support. Kampala's extensive role in the war has clearly affected its capacity to support the SPLA, both in terms of personnel and materiel.

A further unforeseen advantage accruing from the DRC conflict has been the fracture of the alliance between Uganda and Rwanda. From Khartoum's perspective the continued competition for supremacy between the two powerful former allies negates the possibility of a joint strike in southern Sudan on behalf of the SPLA.

Despite the denials, it is estimated that Sudan has between 500 and 2,000 troops in DRC at any one time. RCD rebels claim to have captured Sudanese soldiers fighting with pro-Kabila forces. More seriously, as already mentioned, Uganda has accused Sudan, without impartial verification, of bombing villages under rebel control in northern DRC, killing around 500 people.[22]

Angola

For Kabila, Angola's intervention was key. The influx of well-trained and battle-hardened troops from the Forças Armadas Angolanas (FAA) supported by Angolan air power swung the balance of the war in the west of DRC. The FAA forces deployed on 21 August 1998, a day after those of Zimbabwe. By 28 August rebel forces were defeated in Kinshasa and by 30 August Angolan troops had recaptured Inga and Matadi.

Angola joined Zimbabwe and Namibia in citing the flawed justifications of the SADC Organ for Politics, Defence and Security and the ISDSC decision as legitimising the intervention. Deputy Foreign Minister Jorge Chicoti told a press conference in Luanda that Angolan special troops had crossed the border to back Kabila's 'legitimate government' against a 'foreign invasion' led by Rwanda and Uganda. He added, 'we cannot accept that a neighbouring country be invaded'.[23] The official *Journal de Angola* further justified the operation in stating the need 'to defend our borders as the instability in DRC posed a great threat to our country'.[24] However, a week into the campaign the tone of Angolan media reporting took on a jubilant note. Official Angolan radio announced 'the triumphal march' of the FAA in west DRC.[25]

Angola had been a vital and staunch ally of Rwanda and Uganda during the first rebellion that brought Kabila to power. The decision to oppose its former allies was essentially based on the need to prevent UNITA from reconstructing supply lines in south-west DRC. The fateful decision by the rebel alliance in the DRC to accept UNITA support ensured Angolan intervention.

A further motivation was the overture made by DRC rebel leader Arthur Z'Ahidi Ngoma to Henrigues Nzita Tiago, leader of the Angolan secessionist movement Frente de Libertaçao do Enclave de Cabinda (FLEC). Ngoma reportedly offered, once in power, to support FLEC in return for DRC access to Cabinda's oil reserves and access to the sea.[26]

UNITA's strategic response to the Angolan intervention was swift. Sensing that Angola would be over-stretched in DRC, UNITA's leader, Jonas Savimbi, denounced the official ceasefire observers from Portugal, United States and Russia in Angola, effectively reigniting the civil war. By mid-February 1999 most of the FAA interventionist forces were forced to return to Angola. As with its entry into the conflict, Angola's retreat from DRC had profound effects on the other combatants. Not only were Kabila's Congolese forces left exposed, but the Namibian and Zimbabwean contingents were also left vulnerable since Angola had been providing much of the logistical support for the pro-Kabila coalition. As a result strategic advantage swung away from Kabila and towards a stalemate. Richard Cornwell of the South African-based Institute of Strategic Studies realigned the emphasis – 'They [Kabila's ministers] are no longer saying: "We'll smash you." Now the tone indicates something like: "We'll settle for a draw"'.[27]

After a year of reverses the FAA, at times supported by Namibian and Zimbabwean troops, began to reassert superiority over UNITA in Angola. Nonetheless, a small number of Angolan troops remained in DRC. In November 2000 Angolan Defence Minister Kundi Paihama stated that 'the allies should continue to work towards driving foreign forces out of the Congolese territory, as they are the main cause for the current climate of instability'.[28] However, although Angolan troop levels in DRC had become purely symbolic, Angola still underwrote much of the costs for the pro-Kabila alliance, including those of Namibia and Zimbabwe.[29]

Despite official announcements from Luanda, it appears that Angola is reappraising its strategy against UNITA vis à vis DRC. Along with its allies Angola has come to the conclusion that there is little value in maintaining support for the maverick Kabila. Defence spending has spiralled to 16.5 per cent of GDP in 1999. The Angolan government has signalled that it wants to normalise its economy and revive IMF lending.[30] Moreover, Luanda has received intelligence that UNITA has been allowed, at a premium, to trade 'rogue' diamonds in Kinshasa. As Kabila comes under sustained pressure from the international community and his own allies to accept a negotiated settlement, Luanda has engaged in a series of meetings with senior Ugandan officials. In November 2000 the Ugandan army commander Major-General Jeje Odongo visited Angola to assure President José Eduardo dos Santos that his forces were no longer fighting alongside UNITA.[31] If a climate of mutual trust can be created these two former allies may yet work together to ensure compliance with the Lusaka Agreement, a peace accord negotiated by President Chiluba of Zambia in July/August 1999, with the backing of SADC, the OAU, UN and EU. However, its provisions have still not been implemented to date, and fighting continues in many parts.

Summary

The consequences of the war have also spilled over into Congo-Brazzaville, Central African Republic and Zambia, in the form of refugees and military stragglers, armed bandit groups etc. It has disrupted trade and added to the general state of political and economic instability throughout this region.

This war is now primarily about control of mineral wealth. Both sides use diamonds to fund their forces and the most intense fighting has centred on these mining areas. There is also a suggestion of involvement from North Korea and China. The North Koreans are allegedly training and equipping Congolese troops for Kabila in return for access to the uranium from the Tshinkolbwe mine for its missile programme. North Koreans trained the Zimbabwe 5th brigade in the early 1980s and two officers from that unit, generals Chiwenga and Zvinavashe, are now in the DRC. Both have sat on the board of Zimbabwe Defence Industries which has close links with Norinco, the Chinese state arms manufacturer and supplier to both Kabila and Zimbabwe. Such connections are of concern to the United States and will obviously affect their relations with Zimbabwe and Kabila. Although a peace agreement has been signed in Lusaka, it would appear that the fighting has not finished entirely. Many issues remain unresolved concerning the domestic politics of the DRC and the interests of outside parties. The policing of any agreement will have to be done by African states themselves with South Africa playing a prominent role. However this will be an enormous task and if the consent of all the belligerents is not forthcoming then it will be quite beyond the capacity of African states even with the full participation of South Africa.

As of November 2000 both the peace agreement and the UN intervention seem moribund. Fighting continues in the interior. Kabila has stirred up ethnic hatred against Congolese Tutsis leading to vicious ethnic clashes in August in the east. The DRC itself appears to be rearming, buying ten Su25 ground attack jets from Russia. The presence of foreign mercenary specialists, especially pilots, was confirmed when two Ukrainian pilots were killed when a government transport plane crashed at Mbandaka in January 2000.

The consequences of this conflict will linger for many years especially for those states that have been heavily involved. The principal winners have been, as usual, greedy individuals; the major losers are the ordinary people of the countries involved, especially in the DRC where they are always the most vulnerable. It would be nice to think that the quagmire of the DRC might have cured Africa's leaders of the desire for military adventurism. However, as long as so many of Africa's leaders treat their countries as their personal fiefdoms to do with as they please, then this view will have to be regarded as wildly optimistic.

Notes

1 Berman, Eric G. and Sams, Katie E. (2000), *Peacekeeping in Africa: Capabilities and Culpabilities*, United Nations Publications: Geneva, pp. 160-178.
2 *Business Day*, 8 November 1999.
3 *N'Djaména Hebdo*, 1 October 1998.
4 BBC Monitoring Service, 'Chad: Government spokesman on reason for sending troops to DRC', 1 October 1998.
5 Economist Intelligence Unit (1999), *Country Report: Libya*, 2nd Quarter, p. 15.
6 Economist Intelligence Unit (1999), *Country Report: Chad*, 1st Quarter, p. 37.
7 *N'Djaména Hebdo*, 1 October 1998.
8 BBC Monitoring Service, 'Chad: Government spokesman on reason for sending troops to DRC', 1 October 1998.
9 *N'Djaména Hebdo*, 12 November 1998.
10 Economist Intelligence Unit (1999), *Country Report: Chad*, 1st Quarter, p. 37.
11 Interview with Major-General Abubaker Jeje Odongo, Army Commander of the Ugandan Peoples Defence Force (UPDF), Kampala, February 1999.
12 *N'Djaména Hebdo*, 12 November 1998.
13 *N'Djaména Hebdo*, 12 November 1998.
14 *N'Djaména Hebdo*, 19 November 1998.
15 *The Namibian*, 30 April 1999.
16 BBC Online Network, 'Namibia confirms its troops are fighting with Kabila' www.news.bbc.co.uk, 27 August 1998.
17 Namibian Press Association <www.nampa.org> 21 November 2000.

18 Economist Intelligence Unit (1999), *Country Report: Namibia*, 1st Quarter, p. 12.
19 *The Namibian*, 23 April 1999.
20 Economist Intelligence Unit (1999), *Country Report: Namibia*, 1st Quarter, p. 12.
21 Economist Intelligence Unit (2000), *Country Report: Namibia*, April, p. 18.
22 Economist Intelligence Unit (1999), *Country Report: Sudan*, 4th Quarter, p. 20.
23 Quoted by Agence France Presse International, 26 August 1998.
24 Quoted by Agence France Presse International, 28 August 1998.
25 Quoted by Agence France Presse International, 28 August 1998.
26 Economist Intelligence Unit (1999), *Country Report: Democratic Republic of Congo*, 4th Quarter, p. 24.
27 Quoted in *Daily Mail* and *Guardian*, 19 February 1999.
28 Integrated Regional Information Networks (IRIN), 13 November 2000.
29 *Africa Confidential*, 41/20, 10 October 2000.
30 Stevenson, Jonathon (2000), 'Prospects for Peace in the Congo', *Institute of International Strategic Studies: Strategic Pointers*, 25 October.
31 Indian Ocean Newsletter, 4 November 2000.

11 Sierra Leone: a Victim of Intervention

Gerry Cleaver

Introduction

It may safely be said that, in the case of Sierra Leone, the last ten years have been a decade of interventions. This one small West African state has been subjected to military interventions by a whole variety of actors. These have included externally sponsored rebels, mercenaries, private security companies, neighbouring states, regional and global international organisations and the former colonial power.

In many ways the recent history of Sierra Leone can be considered a catalogue of the ailments afflicting contemporary sub-Saharan Africa. These are typified by the effective collapse of the power of the state, chronic economic failure and loss of economic sovereignty, permeable borders, both geographic and political, apparently interminable conflict, centred on the exploitation of natural resources, with civilians as the primary victims. To this recipe for disaster the following additional ingredients can be added: the phenomenon of child soldiers, systemic corruption, infrastructure collapse, a dysfunctional military and almost inconceivable barbarities perpetrated, in the main, by the rebel Revolutionary United Front (RUF).

Many of the interventions discussed in this chapter have either exacerbated existing problems or created new ones. Some interventions have been motivated by the best of intentions but little concrete progress appears to have been made. Perhaps not as collapsed as Somalia but at least as bad as the Democratic Republic of Congo and Angola, Sierra Leone remains in a mess – a classic African basket case, at least to the casual observer. However a glimmer of hope may be discerned in the recent operations in Sierra Leone by the British army in support of the United Nations. The international community appears unwilling to give up completely on Sierra Leone just yet.

The principal objective of this chapter is to provide a general overview of the main military interventions in Sierra Leone since 1991. After an examination of the political, historical and economic factors that have shaped the recent history of Sierra Leone, this chapter will concentrate on five main types of military intervention in Sierra Leone. Firstly I will look at the RUF - an externally sponsored, some might argue manufactured, 'rebel' movement - whose actions have been the prime cause of most of Sierra Leone's present woes. Next there will be an examination of the interventions, both overt and covert, by other African states. Thirdly the role of international organisations, principally ECOMOG and the United Nations, will be discussed. Fourthly I will discuss the crucial role played by private security companies such as Executive Outcomes and Sandline in the Sierra Leonean conflict. Finally I will discuss the impact that the actions of the former colonial power, Britain, have had, especially since the coming to power of the New Labour government in 1997. At the end I will attempt to draw some conclusions from Sierra Leone's experience of being intervened in.

Background

Sierra Leone gained its independence form Britain on 27 April 1961.[1] Its post independence political history mirrored that of many of its neighbours. Lacklustre civilian regimes were ousted by military coups. The nation's resources were squandered as patrimonialism and corruption became the prime tools of government. The country slid into single party rule under the All People's Congress (APC) with the dominant political figure of this period being its leader, Siaka Stevens. He was replaced in 1985 by the military leader Joseph Momoh, whose talents, if he had any at all, did not lie in political leadership.[2] Under his administration the circumstances of the country deteriorated even further. He was still nominally in charge when Sierra Leone's present troubles really began in earnest in March 1991, with the invasion by the RUF. This latter event effectively helped scupper a fledgling attempt at a return to multiparty politics.

Since 1991 the politics of Sierra Leone have been dominated by the war. Briefly, Momoh was ousted in a coup in 1992 by Captain Valentine Strasser, who was in turn removed by his deputy, Julius Maada Bio, in January 1996. There were several attempted coups during this period that saw the banning of political parties. A change in circumstances in the civil war enabled the holding of multiparty elections in February 1996. Ahmed

Tejan Kabbah of the Sierra Leone People's Party became President. He organised a coalition government that negotiated a cease-fire with the RUF in the November of that year. However as is unfortunately all too typical in contemporary sub-Saharan Africa, this particular cease-fire was honoured more in the breach than in the observance. In May 1997 units of the Sierra Leone army seized power and formed an Armed Forces Revolutionary Council (AFRC) headed by Major Johnny Paul Koroma. He immediately formed an alliance with the RUF confirming long held suspicions that these erstwhile military adversaries were, in many cases, cooperating to exploit Sierra Leone's diamond resources under the cover of the confusion generated by the civil war.[3]

This junta operated more like a criminal gang than a government. Shunned by the international community it perpetrated numerous atrocities against the civil population. It was eventually removed in March 1998 by Nigerian-led forces of ECOMOG with the assistance of the Kamajor militia and arms and mercenaries supplied by Sandline.[4] Like previous governments, the restored Kabbah regime was unable to secure control of the whole of the countryside. The RUF came dangerously close to winning control of Freetown in January 1999, in the process committing even more atrocities against civilians. ECOMOG forces eventually forced them out but were unable to defeat them completely. The ongoing military stalemate and increasing international pressure led firstly to a cease-fire in May 1999 and then to the unsatisfactory Lomé Peace Agreement in July 1999.[5]

This peace agreement provided for the inclusion of the RUF and its leader, Foday Sankoh, in the government of Sierra Leone.[6] The agreement also provided for the disarming of warring factions, restructuring of the army and the restoration of peace and security. Facilitated by Britain, the United States and the United Nations' compliance with the agreement was to be monitored by a United Nations peacekeeping force.[7] Preoccupied with the now legalised plundering of the country's diamonds, Sankoh and the RUF showed little enthusiasm for the other elements of the agreement. They sought confrontation with the United Nations, culminating in the murder and kidnapping of hundreds of United Nations observers in May 2000.[8] This resulted in the direct military intervention of British forces and a massive reinforcement of the United Nations mission. At the time of writing the civil war persists but the RUF have suffered a number of reverses, especially the capture of Sankoh. The Sierra Leone army and its allies have moved onto the offensive and the United Nations mission has taken on more of a peace enforcement role.[9]

Apart from agricultural products Sierra Leone's economic wealth lies in its minerals. These include bauxite, the titanium ore rutile and some gold. However the main and most easily accessible mineral wealth of Sierra Leone are its deposits of alluvial diamonds. The regulation of this industry has always been problematical given the relative ease of extraction of these diamonds, their 'smugglability' and the availability of markets in which to sell them. As in other African wars, for example Angola and the Democratic Republic of the Congo, the belligerent parties in Sierra Leone have sought control of the nation's mineral resources, especially the diamonds, in order to finance their military operations and to fill their own bank accounts.

In the case of Sierra Leone it has been suggested that the army and the RUF have, in the past cooperated to plunder the diamond mining areas, using the war as a smokescreen. Despite the apparently tight control of the international diamond market by De Beers, groups such as the RUF and UNITA have had little difficulty in finding buyers for their illegally obtained stones. This trade has led to the coining of a new expression – 'conflict diamonds' and strenuous attempts by both the diamond industry and the United Nations to ban the trade in illegal gems.[10]

At independence Sierra Leone inherited an army based on the British model. The colonial forces of British West Africa had earned an enviable reputation in combat in World War Two, particularly in Burma. However post-independence involvement in politics, arrears of pay and failure to modernise, meant that by 1991 the Sierra Leone army was a poor shadow of the force left by Britain. The army proved totally incapable of dealing with a guerrilla incursion that should have been easily defeated. In the ensuing years the Sierra Leone army disintegrated as an effective military force leading to successive governments in Freetown having to rely on various rural militias such as the Kamajors, ECOMOG troops, especially the Nigerians and private security companies. In some instances it became so difficult to distinguish between government soldiers and RUF rebels that civilians took to referring to them as 'Sobels'.

The coup of May 1997 led to a schism in the army between those who stayed loyal to the Kabbah government and those who supported Koroma and the AFRC. The situation still remains complicated. It would appear that following the Lomé agreement Koroma began to distance himself from the RUF with whom he had openly allied. 'Government' forces today comprise a motley collection of independent militias such as the West Side Boys, AFRC supporters, Kamajors and the regular Sierra Leone army which is in the process of being reequipped and trained by Britain.[11] It has to be said that with the exception of the British-trained units, the military effectiveness of the forces available to the Sierra Leone government is highly questionable and the RUF remains to be finally defeated in the field. The Freetown regime is still dependent for its security upon the intervention of outside forces such as the United Nations, Britain and mercenaries.

Finally in this section it is necessary to place Sierra Leone's war in the broader context of the Liberian civil war. Sierra Leone was a supporter of and initial contributor to, the Nigerian-led ECOMOG force that intervened in Monrovia in August 1990. This intervention was opposed by Charles Taylor and his National Patriotic Front of Liberia (NPFL) who considered that the Nigerians had cheated him of his impending victory over the incumbent President, Samuel Doe.[12] As the Liberia conflict continued and escalated to an effective war between the NPFL and ECOMOG Taylor looked to open up a 'second front' as it were, against ECOMOG. The most obvious choice was Sierra Leone since this was the major logistical supply route for ECOMOG and Lungi airport in Freetown was being used by Nigerian air force planes for bombing missions against the NPFL in Liberia.[13] It was thus that Taylor helped instigate the RUF invasion which he has continued to support ever since, despite public denials to the contrary. Since he became President of Liberia in 1997, Taylor's continuing support for the RUF has been a crucial factor in the continuance of the Sierra Leone civil war.

Interventions

The Revolutionary United Front

I believe that it is justifiable to consider the RUF campaign as an external intervention since the RUF can be viewed as the artificial creation of a external power much as RENAMO was in Mozambique. In the case of the RUF its creator was not a nation state but another rebel movement, Charles Taylor's NPFL in Liberia. However at the time the NPFL had effective control over much of the Liberian hinterland. The so-called invasion of 1991 comprised only 100 fighters, including a number a mercenaries from Burkina Faso.[14] There have also been suggestions that Liberians have been fighting alongside the RUF as well as more recent 'sightings' of white mercenaries among their ranks especially during the fighting in Freetown in January 1999.[15]

The self-appointed leader of the RUF, Foday Sankoh, is an ex-army sergeant and semi-professional photographer. As with other such groups it is questionable as to how much control he has ever exercised over his field forces, which seem to give primary allegiance to their local 'commanders'. The ideology of the RUF is virtually non-existent and their 'evolution' since 1991 has taken them from being auxiliaries of the NPFL to the status of an armed criminal gang whose purpose is to loot the assets of Sierra Leone and whose members appear to engage in violence for its own sake.

Militarily the RUF are ineffective against trained and motivated opposition. This has been demonstrated by Executive Outcomes, the Kamajors and more recently by British paratroopers. However their drugged and often extremely young fighters cannot be totally dismissed. Intoxication, ignorance of military reality and a belief in the protective powers of magic, can turn these individuals into fearsome opponents. In nearly ten years of combat the RUF has, of course, learnt many useful tactics for the conduct of bush warfare; however their morale remains fragile and their popular support base non existent. They have however benefited from a safe haven in Liberia to which they can retreat and regroup after suffering defeats. They have also all too often been opposed by timid, ill equipped or under-strength opponents who have been unable to press home any military advantage obtained over the RUF.

The RUF have also been the principal beneficiaries of the collapse of the Sierra Leone army, forming alliances with some units to loot the diamond fields. At one stage the leader of the Freetown junta, Julius Maada Bio, had a sister in the upper echelons of the RUF.[16] This convergence of interests between rebels and soldiers reached its apogee following Koroma's coup in May 1997. He cited Sankoh as the ideological inspiration for the coup and invited the RUF to merge with his junta and form a 'People's Army'.[17] This marriage of convenience has not endured and nominally at least, Koroma and his AFRC faction are now once again fighting the RUF.

Finally mention must be made of the appalling record of atrocities by the RUF. It is an unpleasant fact of life in contemporary sub-Saharan Africa that civilians remain the prime targets in conflicts and atrocities against them are depressingly common. However by whatever warped yardstick one might have to use to measure these things, the RUF would have to emerge as the worst offenders on the continent. Rape, murder, robbery, the abduction of children for military and sexual purposes are but the prelude to their worst offence, the deliberate maiming of civilians. Hands and arms are cut off to prevent their owners from voting and this practice extends even to babies. The RUF use terror very effectively, but these acts of barbarity mean that they can not be considered to be anything more than a collection of psychotic criminals and most certainly not any form of political association.

Neighbouring States

The involvement of Sierra Leone's neighbours in its affairs has taken a number of forms. They have either acted individually in pursuit of their particular agendas or sometimes collectively through ECOMOG. The main protagonists have been Nigeria and Liberia, especially since Charles Taylor became President in 1997. The conflict between Taylor and Nigeria in Sierra Leone is an extension of their confrontation in Liberia which in turn is connected to a broader antagonism between the Anglophone and Francophone members of ECOWAS. Taylor received a great deal of support both political and practical from the Francophone countries of ECOWAS, especially Ivory Coast and Burkina Faso. They acted in response to what they perceived as Nigeria's hegemonic ambitions in Liberia.[18] There are several examples of Liberian fighters operating alongside the RUF, doubtless with the approval of the Liberian government. Recent reports indicate that this policy of supplying men and equipment is continuing.[19] Liberia also stands accused of aiding the RUF in selling illegally obtained diamonds for arms.[20]

The RUF have consistently received support from Burkina Faso in the form of mercenary fighters and allegations persist that it has acted as a conduit for arms shipments to the RUF from Bulgaria and the Ukraine, an activity undertaken in alliance with Liberia and Libya. Burkinabe government aircraft have been used to fly arms into RUF held areas of Sierra Leone.[21] The arms are shipped from the Ukraine to Libya and then onto Burkina Faso. Libyan planes have also been traced making supply runs into Sierra Leone.[22] However, despite the activity of these states, it does appear that the majority of governments in West Africa are genuinely revolted by the actions of the RUF and would dearly like to see an end to this conflict.

Nigeria initially moved its forces into Sierra Leone in order to protect ECOMOG's supply lines into Liberia. Subsequently Nigeria became deeply involved in the conflict as the main contingent of the ECOMOG force. Nigerian forces even found themselves in action alongside the South African based Executive Outcomes against the RUF.[23] However recent military cutbacks in Nigeria have led to the withdrawal of the majority of

Nigerian troops from Sierra Leone. Some remain as part of the United Nations mission and their past effectiveness has led to American proposals to help finance the return of Nigerian soldiers to Sierra Leone.[24]

International Organisations

Both ECOWAS and the United Nations have become involved in the Sierra Leone conflict. The former as a result of its operations in Liberia and the latter more recently in what could be interpreted as an attempt to restore its somewhat tarnished reputation in Africa. The interventions of both organisations have been more attempts at preventing the collapse of the Sierra Leonean state than efforts to bring the war to a conclusion. A partial explanation of this may lie in the reluctance by international organisations to face the unpalatable truth, that in certain circumstances the military option is the only way forward. There are, of course, other factors involved in limiting the effectiveness of these interventions. Neither organisation is possessed of extensive resources, either military or financial. Their activities in Sierra Leone have been affected by other calls on their resources and in the case of the United Nations by the general reluctance of the Western powers to become actively involved themselves. Both organisations have of course to maintain a consensus amongst their members for action, which is never an easy task.

ECOMOG became embroiled in the Sierra Leone war as a result of the threat posed to its lines of communication into Liberia. Initially Nigerian forces deployed to Sierra Leone in large numbers in the spring of 1993 although there had been a Nigerian military presence of sorts in the country for a number of years.[25] The ECOMOG involvement became deeper after the coup in May 1997 that brought Koroma's junta into power. After an initially unsuccessful attempt by Nigerian and Guinean troops to overthrow the junta by force, the ECOMOG forces settled down effectively to laying siege to Freetown and to cooperating with the pro-Kabbah Kamajor militias in the countryside. In this ECOMOG was assisted by the international isolation of the junta and the imposition of extensive sanctions.[26] This situation persisted until the following February when reinforced ECOMOG forces attacked Freetown and ousted the junta, leading members of which were arrested by ECOMOG inside Liberia.[27]

ECOMOG became the de facto government in Freetown until the return of President Kabbah from exile in Guinea. However it proved impossible for the ECOMOG forces to wrest total control of the Sierra Leone countryside from the RUF and the AFRC forces and for the remainder of

1998 the war settled into something of a stalemate. This state of affairs abruptly changed on 6 January 1999 when RUF rebels successfully infiltrated Freetown and occupied large areas of it. They embarked on an orgy of murder and mutilation and were only evicted from the city after some hard fighting by ECOMOG forces.[28] Once again they were unable to inflict a total defeat on the RUF. This military impasse together with a desire by Nigeria to reduce its overseas military commitments were instrumental in putting pressure on the Freetown government to sign the Lomé Agreement with the RUF. The signing of this agreement led to the withdrawal of most of the ECOMOG forces and their replacement by a United Nations force.

The United Nations Mission in Sierra Leone (UNAMSIL) began life as a small observer mission in June 1998 entitled UNOMSIL. It consisted of some 50 military observers whose purpose was to monitor the progress of the disarmament programmes underway then, theoretically at least. Their work was effectively brought to an end by the RUF's January offensive. The signatories to the Lomé agreement called for an expanded role for the United Nations and initially the Security Council authorised an expansion of UNOMSIL to some 200 observers. However in October 1999, the Security Council again decided to expand the mission even further to a force of some 6,000 military personnel to assist in the carrying out of the provisions of the Lomé Agreement. Thus UNOMSIL became UNAMSIL and it was further enlarged in February 2000 by Security Council resolution 1289 to a maximum strength of 11,100.[29]

Deployment of the force has met with considerable opposition and obstruction from the RUF and the build-up of United Nations forces was slow.[30] In addition some of the units provided were not up to the required standard. To this must be added flagrant breaches of the peace agreement by the RUF and little real progress towards general disarmament in the country. There was also a general public dissatisfaction with a settlement that made no provision for the punishment of the perpetrators of atrocities and that included their chief architect, Foday Sankoh, in the government. The omens for the continuation of the peace agreement and the success of the United Nations mission were not good and matters came to a head in May 2000 with the killing of a number of United Nations personnel and the kidnapping of several hundred others by the RUF.

Robust intervention by British forces and a significant reinforcement of UNAMSIL has led to the freeing of all these hostages and the inflicting of a number of reverses on the RUF. Security Council resolution 1299 of 19 May 2000 increased the strength of UNAMSIL to 13,000, the majority of which have now been deployed.[31] Their mandate is still technically, to help carry out the provisions of the Lomé Agreement, however they have become more robust in their dealings with transgressors and this has led to a general improvement in the security situation.

Private Security Companies and Mercenaries

The activities of two of the main private security companies involved in Sierra Leone, Sandline and Executive Outcomes, have been explored in some detail elsewhere in this volume.[32] In this section I merely wish to highlight the extent to which private security companies and mercenaries have played an important role in the Sierra Leone civil war. Both main parties to the conflict, the Sierra Leone government and the RUF have employed 'hired help' and even international organisations have found it expedient to operate alongside them. The RUF employed mercenaries at the start of the war and have been helped in the latest outbreak of combat by fighters from Liberia. There have been shadowy reports in the past of sightings of 'white men' fighting alongside the RUF and the BBC has uncovered a recent Sierra Leone police report suggesting that Serbian snipers had been hired by the RUF.[33]

The effective collapse of the Sierra Leone Army in 1994/5 forced the regime of Valentine Strasser to rely to a great degree on foreign troops, initially the Nigerian forces based in Freetown. However an increasingly desperate military situation compelled him to seek additional assistance elsewhere. At first he turned to a private military company based in the Channel Islands that employed former Gurkhas from the British army. The Gurkha Security Group however proved to be less effective than Strasser hoped, especially after the death of their commander in an ambush shortly after their arrival. Strasser next turned to the South African-based Executive Outcomes. With their vast experience of Africa's wars, gained whilst employed by the apartheid regime, they proved to be very effective in dealing with the RUF.[34]

Throughout 1995 and 1996 Executive Outcomes recaptured the diamond and rutile mining areas from the RUF and in cooperation with the Nigerian forces and the Kamajors, effectively forced the RUF to the negotiating table. Their actions had created the environment, which permitted the holding of elections in February 1996 that led to the installation of the Kabbah government. Their services, of course, came with a significant price tag, not only a monthly fee but also the expansion of the mining activities of Branch Energy, a company with which Executive Outcomes had corporate links.[35]

The moral issues raised by the employment of private military companies by sovereign states have been discussed elsewhere. Whatever one's opinions might be, the fact remains that Executive Outcomes effectively defeated the RUF in the field and proved that a relatively small force of well trained, equipped and motivated troops could defeat what was in reality little more than a criminal rabble. The effectiveness of Executive Outcomes was not lost on the RUF who made it a condition of the November 1996 peace agreement that Executive Outcomes should leave Sierra Leone.

That did not mark the end of the involvement of private military companies in Sierra Leone. Lifeguard, a company closely affiliated to Executive Outcomes, continued to provide security for mining company personnel and were prominent in the defence of the Mammy Yoko Hotel after the May 1997 coup.[36] It is believed that this company may still be active in Sierra Leone and may well be employing former Executive Outcomes personnel following that company's closure in January 1999. Sandline and Defence Systems Ltd are believed to be still active on one level or another in Sierra Leone. The activities of Sandline in helping to restore the Kabbah government following that coup have been examined in the chapter on private security companies. Sandline's efforts may or may not have been crucial to that restoration but they did signify a willingness on the part of the British government to use a private military company to pursue foreign policy objectives. The accompanying political fuss in Britain was more concerned with the means employed than the ends achieved, which were generally regarded in a favourable light.[37]

Apart from the private military companies, individual mercenaries have found Sierra Leone to be a lucrative market for their services. Foreigners operate the government's only helicopter gunships, their most effective weapon against the RUF. The pilots are South African and many of the technicians East European. A number of mercenaries, mostly former employees of Executive Outcomes, are operating in Liberia in support of the RUF. In the past the government of President Kabbah hired an Israeli mercenary as a military adviser unaware of his activities as a gunrunner for the RUF.[38]

The continued involvement of private military companies in Sierra Leone highlights the persistent deficiencies in the Sierra Leone Army. Currently a British military training team is in Sierra Leone trying to improve the quality of what has been a rather ramshackle force. However unless the soldiers are paid regularly, equipped and led properly the benefits of this training could be short lived, forcing a future Sierra Leone government to rely once again on private military companies and mercenaries.

Britain's Involvement

Britain has a long standing connection with Sierra Leone due to its former role as the colonial power. More recently Freetown became a staging area during the campaign to retake the Falklands in 1982. The British government in the person of the High Commissioner was active in assisting with the restoration of the Kabbah regime. Although his involvement with Sandline earned him some unjustified opprobrium from his political masters in London, his actions made him very popular in Sierra Leone. The British government was also very active in promoting the Lomé agreement despite its many obvious shortcomings. Britain contributed a number of military observers to UNAMSIL and provided logistical assistance towards its deployment.

However the most dramatic indication of an increased commitment to Sierra Leone came in the form of Operation Palliser which was launched on 6 May 2000 in response to the murder and kidnapping of United Nations personnel by the RUF. At its height Operation Palliser involved 4,500 military personnel and extensive air and naval assets. It was the largest deployment of British forces outside of the NATO area since the Falklands campaign of 1982.[39] Although initially portrayed as an operation to facilitate the evacuation of foreign nationals, it soon became clear that the forces were being deployed to bolster and help reinforce UNAMSIL. The forces deployed included Paratroopers, the SAS, Royal Marines, an aircraft carrier and Harrier jets. A number of encounters with the RUF took place in which the latter came off worse. The presence of the British forces with their robust rules of engagement stabilised a deteriorating situation and enabled UNAMSIL to be reinforced. It also provided the boost to morale that enabled the Sierra Leone Army to take the fighting to the RUF. Although the operation has been scaled down British military assets remain available for use in Sierra Leone, as was demonstrated in the successful evacuation of United Nations personnel besieged by the RUF in Kailahun.[40]

Britain has supplied weapons and ammunition to the Sierra Leone Army and a 180-man training team is currently training Sierra Leone troops in the use of this equipment as well as raising their overall level of military proficiency. This programme has proved so successful that a second

British military training team will replace the current one when its tour of duty is finished. Britain is also helping to organise an International Military Advisory and Training Team to assist with the long-term reformation of the Sierra Leone Army and Canada has agreed to cooperate in this programme.[41] A number of junior officers have been sent to Ghana for training by the British military team there. The British government has also been very active in promoting a ban in the trade in so called 'conflict diamonds', the effectiveness of which has yet to be seen. On the surface at least the commitment of the present British government to Sierra Leone appears to be long term.

Conclusions

The problems of military intervention in Sierra Leone cannot be dealt with in isolation. They have to been seen in the context of both the West African region and the continent as a whole. The Sierra Leone civil war started as a result of the conflict in Liberia and has spread to threaten the stability of number of neighbouring states, especially Guinea. It is related to wider geopolitical struggles between would-be hegemonic states and to the persistence in African politics of leaders who view their states as personal fiefdoms and their power as a licence to rob.

The inherent weakness of African states makes them vulnerable to intervention. Their borders are easily permeable and often in dispute. Their military resources are, more often than not, both inadequate and unreliable. The mineral assets, which make African countries potentially very rich, also make them very vulnerable. Foreign companies and states cast covetous eyes on their wealth and unfortunately oil and diamonds can be easily converted into cash and weapons. Once a conflict erupts it becomes very difficult for African states, individually or collectively, to put an end to it. The achievement of a decisive military victory is almost impossible. Thus the governments of enfeebled African states are forced to rely on outside assistance.

Neighbouring states may well offer help but this usually comes with a political price tag. Nigeria's assistance to Sierra Leone over the years had a number of motivations, many to do with domestic Nigerian politics. After the restoration of the Kabbah government in February 1998 the Nigerians virtually occupied Freetown and took over what was left of the Sierra Leone Army. Dependence upon an ally exposes a state's weakness, especially if the ally decides that it wants to reduce its commitment to it. This has certainly been the case with Sierra Leone, regarding Nigeria.

The international community, in the shape of the United Nations, can often offer little real help to a country such as Sierra Leone. The marginalisation of Africa in the last decade or so and the effective disengagement of the United States from participating in United Nations peacekeeping operations, has left the latter organisation hamstrung. The United Nations finds it increasingly difficult to deploy effective numbers of troops quickly. Its recent track record in Africa is less than impressive, particularly in Somalia, Rwanda and Angola. Many of the units committed by member states to United Nations operations are below the required standard. The United Nations also appears reluctant to provide its forces with sufficiently robust mandates. Traditional 'blue helmet' United Nations peacekeeping requires the consent of the belligerent parties. In contemporary African conflicts this is usually absent. In these circumstances, such as exist in Sierra Leone, United Nations forces need to be equipped and prepared for combat if the need arises. It was only after the intervention of British forces and the 'beefing up' of UNAMSIL that action could be taken against the RUF who had taken United Nations personnel hostage. UNAMSIL has now taken a more robust stance with regard to the RUF, however with the civil war still in full swing, one might question the purpose of the United Nations operation in Sierra Leone.

In the absence of reliable domestic forces, with uncertain allies and a hesitant international community, it is no wonder that states such as Sierra Leone turn to private military companies for their security needs. These organisations are expensive to employ but they generally achieve immediate military results. Individual mercenaries are more likely, these days, to be weapons specialists and technicians rather than front line fighters. Whatever the moral questions associated with the employment of these organisations, desperate regimes have no choice. Increasingly Western governments see private military companies as a means of 'doing something', as demanded by their public, without risking their own forces in a long-drawn out war. During the crisis that afflicted the United Nations in Sierra Leone in May 2000, there were calls from some writers in the Western press for the employment of private military companies as an alternative.

Sierra Leone offers an example of a state at the mercy of military interventions of one type or another. It would appear to have benefited little from any of them. To be sure, the RUF have not taken control of the country and that must be counted as some sort of achievement. But neither have they been totally defeated and the war carries on. The Sierra Leone war is not really about politics but about assets, in this case diamonds. The prime motivator for many of the belligerents since 1991 has been greed. Not necessarily for political power as an end in itself, but as a method of accessing the nation's mineral wealth. This has been a motivator for the RUF, the military juntas that have ruled Sierra Leone, the Nigerians and the private military companies and the corporate allies. It is only very recently that real efforts have been to regulate the international diamond trade so as to curb this incentive to conflict.

Despite the achievements of the British forces and the United Nations since May 2000, Sierra Leone remains vulnerable. The underlying problems of that country have yet to be tackled and cannot be addressed so long as the civil war continues. In this respect Sierra Leone is like many other African states and while these circumstances persist military interventions of one sort or another will plague the continent.

Notes

1 Chazan,N., Mortimer, R., Ravenhill, J. and Rothchild, D. (1992), *Politics and Society in Contemporary Africa,* 2nd Edition, MacMillan, p. 463.

2 Africa Confidential Special Reports Chronology of Sierra Leone, 'How Diamonds fuelled the conflict', available at: www.africa-confidential.com /special.htm.

3 Africa Confidential Special Reports Chronology of Sierra Leone, 'How Diamonds fuelled the conflict', available at: www.africa-confidential.com /special.htm.

4 Musah, Abdel-Fatau and Fayemi, J.'Kayode (eds) (2000), *Mercenaries: An African Security Dilemma,* Pluto Press: London, p. 99.

5 Foreign & Commonwealth office Background Briefing on Sierra Leone Accessible at www.fco.government.uk/news/dynpage.asp?Page=10054 Theme=16.

6 Sierra Leone timeline. Accessible at http://www.bbc.co.uk.

7 Foreign & Commonwealth office Background Briefing on Sierra Leone, accessible www.fco.government.uk/news/dynpage.asp?Page=10054& Theme =16.

8 'Sierra Leone rebels humiliate United Nations hostages', *Sunday Telegraph*, 7 May 2000.

9 'Setbacks for Sierra Leone rebels', BBC World News – Africa 14 July 2000. Accessible at www.bbc.co.uk/news/world/africa.

10 'Dealers to outlaw 'conflict diamonds' ', *The Guardian*, 18 July 2000.

11 Debay, Y. (2000), 'Folly in Masiaka', *Combat and Survival*, Vol. 12, No. 5, August.

12 Cleaver, G. (1998), 'Liberia: lessons for the future from the experience of ECOMOG', in Furley, O. and May, R. (eds), *Peacekeeping in Africa*, Ashgate: Aldershot.

13 Africa Confidential Special Reports Chronology of Sierra Leone, 'How Diamonds fuelled the conflict'. Available at: www.africa-confidential.com/special.htm.

14 Africa Confidential Special Reports Chronology of Sierra Leone, 'How Diamonds fuelled the conflict'. Available at: www.africa-confidential.com/special.htm.

15 Musah, Abdel-Fatau, and Fayemi, J.'Kayode (eds) (2000), *Mercenaries: An African Security Dilemma,* Pluto Press: London, p. 106.

16 Africa Confidential Special Reports Chronology of Sierra Leone, 'How Diamonds fuelled the conflict'. Available at: www.africa-confidential.com/special.htm.

17 Africa Confidential Special Reports Chronology of Sierra Leone, 'How Diamonds fuelled the conflict'. Available at: www.africa-confidential.com/special.htm.

18 Cleaver, G. (1998), 'Liberia: lessons for the future from the experience of ECOMOG', in Furley, O. and May, R. (eds) *Peacekeeping in Africa,* Ashgate: Aldershot.

19 'Sierra Leone Document Two', www.bbc.co.uk/news/world/africa, 18 July 2000.

20 'United Nations gets evidence of war-zone diamonds trade', *The Guardian*, 1 August 2000.

21 Musah, Abdel-Fatau, and Fayemi, J.'Kayode (eds) (2000), *Mercenaries: An African Security Dilemma,* Pluto Press: London, p. 106.
Africa Confidential Special Reports Chronology of Sierra Leone, 'How Diamonds fuelled the conflict'. Available at: www.africa-confidential.com/special.htm.

22 Venter, A. (2000), 'Third World Turmoil', *Combat and Survival*, Vol. 12, No. 4 , July.

23 Africa Confidential Special Reports Chronology of Sierra Leone, 'How Diamonds fuelled the conflict'. Available at: www.africa-confidential.com/special.htm.

24 'Sierra Leone: the balance of forces', accessible at www.bbc.co.uk /news/world/africa, 10 May 2000.

25 Africa Confidential Special Reports Chronology of Sierra Leone, 'How Diamonds fuelled the conflict'. Available at: www.africa-confidential.com/special.htm.

26 'West African force at alert in Sierra Leone', Panafrican News Agency, 5 August 1997.

'Coup in Freetown?', *West Africa*, 2-8 June 1997, pp. 887-888.

27 Africa Confidential Special Reports Chronology of Sierra Leone, 'How Diamonds fuelled the conflict'. Available at: www.africa-confidential.com/special.htm.

28 Musah, Abdel-Fatau and Fayemi, J.'Kayode, (eds) (2000), *Mercenaries: An African Security Dilemma,* Pluto Press: London, p. 105.

29 UNAMSIL United Nations mission in Sierra Leone briefing paper, United Nations department of public information, Peace and security section, 30 June 2000.

30 Foreign and Commonwealth Office Background Briefing on Sierra Leone. Accessible at: www.fco.government.uk/news/dynpage.asp?Page=10054&Theme=16.

31 'United Nations troops reach safety', 16 July 2000. Accessible at www.bbc.co.uk/news/world/africa.

32 Cleaver, G., 'Interventionist Companies: Privatising the military option', in this volume.

33 'Sierra Leone Document One', www.bbc.co.uk/news/world/africa, 18 July 2000.

34 Africa Confidential Special Reports Chronology of Sierra Leone, 'How Diamonds fuelled the conflict'. Available at: www.africa-confidential.com/special.htm.

35 Cleaver, G., 'Interventionist Companies: Privatising the military option', in this volume.

36 Africa Confidential Special Reports Chronology of Sierra Leone, 'How Diamonds fuelled the conflict'. Available at: www.africa-confidential.com/special.htm.

37 Musah, Abdel-Fatau and Fayemi, J.'Kayode (eds) (2000), *Mercenaries: An African Security Dilemma,* Pluto Press: London, p. 105.

38 Musah, Abdel-Fatau and Fayemi, J.'Kayode (eds) (2000), *Mercenaries: An African Security Dilemma,* Pluto Press: London, pp. 105-106.
Venter, A. (2000), 'Third World Turmoil', *Combat and Survival*, Vol. 12, No. 4, July.

39 *Combat and Survival*, Operation Palliser Sierra Leone special, Vol. 12, No. 5, August 2000.

40 'United Nations troops reach safety', 16 July 2000. Accessible at www.bbc.co.uk/news/world/africa.

41 Sierra Leone Current Situation, 24 July 2000, Ministry of Defence website www.mod.uk.

12 Intervention in Guinea-Bissau

Simon Massey

An exchange of gunfire in Bissau city between soldiers loyal to President João Bernardo 'Nino' Vieira and mutinous troops supporting the recently dismissed army chief of staff Brigadier Ansumane Mané in the early morning of 7 June 1998 heralded the start of 11 months of civil conflict. 'It was not a huge war', the *Economist* noted, 'but for the 1m people ... of Guinea-Bissau, it was devastating...Hundreds of people were killed, the city was destroyed and hundreds of thousands fled into the countryside'.[1] The primary reason for the fighting - irrevocable splits within the government and leading *Partido Africano da Independencia da Guiné-Bissau e Cabo Verde* (PAIGC) - sat amidst a web of geopolitical machinations and posturing. Guinea-Bissau became the locus for intervention based on political opportunism, as well as a humanitarian intervention that, nonetheless, was marked by strong political impulses.

The Background to Civil War

By 1998, Guinea-Bissau had moved far away from the original revolutionary vision of political society articulated by cofounder of the PAIGC Aristides Perreira - 'the model which our party builds is one in which participation at the base is guaranteed in all decisions, and at every level, by a democratic organization and method'.[2] A disparate population had disengaged from a dependent state. Lars Rudebeck's long-term research in the Bissauan village of Kandjadja underscores the sense of post-election frustration – 'in spite of democratisation, the gap between society and state is as deep as ever. In a way it is even deeper, as new hopes and expectations have been called forth and quickly betrayed'.[3]

Beyond widespread popular unrest, Guinea-Bissau's foreign relations add a further key causal factor underlying the civil war. Bissauan foreign policy has concentrated on two interlinked spheres, relations with Portugal and France and regional geopolitical dynamics. As one the world's poorest countries Guinea-Bissau relies heavily on external aid. Clapham makes the point that, 'beneath a veneer of rhetoric designed to maintain the appearance of commitment to moral principles ... a clientelist domestic political structure entailed a clientelist foreign policy'.[4] Conditional aid from multilateral donors instigated economic and, latterly, political liberalisation. Both sets of conditions adversely affected Vieira's security of tenure. Stringent fiscal policy deepened deprivation, whilst democratisation seemed to offer, then thwart, opportunity for change.

The troubled relationship with Senegal merges Guinea-Bissau's *extra*-continental and regional policies. Since its independence, France has looked to Senegal to protect its interests in the sub-region. Senegal's first president, Leopold Senghor, was pro-Western and wary of the PAIGC's socialist ideology. Unlike Sekou Touré in Guinea, Senghor offered no support for the PAIGC during the liberation struggle. After 1974 Dakar perceived the border between the two countries as a front line in the Cold War.

Mistrust of Bissau's intentions intensified following the outbreak of secessionist violence in the Casamance region of southern Senegal in 1982. There was an affinity between Guinea-Bissau and the Casamance secessionists as a result of the provision of rear bases by the Casamançais during the war of liberation. Even so, Bissau frequently sought to reassure Dakar that it was not supporting the rebel *Mouvement des forces démocratiques de la Casamance* (MFDC).[5] Nonetheless, conservative Senegal saw parallels in Guinea-Bissau's revolutionary origins and the rebellion in Casamance. A strong physical, cultural and historical conjunction exists across the fluid border between the two countries based on Jola ethnicity and a shared history of the Mandinka Kingdom of Gabu.[6] Jean-Claude Marut conjures the 'spectre d'union des 3Bs' (a territorial aggregation along the axis of Bissau, Bignona in Casamance and Banjul) as a strategic preoccupation in Dakar.[7] Finally, growing conflict in Casamance offered the potential for impoverished Bissauan and Senegalese army officers and well placed government officials to benefit financially through extensive smuggling of arms to the rebels.

Tension continued throughout the 1990s. In December 1992 following an attack by the MFDC that killed two soldiers, Senegalese aircraft strafed border villages killing two Bissauans.[8] Two years later, the Senegalese Air Force bombed the border village of Ponta Rosa and shelled the village of Ingore.[9] In the ensuing diplomatic round, *realpolitik* triumphed. A politico-military accord was framed with Senegal. Bissau moved closer to Paris with Vieira signalling Guinea-Bissau's entry into the Franc Zone.

Following the disappearance of four French tourists in Casamance in 1995, joint exercises, with French logistical support, were conducted. Whilst Guinea-Bissau was legally neutral, the Senegalese saw the exercises as a basis for a full scale offensive against the rebels. An agreed zone of 'hot pursuit' was created giving Senegalese troops access to a strip of Bissauan territory, seven kilometres wide, along the border. The result of the new politico-military *rapprochement* was the militarisation of the border area and a small-scale refugee crisis as displaced civilians moved into the Casamance and Guinea-Bissau hinterlands. Vieira had accepted a '*frontière élastique*'.[10] By January 1998 the MFDC was accusing Guinea-Bissau of lending military support to the Senegalese. At the same time, Senegal voiced suspicions that arms continued to flow from the Guinea-Bissau army to the rebels.

Bilateral Intervention: *Opération Gabou*

Since 1990, the MFDC has significantly upgraded its arsenal. Senegal surmised that arms had been obtained from suppliers in the region from Liberian, Gambian and Mauritanian sources, as well as through illegal international smuggling. Sources in Guinea-Bissau had also long been suspect. In late January 1998 a shipment of weapons from the Bissauan army was seized *en route* to Casamance. Vieira and prime minister Correia were abroad when the scandal broke. The government denied responsibility. The immediate response was the arrest of about twenty low ranking soldiers, and the suspension of Mané, from his post for dereliction of duty.[11]

Opposition parties in Bissau made political capital from the affair. Citing structural failure in the chain of command in government and armed forces, and a breakdown of trust between the two institutions, the National Assembly established a committee to investigate arms trafficking. Although due to report in June 1998, the findings would not be disclosed until 13 April 1999. However, core findings and the tenor of the report became common knowledge in Bissau. Far from endorsing the suspension of Mané, the report blamed high ranking officers in the security forces and implied that the president was aware of the trade, but was unable, or unwilling, to intervene.

Mané's response to suspension was to pre-empt the report and publicly accuse the president of agreeing to arms smuggling. Vieira's fateful decision to confront Mané meant challenging a former protégé, comrade in arms, and friend. Mané, a Mandinka from Gambia, moved to Guinea-Bissau when he was sixteen where he served under Vieira in the liberation struggle. Self-taught, Mané had been considered more soldier than politician. Throughout the crisis he stated that he did not harbour political ambitions, only a desire to clear his name.[12] On 6 June 1999 Brigadier-General Humbert Gomes replaced him as chief of staff. The day after, and a day before the parliamentary report on arms trafficking was due to be published, about 400 rebel soldiers attacked the Bra barracks complex and the airport in Bissau. A stalemate developed. Vieira blamed opposition parties for fomenting the revolt and predicted imminent defeat for the rebels. Mané proclaimed himself head of an interim military council, the *Junta Militar*, called for free and transparent elections and counter-claimed that only the risk of heavy casualties prevented him taking the capital.[13]

After three days of fighting a dual intervention took place from neighbouring Senegal and Guinea. Senegal's immediate diplomatic justification, circulated to regional governments, was based on a humanitarian imperative. This rationale was superseded by the explanation that Vieira had invoked mutual defence pacts signed in 1965 (Senegal) and 1997 (Senegal, Guinea-Bissau, Guinea and Gambia). These 'secret' pacts were of questionable legality. From a Gambian perspective at least, the 1997 pact was a collective security arrangement that precluded intervention in the internal affairs of the other signatories.[14] Senegal and Guinea dispatched 1,300 and 500 troops respectively as part of an intervention that the Senegalese dubbed *Opération Gabou*. The arrival of foreign forces inflamed the conflict. Within ten days the 300,000 residents of Bissau had nearly all quit the city. Most of Bissau was destroyed. Foreign diplomatic missions had been evacuated, and the American embassy demolished.[15] The conflict expanded. After nearly a month of fighting, international agencies were predicting a humanitarian cataclysm. Fighting intensified in Mansoa, whilst the rebels took the towns of Ingore, Bula, and Bigene on the Casamance border.

Senegalese forces of the *Forces expéditionnaire sénégalese en Guinée-Bissau* (Forex) under the command of Colonel Abdoulaye Fall landed on 10 June. Fall saw his objectives as the consolidation of a bridgehead at the new port, control of approach roads to Bissau and Bra and, finally, to secure the airport.[16] Fiercest fighting was at Bra. On 13 June, following heavy artillery bombardment, the central magazine exploded. Reports that the rebel offensive in Bissau was at the point of collapse proved premature.

Two days later, a Dakar daily newspaper described a counter-offensive by rebel forces. *Le Soleil* speculated that troops loyal to the *Junta Militar* received an injection of logistical supplies from an Antonov transport aircraft of unknown provenance that landed at the rebel-controlled airport in the early hours of 15 June. The newspaper reported unsubstantiated Forex claims that fighters from *Atika* (the armed wing of the MFDC) had been seen fighting with *Junta Militar* forces.[17] Most significantly, it was becoming clear that, the Presidential Guard apart, most Bisauan troops were siding with the rebels. Out of an army whose strength was assessed as 6,800 troops only a few hundred remained loyal. At the start of the conflict Vieira was forced to request external help to replace the uniforms of loyalist troops in order to distinguish them on the battlefield.[18] This problem was short-lived since within weeks most troops fighting on the loyalist side were Senegalese or Guinean. One refugee, quoted by the Missionary News Agency (MISNA), noted that 'we do not see national troops on the government side'.[19] Moreover, many veteran troops from the liberation era chose to return to arms to fight for the *Junta*.

The intervention developed into a military disaster for Senegal. At the end of June, Senegalese forces were split, with those reinforcements landed at Buba in the south unable to join the exhausted expeditionary force in Bissau. Moreover, the reinforcements comprised young, trainee conscripts. The Senegalese troops were seen by almost all the Bissauan population as 'nothing but an invasion', and 'the biggest impediment to peace negotiations'.[20] In Dakar opposition leaders loudly complained at the manner in which the intervention had been conducted. The main opposition leader, Iba Der Thiam, accused the Senegalese government of Abdou Diouf of acting without recourse to parliament.[21] However, although, he referred to the intervention as 'totally unacceptable', few Senegalese politicians objected to the underlying goal of the intervention – to create conditions for a direct assault on MFDC rear bases in Guinea-Bissau.

Suffering amongst the civilian population and the numbers of refugees fleeing the Bissau area soon developed into a major humanitarian catastrophe. If early artillery exchanges between the rival armies did not target the civilian population, they were marked by a high proportion of stray ordnance. Most of the capital's inhabitants escaped to the east and north of the country. Senegal initially closed its borders, but 13,000 Bissauans crossed into Guinea. UN High Commissioner for Refugees, Sadako Ogata, issued an emergency statement warning that, 'immediate consequences could be famine, refugee outflow into neighbouring countries and threats to the safety of the 5,000 Senegalese refugees who have been living in Guinea Bissau since 1992'.[22] Launching an appeal for aid a group of Bissauan exiles summarised the fears of humanitarian organisations – 'the unexpected arrival of this human mass has increased the demographic pressure on the weak infrastructure in these areas as well as on the environment and the food stocks ... emerging information speaks of many people dying of hunger, thirst or sickness'.[23] The UN issued an interim inter-agency appeal. Despite Senegalese reluctance to assist, UNHCR convoys from Senegal began arriving in Bafata and Gabu after the border was opened for the delivery of humanitarian aid on 14 July. The operation proved belated and inadequate. Although mosquito nets were distributed in Bafata with the assistance of the ICRC, the distribution of 150 tons of non-food aid from stocks in Niger would not take place until mid-September. At the end of the year UNHCR still recognised 202,200 people as being refugees or of concern. The vast majority (195,600 people) were internally displaced persons (IDPs) falling under the UNHCR mandate.[24]

Amnesty International documented a series of human rights abuses, including arbitrary arrests, torture, and extrajudicial executions, by Senegalese troops and loyal Guinea-Bissau forces.[25] Likewise, the US Department of State Bureau of Democracy, Human Rights and Labour, reported loyalist troops as having 'killed an unknown number of civilians', whilst 'Senegalese troops reportedly killed and beat a number of civilians'.[26] Guinean troops were accused of arbitrary beating of civilians. *Junta Militar* forces were also accused of extrajudicial killings and human rights abuse. However, given that the civil war in Guinea-Bissau was essentially a conventional war between relatively disciplined armed forces, human rights abuse, egregious in itself, did not approach the scale of atrocity of the contemporaneous civil conflict in Sierra Leone.

Mediation

Despite apparent popular support, and the marshalling of the vast majority of the armed forces behind the rebellion, the international community condemned the rebellion. The Organisation of African Unity (OAU), Economic Community of West African States (ECOWAS), European Union (EU) and the international organisation for lusophone states the *Communidade de Paises de Lingua Franca Portuguese* (CPLP) each demanded a return to constitutional government. It became clear that the

OAU intended to assume a secondary role behind ECOWAS in conflict resolution efforts. When the OAU's Central Organ of the Mechanism for Conflict Prevention, Management and Resolution met on 13 July, stress was placed on endorsing the ECOWAS position in general, and the intervention by Senegal and Guinea in particular.[27] In calling for the UN Security Council to reinforce this stance, the Central Organ warned 'the international community at large, to desist from according support, in whatever form, to the mutineers'.[28]

On 16 June, President Yahya Jammeh of Gambia and his foreign minister, Lamine Sadat Jobe, met with regional leaders and Mané in a fruitless effort to arrange a cease-fire and mediation talks between the two sides in Banjul. These twin initiatives heralded a sustained drive by Gambia to find a solution to the crisis. Historical, ethnic and personal links, as well as humanitarian concern, prompted Gambia's diplomatic intervention. However, the prime motivation was a need for regional security. Banjul saw a firm link between the secessionist campaign in Casamance and the war in Bissau. Given the proximity, the potential for cross-border contagion, and the possibility of serious refugee flows Gambia clearly had a stake in ensuring a swift resolution to the conflict. Officials emphasise Gambia's leading role in mediating both crises as part of a 'comprehensive peace strategy'.[29]

On 3 July ECOWAS ministers of foreign affairs and defence met in Abidjan to discuss the crisis.[30] Vieira requested that ECOMOG's mandate should be extended beyond its application in Liberia and Sierra Leone to Guinea-Bissau. Claiming that the mutineers showed 'a fierce determination', he argued that the rebellion 'threatens peace, security and stability' in the country.[31] ECOWAS ministers agreed. Whilst stressing the need for negotiation, the ministers accepted that interventionist measures, including the imposition of sanctions and the use of force, could not be ruled out. At the time, a senior Western diplomat was reported as describing an intervention as 'secondary', adding that ECOMOG could only realistically intervene following a negotiated settlement and doubting the willingness of Western donors to fund the logistics needed for a meaningful peacekeeping intervention.[32] Nonetheless, an implementing mechanism, the Committee of Seven, was constituted.[33] The meeting concluded by calling on the Committee to seek support for ECOWAS from the UN Security Council.

Conflict in Guinea-Bissau gave Portugal the opportunity to revive the dormant CPLP.[34] The organisation took a key role in the mediation effort at the second summit of the CPLP held in Cape Verde on 13-17 July. A Contact Group, chaired by the foreign minister of Cape Verde, was established.[35]

A climate of mutual suspicion enveloped these respective diplomatic initiatives, described by one participant as 'sheer rivalry'.[36] Franco-Portuguese regional competition formed the basis for mistrust. Portugal fostered a belief amongst CPLP members that, with Nigeria distracted by domestic considerations and military commitment in Sierra Leone, Senegal and Guinea were in a position to manipulate support for the francophone position within ECOWAS. ECOWAS executive secretary, Lansana Kouyate, responded by alluding to Portugal's 'neo-colonial behaviour'.[37] Whilst briefing the UN Security Council in mid-July, ECOWAS ambassadors 'appealed to the Council to stop Portugal from undermining regional efforts in resolving the conflict as well as to avoid supplying arms to the rebels', given that, 'reports from Guinea-Bissau indicated that Portugal had already supplied sophisticated satellite communications technology to the rebels'.[38] ECOWAS argued that with Senegalese and Guinean troops on the ground, the focus for conflict resolution should remain in the region. After five weeks of fighting a senior Western diplomatic source stated that efforts to find a peaceful solution to the conflict had 'stalled', and that ECOWAS had resolved to defeat the rebels by force.[39]

In the event, the first of a series of fragile truces was only two weeks away. A military stalemate obtained in the capital. Losses were increasing on both sides, and opposition pressure against the intervention was growing in Dakar. A renewed effort by the CPLP following the Cape Verde summit produced results. Signed on 26 July, the Memorandum of Understanding 'called for formal negotiations to start within eight days'.[40] An appendix to the memorandum foresaw the rival forces maintaining their relative positions at the start of the truce.[41] However, the most contentious issue, the withdrawal of Senegalese and Guinean forces (formally a *Junta Militar* precondition for negotiation) was not explicitly mentioned in the agreement.

Hostilities never fully ceased. The evening after the signing of the truce, the Senegalese minister of defence, Samba Lamine Mané, announced on television that the rebels had already broken the truce. For their part the *Junta Militar* accused government troops of destroying a bridge outside Bafata. However, neither side rescinded the agreement.[42]

CPLP success in mediation caused ECOWAS to review its own strategy. On 4 August the Committee of Seven met in Accra, Ghana. The meeting reaffirmed support for the role of Senegal and Guinea. The tenor of discourse towards the *Junta Militar*, and the CPLP, was more conciliatory, as the ministers sought to reassert ECOWAS primacy in seeking a resolution to the conflict. A joint ECOWAS/CPLP Consultative Meeting was held on 25 August at Praia. As a result the truce of 25 July became a formal cease-fire. A Cease-fire Agreement was drafted providing for 'the reopening of the airport to allow in humanitarian assistance, an international observer force and a buffer zone along the border with Senegal'.[43]

Senegal sought to justify its intervention on an international stage at the 53rd Session of the UN General Assembly. Jacques Baudin, Senegal's foreign minister, reconfirmed Senegal's adherence to the dubious bilateral defence pact with Guinea-Bissau. He added that Senegal's aim was to secure peace and end 'the threat to public security and to foreigners, and contribute to reinforcing stability and security in the sub-region and in Africa'.[44] Meanwhile, tension between the two parties remained high. On 14 October fierce fighting resumed in Bafata, and then in Bissau and Gabu.

Within days *Junta Militar* had fought to within 500 yards of the presidential palace in Bissau, inflicting serious casualties on loyalist troops, as well as Senegalese and Guinean forces. As the fighting intensified the capital city emptied once more, with over 50,000 people fleeing to Safim, Nhacra, and Bissora to the north and Prabis to the west, as well as leaving in boats for the Bijagos Islands. Smaller numbers of refugees crossed into Guinea. The UN World Food programme (WFP) announced that renewed fighting would halt the ongoing delivery of rice to the scattered displaced persons from the initial exodus. On 21 October Vieira declared a unilateral cease-fire. Two days later, with the whole country except central Bissau in their hands, the *Junta* accepted a truce.

Multilateral Intervention: ECOMOG

The Treaty of ECOWAS signed in Cotonou in July 1993, requires member states 'to employ where appropriate, good offices, conciliation, mediation and other methods of peaceful settlement of disputes', as well as establishing 'a regional peace and security observation system and peacekeeping forces where appropriate'.[45]

Once more Gambia led mediation efforts. Between 25 October and 30 October a series of meetings were held in Banjul between Vieira and Mané, during which, according to a senior Gambian official, there was much 'tough talking' by the hosts.[46] The key obstacles remained Senegalese fears over the security of its southern border, and the *Junta*'s determination that foreign troops leave Guinea-Bissau. With an agreement pending, the Gambian mediators arranged for the two sides to be flown to Abuja where a summit meeting of ECOWAS foreign ministers was being held. Henceforward, the CPLP would take a nominal role.

On 1 November 1998, Vieira and Mané signed an agreement, the Abuja accords.[47] A peace plan was framed reaffirming the 26 August agreement in Praia. Senegalese and Guinean troops would be replaced by ECOMOG troops. The accords required the formation of a government of national unity to include members of the *Junta Militar* to be followed in March 1999 by legislative and presidential elections to be monitored by ECOWAS, the CPLP and the international community.

Sovereignty and Intervention

The legality in international law of the operation in Guinea-Bissau lent heavily on lessons learnt from the two previous ECOMOG interventions in Liberia and Sierra Leone. In both cases support from the UN, the ultimate authority, was tacit rather than explicit. The original intervention, in Liberia in August 1990, was widely criticised for ignoring international norms of non-intervention in the internal affairs of sovereign states. Anthony Ofodile's comprehensive analysis of ECOMOG in Liberia demonstrates that the intervention did not have 'any solid anchor in international law'.[48]

However, a pre-existing, albeit weak, cease-fire made the framing of a resolution and mandate for the Guinea-Bissau intervention seemingly less indeterminate. There was also, to a degree, consent on both sides. The UN Security Council adopted Resolution 1216 (1998) on 21 December. After commending the efforts of ECOWAS and the CPLP the Security Council approved 'the implementation by the ECOMOG interposition force of its mandate ... in a neutral and impartial way and in conformity with UN peacekeeping standards to achieve its objective to facilitate the return to peace and security by monitoring the implementation of the Abuja Agreement'.[49]

ECOWAS' decision to embark on a third intervention, especially as the difficult operation in Sierra Leone was still in progress, implies a willingness to reassess attitudes to state sovereignty. Richard Jackson notes,

> Old principles of international behaviour are changing rapidly, and as a consequence, Africa's leaders now appear increasingly inclined to allow regional and global multilateral organisations wider scope in intervening in threatening internal conflicts. That is, the once sacrosanct concept of state sovereignty that hamstrung conflict management effort in Africa for 30 years is now being reconsidered, and an effort is under way to clearly articulate new norms of external intervention where severe internal insecurity exists.[50]

However, Jackson enters a caveat. He points out that all ECOMOG interventions have been conducted essentially as attempts to preserve sitting governments – 'states of dubious legitimacy fighting to preserve other regimes of dubious legitimacy'.[51] To this extent, states might surrender a measure of sovereignty to an interventionist sub-regional organisation by way of 'a necessary survival strategy in the post-Cold War world'[52] As superpower patronage dissolves, such subregional economic and political strategies emerge 'to preserve the position of ruling African elites in an era of increasing external and internal pressures'.[53] Such a mutual self-preservation role underpinned much of the pro-interventionist discourse during the Guinea-Bissau mediation. However, clearly, Mané would not willingly allow a robust ECOMOG force to undermine his position on the ground, and allow Vieira to shore up his tenuous grip on power. Likewise, the civilian opposition leader, Kumba Yalla voiced opposition to the intervention. 'To be frank', he commented, 'I do not believe in ECOWAS because it has never succeeded in settling any problem … ECOWAS cannot become a defence union for presidents in the sub-region'.[54]

Mandate

Whilst the Abuja accords framed a comprehensive, potentially extensive mandate for ECOMOG, the proposed force would not replicate the peace enforcement role attempted by ECOMOG in Liberia and Sierra Leone. The mandate agreed at Abuja established three tasks for the force:

1. ECOMOG forces to guarantee the border between Senegal and Guinea-Bissau;

2. To maintain peace between rebel troops and troops loyal to the Vieira government;

3. To allow humanitarian organisations safe access to the civilian population. To this end Bissau international airport would be reopened.

Each of these stated aims presented inherent difficulties for the force. Securing Guinea-Bissau's northern border would require engagement in a zone of conflict of ten years duration. Acting as a buffer between the warring parties might involve conflict in terrain, and against troops, that had already defeated the Portuguese and inflicted serious casualties on the Senegalese and Guinean armed forces. The need to prevent leakage in the distribution of humanitarian aid would bring into question the neutrality of ECOMOG's component contingents.

Furthermore, the parties involved in the conflict each harboured a different interpretation of the mandate. For Vieira, the Abuja accords provided a hiatus during which he could attempt to regroup his forces. Beyond this respite, Vieira looked to the intervention force to add a physical dimension to the diplomatic support that his government had already received from the international community, in particular ECOWAS. Given his overwhelming superiority on the ground, but aware of the increasing number of Bissauan casualties and destruction of infrastructure, Mané perceived the suspension of fighting as a necessary diplomatic step that would be unlikely to harm his overall position. However, in light of the line taken by ECOWAS throughout the conflict, he was acutely suspicious of the proposed force, insisting that ECOMOG's neutrality should be transparent, and emphasising the humanitarian aspect of the mandate.

The UN Security Council's requirement that ECOMOG should act in a 'neutral and impartial way' was incorporated in the enabling resolution for the sake of form.[55] The UN had, however tacitly, supported the ECOMOG position in Liberia and Sierra Leone. 'The effect of this', in Jackson's words, 'was to compromise the perceived neutrality of the world body'.[56] Even if the desired outcome, the preservation of the Vieira presidency, was more a matter of hope than expectation, the UN clearly wanted the intervention to maintain the status quo until elections could be held. Likewise, from ECOWAS' standpoint there was an intrinsic partiality towards the defence of an existing regime against a mutiny, with the restitution of democratic institutions as a secondary consideration.[57]

Did the ECOMOG force have a further unofficial mandate? From the start of their respective interventions, Senegal and Guinea suffered heavy casualties. Neither country has produced definitive numbers of dead and wounded, but reliable accounts describe a series of routs. In early November, the *Junta* leader in Bambadinca reported forty-seven Guinean soldiers had been killed and several dozen wounded or captured.[58] Senegal's losses were greater still. An unidentified MFDC rebel fighting with *Junta* forces, referring to actions against Forex reinforcements commented – 'we were just hosing them down, they were kids.'[59] The extrication of Senegal and Guinea from an intervention over which they had lost control became a prime concern not only in Dakar and Conakry, but also within the ECOWAS executive secretariat in Abuja and amongst diplomats in the African section at the *Quai d'Orsay* in Paris.

Senegal was the party most grateful for a break in hostilities. The renewal of the cease-fire allowed Dakar the chance to reassess its strategy in Guinea-Bissau. Henceforward the Diouf government would need to align an imperative to withdraw its troops from Guinea-Bissau without any further significant losses with the abiding obligation to deal with the security dilemma on the Casamance border. From Senegal's perspective if ECOMOG would not, or could not, secure the border, the least it could achieve was to allow a relatively dignified Senegalese (and Guinean) retreat from Guinea-Bissau. The MFDC saw the Abuja accords as a victory for the people of Guinea-Bissau over the 'forces of evil'.[60]

Tension between *Junta Militar* troops and the pro-government alliance endured. In mid-January a Western diplomat reported that 'the atmosphere in Bissau was potentially dangerous because Senegalese and *Junta* forces were facing off not too far from each other'.[61] On 31 January, with the first large-scale contingent of ECOMOG troops *en route*, heavy fighting erupted along this front line. A further flux of refugees ensued. The ICRC reported at least one hundred dead civilians and an outflow of thirty thousand people from the capital between 31 January and 3 February.[62] The *Junta* reportedly suffered heavily from land and sea artillery barrages during this round of fighting.[63] A truce was only brokered following mediation from Togolese foreign minister, Joseph Kokou Koffigou, representing the chair of ECOWAS.

Finance and Logistics

The *Junta* did not want to see a sizeable ECOMOG force fulfilling the conditions of the Abuja accords. Although the *Junta*'s key objective, the withdrawal of Senegalese and Guinean forces, would clearly be expedited by the deployment of ECOMOG, Mané considered a force of 750 troops to be sufficient to carry out the mandate. Lansana Kouyate on behalf of the ECOWAS secretariat mooted a figure of 1,450 troops. Vieira and Senegal demanded a force of no less than 4,000 troops.[64] A rough timetable had envisaged peacekeepers on the ground by the end of November, but this proved optimistic. Troop-contributing states had yet to make their contingents available for transportation. Moreover, ECOWAS did not have the resources immediately available for their transport, and negotiations were continuing with external donors for financial and logistical support.

The onus for constructing the force had fallen on Togo as current chair of ECOWAS. An appeal for troop-contributing states resulted in immediate responses from Togo, Niger, Bénin and Gambia. Togo would supply the force commander, Colonel Gnakoude Berena. Slow diplomatic progress and uncertainty over funding delayed the finalisation of the force's composition. In the case of Gambia, President Jammeh sent his official response only on 29 December. In his letter to President Eyadéma, Jammeh expressed the need for ECOWAS 'to act in concert, and this at the earliest possible opportunity to consolidate the very fragile peace achieved during the 21st Summit of our sub-regional organisation'.[65]

Nigeria's inability to supply funding, manpower or logistics was reiterated in early February 1999 as the main ECOMOG force was landing in Bissau. The definitive announcement came after talks in Dakar. If Diouf had requested a strong Nigerian presence in the intervention force then he was to be disappointed. Abubakar restated Nigeria's position – 'its hands were full'.[66]

France was quicker to react. Soon after the Abuja accords were concluded, the French deputy chief of staff, Jean-Paul Raffenne told Reuters that 'talks were already underway for us to play a role in this force'.[67] On 27 January the French ambassador to Guinea-Bissau, M. François Chappellet announced that France had arranged a package of logistic and financial aid with the troop-contributing states.[68] The basis for the support was France's ongoing conflict resolution initiative in West Africa, the *Renforcement des capacités africaines de maintien de la paix* (RECAMP). Conforming to the RECAMP programme, logistical equipment for use in peacekeeping scenarios had been prepositioned in Dakar. These resources had already been partially utilised during the peacekeeping exercise *Guidimakha* in February 1998 and by the UN mission in the Central African Republic (MINURCA).

On 20 January Executive Secretary Kouyate sent a letter to the heads of state of the four troop-contributing countries assessing the current state of preparedness of the mission and detailing the extent of French assistance as agreed by the French roving ambassador in the region, M. Bellescize.[69] ECOWAS had received pledges for an intervention force of 1,450 men.[70] In the event, the French military transported a six-hundred-man battalion of RECAMP strength.[71] France would also provide logistical support.[72] Furthermore, France agreed to pay an allowance of FFr100 per man per day of the intended six month duration of the operation, the same amount as was paid to troops serving in MINURCA.[73]

Why France? Paris had much to gain from funding the operation. It could conceivably exercise a degree of influence over the possible outcome of both the conflict in Guinea-Bissau and the conduct of the peacekeeping operation, as well as test the extent to which RECAMP could act as a proxy for French interests in the region. Moreover, there were no pressing offers of support from other international donors capable of underwriting an operation of this size. With Nigeria unable to commit resources, the prepositioned French garrison in Dakar was the only viable source of logistical support necessary for the operation to proceed.

Deployment and 'Command and Control'

Although the French warship *Siroco* reached Guinea-Bissau's territorial waters on 31 January the renewal of fighting meant that the proposed landing could not take place. On 4 February, after the restoration of the cease-fire, three hundred troops from Niger and Bénin disembarked. Finally, on 8 February the remainder of the force was shuttled to Bissau.[74]

Yet, the troops that arrived on 4 February were not the first ECOMOG soldiers to arrive in the country. On 26 December Togo sent about eighty troops to Bissau. These were followed by a further thirty troops a few days later. *Radio France Internationale* reported that the Togolese troops had orders to reopen Bissau airport. However, these orders apparently did not come from ECOWAS. Senior officials in the Gambian government have pointed out that the deployment was not part of a prearranged joint strategy between the contributing nations or the ECOWAS secretariat.[75] A meeting to discuss final plans for the main deployment did not take place until 19 January. General Eyadéma, as chair of ECOWAS, might have felt compelled to give impetus to a sluggish process. Moreover, in the light of a series of poor human rights reports, the premature dispatch of the contingent could be construed as part of an ongoing 'charm offensive' by Lomé to capture a modicum of favourable international attention.[76] However, viewed from a wider geopolitical perspective, the early deployment had potential advantages for the pro-Vieira lobby. Togo's surprise election as chair of ECOWAS placed Eyadéma in a pivotal position as negotiations continued. President Chirac met Eyadéma before the 20th Franco-African summit in late November. The impetus for a predominantly francophone composition of the peacekeeping force came from this meeting.[77] Clearly, *Junta* fighters would not simply abandon their positions at such a key installation as the airport to troops about whom they had already expressed antipathy. Nonetheless, the early presence of a contingent with open channels to Paris, and hence Dakar and Conakry, offered some strategic leverage.

ECOMOG's arrival moved the conflict into endgame. The force had two immediate security goals. In order to fulfil its role as an interposition force, and thus enable the Senegalese and Guineans to withdraw, ECOMOG needed to construct a working relationship between themselves and the warring parties.

It is estimated that there were about 2,500 Senegalese and 500 Guinean soldiers in Guinea-Bissau by this time. The eventual size of the ECOMOG force became a central issue. It became clear that far from the 4,000 ECOMOG troops demanded by Vieira, the force would not exceed the 600 troops that France had agreed to support. As the deadline for the departure of Vieira's military shield approached the parties engaged in a round of accusation and counter-accusation. On 9 February, an EU diplomat from a delegation that met the Senegalese president reported that the withdrawal 'would not take place soon'.[78] Although Senegal needed to ensure that its intervention did not descend into further carnage, withdrawal on existing terms meant a serious setback to its Casamance strategy. For Vieira the withdrawal of foreign troops signified disaster. Remaining loyalist forces would be highly vulnerable to attack. Vieira's anxiety over his personal safety surfaced after a Swedish diplomat in Bissau was rebuked for disclosing that the president had asked Senegal to provide 200 troops for his own protection.[79] Fears persisted within the *Junta* of collusion between ECOWAS, Vieira and Senegal over claims that the late deployment of

ECOMOG troops was intended to give loyalist forces time to regroup. ECOWAS proposals to oversee elections and help to reunify the Guinea-Bissau armed forces caused further disquiet.

Nonetheless, on 10 February a joint military commission comprising government loyalists, the *Junta* and ECOMOG representatives agreed a calendar for the withdrawal of non-ECOMOG foreign troops from Guinea-Bissau. The first phase of the agreement involved the withdrawal of 1,200 troops by 14 February. The final stage would see the remainder leave by 28 February. The meeting also agreed plans for a pullback of hostile troops, the deployment of ECOMOG to seven 'sensitive points' along the frontline in Bissau and the formation of a combined armed forces.[80] Such a security environment would then allow a phased disarmament and requartering of both sets of troops based on a schedule agreed with the two sides. The details of this schedule were decided at a meeting organised by the EU commissioner for humanitarian affairs, Emma Bonino, on 15 February. After a final extension of the deadline for withdrawal of foreign troops the last Senegalese and Guinean forces left Guinea-Bissau on 15 and 17 March.

From mid-March Vieira depended for his survival on over 600 loyalist troops, surrounding the presidential palace. This force consisted of the remnants of the Presidential Guard together with about 300 *aguenta* soldiers. Aged between fifteen and twenty these troops had been recruited since the outbreak of the conflict and trained in Guinea. The denouement could not be averted for long. On 6 May mortar and light weapons fire was heard in the streets approaching the presidential palace.[81] After twenty-four hours of fighting a spokesman for the army commander, Brigadier Gomes, announced that government forces had surrendered to prevent further bloodshed. The final assault left at least 80 people dead and nearly 300 wounded. The Senegalese embassy was targeted by rockets and destroyed, whilst the French Cultural Centre was besieged by an angry mob. A *Junta* officer escorted Vieira to the Portuguese embassy and relative safety.

According to a report at the time 'soldiers of the West African ECOMOG intervention force were attempting to position themselves between the warring factions'.[82] However, regardless of the predisposition of their respective capitals the various ECOMOG contingents were in no position to prevent a determined push by *Junta* troops. A defence of the presidential palace might have been justifiable under the terms of the mandate, but the military capacity to do so was wholly absent. The EIU point out that the *Junta*'s 'fears of collusion between Mr Vieira's soldiers and ECOMOG were quickly dispelled as [the] peacekeepers ... steered clear of the clashes'.[83]

However, although ECOMOG proved impotent in the face of superior firepower and numbers, there was evidence to suggest that, even at the final juncture, at least one contingent *had* tried to influence the outcome and in the process partially influenced the decision of the *Junta* to exercise the military option. The *Junta*'s official justification for launching their attack was the refusal of loyalist troops to abide by the schedule for disarmament agreed on 15 February. Blame was placed mainly on the desperate intransigence of the loyalist forces, but the *Junta* was reported 'to have been angered by the failure of ECOMOG to disarm the presidential guard'.[84] In particular suspicion fell on the conduct of the Togolese contingent and the Togolese force leader Colonel Berena. The manner in which the Togolese stored and protected weapons taken from both sides by ECOMOG was questioned.[85] Strong rumours circulated that loyalist forces had been allowed access to crates of impounded armaments, or at the least that the Togolese had been perceptibly negligent in protecting the weapons. Reports that loyalist troops were so well armed lend credence to these claims.[86]

Although Mané had frequently claimed to have no personal ambitions he clearly had an interest in ensuring the continued support of his natural constituency who had invested trust in his enterprise – the army, veterans of the independence struggle and the internal opposition within the PAIGC. Mané realised that the overthrow of an elected president would have repercussions in the international community. Moreover, in light of the wider political climate in Guinea-Bissau it was hard to judge the extent to which the *Junta* could influence post-conflict events. However, Mané continued to enjoy an unquantifiable amount of practical support from allies within ECOWAS and beyond. Nigeria's Abubakar had reportedly counselled Mané to curtail the stand-off with a decisive push on loyalist positions.[87] Both Portugal and Sweden could be expected to counter French agitation within the EU. Most importantly the Junta had the unequivocal support of Bissauans. Sweden's representative in the country during the war, Ulla Andrén, squared Sweden's approach to the *Junta*'s assault - 'In the final analysis the military, the ruling party, the parliament and the people had all turned their back on the president'.[88]

External Players

War in Guinea-Bissau was small-scale in comparison with other conflicts taking place on the continent in 1998 and 1999. Nonetheless, the ECOMOG intervention became the object of regional and international manoeuvring. Jeffrey Herbst notes that the first three decades of independence in Africa were marked by few conflicts intended to change borders and, hence, 'within that environment, an assumption that intervention by African countries might be benign was at least plausible'.[89] However, he continues, 'now that at least some African countries appear to be acting in a more traditional manner – whereby they project power to further their own parochial interests – an assumption that intervention can be benign is obviously much more problematic'.[90]

Senegal

Of all the states with an interest in the conflict and the ECOMOG intervention Senegal had the most at stake. Defeat in Bissau meant that Senegal needed to reconstruct a basis for relations with a new regime in a neighbouring country whose foreign policies were vital to its own.

The conflict in Casamance lay at the heart of the conflict. Even prior to the publication of the Guinea-Bissau parliamentary report on arms trafficking, the Diouf government would have been aware that trade with the MFDC had been conducted by many individuals in the Bissau army, including those close to Vieira. There was little confidence in Dakar that Vieira had the will to effectively confront the Casamance rebels. Yet, whilst the schism in the Guinea-Bissau armed forces furnished an opportunity to tackle the MFDC from behind their rear bases, the decision to confront Mané's forces was ill-conceived and conducted on unfavourable terms. The extent of the mutiny was underestimated, whilst Senegal overestimated its capacity to defeat a veteran army on its own unique, harsh terrain. Ill-discipline, combined with its very presence, found the intervention force perceived as an invading army. Defeat was comprehensive.

The renewal of fighting at the end of January was a final opportunity to turn events on the ground. However, from the perspective of the expeditionary force it was clear that Mané could not be defeated. The intervention had become increasingly unpopular. A year before national elections, the intervention had given opposition leaders, such as Iba der

Thiam and Abdoulaye Wade, the opportunity to accuse the Diouf government of ignoring parliamentary process, as well as military failure.[91] In March 2000, Wade defeated Diouf in the second round of the presidential election. A central plank in Wade's electoral platform was to 'bring home the boys from Casamance' implying 'a more diplomatic approach to Guinea-Bissau'.[92]

For Diouf also the essential function of ECOMOG was to provide a feasible pretext for the withdrawal of his troops from the intervention. Dakar supported Vieira's calls for the augmentation of ECOMOG for the sake of form. Its own intervention having signally failed, Dakar realised that the possibility of ECOMOG altering the course of the war was negligible. The intervention had reawakened, in Jean-Claude Marut's words, a '*ressentiment antisénégalais*' amongst a large part of the Bissauan population.[93] The Senegalese Ministry of External Affairs was already preparing for the post-Vieira era. Following Vieira's ouster, Dakar moved quickly to repair relations with Bissau.

Dakar recognised that the imminent victory of the *Junta* would shift the military advantage on the ground towards the MFDC. As Mané launched his final assault on the loyalist stronghold in Bissau, the MFDC shelled Ziguinchor airport as officials from the Senegalese Ministry of Tourism were landing. Although there were no injuries, the incident saw the introduction of 82mm Chinese manufactured shells not previously seen in Casamance.[94] The ordnance was assumed to have come from the *Junta* stockpile. The implication was the *Junta* was both expressing thanks to the MFDC and issuing a warning to the Senegalese government. Senegal's foreign minister, Jacques Baudin, refused to join international condemnation, including that of France, of Mané's assault on the capital. Restricting himself to 'regretting' events in Bissau he asked a rhetorical question: 'Le problème est-il seulement de condamner'? Baudin stressed that with a vital interest in future relations with Bissau, Senegal could not afford the luxury of a trite, distanced condemnation of the coup.[95]

Guinea

Guinea shared the Senegalese need to extricate itself from Bissau. Motivation for the intervention was less apparent than was the case with Senegal and was an amalgam of the economic and strategic. Guinea and Guinea-Bissau shared a history of antagonism since the assassination of Cabral in Conakry. President Lansana Conté opposed Mané over both his

Mandinka ethnicity, as well as his links with the MFDC. The Mandinka have been marginalised in government since the death of Sekou Touré in 1984. A further factor was Guinean opposition to President Charles Taylor during the Liberian civil war. The MFDC reportedly obtain a proportion of their weaponry from Liberian sources.

Opposition leaders in Conakry were as troubled by events in Bissau as their counterparts in Dakar. The Codem opposition grouping publicly condemned the intervention as 'an imperialist venture that Guinea can ill-afford'.[96] The leader of the *Union pour le progrès en Guinée* (UPG), Jean-Marie Doré, complained that the government had deployed troops without a valid defence agreement with Guinea-Bissau and without informing the National Assembly.[97]

The Guinean armed forces have sought to project an 'image of professionalism' in recent years.[98] Yet, it was reported that 200 Guinean troops had deserted from their garrison in Bafata just prior to that town falling to the *Junta* in late October. These soldiers were seen in Conakry a few days later.

Togo

The primary motivation for Togo's involvement in ECOMOG was a pressing need to rehabilitate a severely tarnished reputation. The two targets for this international public relations exercise, the EU and France, had divergent agenda of their own. The EU had frozen aid to Togo since government repression following rioting in 1992. Whilst the EU officially condemned the mutiny in Bissau, it supported the withdrawal of Senegalese and Guinean troops and their replacement by ECOMOG as a neutral interposition force until elections could be conducted.

France was more proactive. Eyadéma's stock had fallen considerably during the Mitterrand presidency. However, relations between Lomé and Paris had improved under Chirac, although the socialist side of the *cohabitation* government was markedly less enthusiastic. In November 1998, the EU Commission, in response to the Togolese failure to address its democratic deficit and human rights abuses, signified that it intended to continue the policy of non-cooperation. At the same time Eyadéma was enjoying privileged access to Chirac as the new chair of ECOWAS during the Franco-African summit. Although Charles Josselin for the government made pro-democracy noises, Chirac used the presidential prerogative to dictate foreign policy to support Togo against the EU. The Togolese led the

ECOMOG intervention, deployed in advance and without the knowledge of the other contingents, and engaged in dubious, and partial, activities during the operation. A lack of capacity, as well as a need to behave with delicacy in the light of wider policies towards the EU and ECOWAS, limited the extent to which the Togolese contingent could act on behalf of France. Nonetheless, it henceforward became a conduit for French policy within ECOMOG.

At the time of the intervention Eyadéma contributed an article to the French journal *défense nationale* on the subject of an all-African peacekeeping force.[99] The article commended the idea of a regional peacekeeping interposition force operating under a UN mandate with *extra-*African funding. Eyadéma envisaged any proposed force operating under a military and politico-legal command situated in a troop-contributing country with a military headquarters established in theatre in the case of intervention. Individual units would be set aside by each state in the region ready to collaborate in the case of crisis. In essence the Eyadéma paper endorses the RECAMP initiative. However, the accent placed on cooperation between the troop-contributing countries and other regional states in the article was belied by Togo's precipitous deployment in Guinea-Bissau.

Gambia

Gambia invested time, diplomatic effort and troops in the ECOMOG intervention. However, as it took the lead in mediation the Gambian government's neutrality came into question. President Jammeh shares his Jola ethnicity with much of the MFDC. Moreover, Mané was born in Gambia. There was some suspicion that Gambia was acting to further the cause of the rebels in both Casamance and Guinea-Bissau either by offering a sympathetic outlet during the mediations, or by enabling convenient cease-fires.[100] Mané's cultural affinity with Gambia - he is still a regular visitor to the country - was no hindrance to the Jammeh initiative. However, Mané is not Gambian. Having left to fight for Guinea-Bissau at the age of seventeen he is a hero amongst veterans of the liberation struggle and within the army. Furthermore, despite a turbulent post-colonial history including the collapse of the short-lived Senegambia confederation, any proven support for the MFDC would be immensely detrimental to Senegal/Gambia relations.

For Gambia the twin motives for its role in the mediation process and ECOMOG intervention were security and economics. Although the Casamance rebellion has not impinged on Gambian territory, civil war in Guinea-Bissau opened the potential for a serious escalation of the conflict with possible consequences including violent contagion and increased refugee flows. Jammeh had been offering to take a more active part in regional conflict mediation for some time. In order to further this ambition Banjul sought to consolidate already close relations with Lagos as senior power in the region and within ECOWAS. This relationship had an unforeseen impact on the ECOMOG intervention when Jammeh dismissed Gambia's chief operations officer, Lieutenant-Colonel Pa Modou Ann, for insubordination. The reason for the dismissal was said to be a refusal by Pa Modou Ann to join the ECOMOG force following a personal slight from a senior Nigerian officer. The EIU reported that the 'sacking was also said to be evidence of Colonel Jammeh's sycophantic attitude towards the Nigerian leadership'. The players in the interventions were francophone. Since the option of a Nigerian contingent did not apply, the presence of an anglophone contingent, albeit small, was useful to Nigeria and other anglophone members of ECOWAS insofar as it gave a modicum of linguistic balance to the ECOMOG force in Guinea-Bissau.

The *Daily Observer* noted that 'Gambia cannot afford not to participate in any project designed to promote the return of stability in a neighbouring state'.[101] However, beyond the regional security dimensions, Gambia had also developed significant economic interests in Bissau. The lorry park in Banjul was dubbed 'Garage Bissau' owing the size of the re-export trade. At the onset of the conflict three trucks *en route* to Bissau were stopped and the cargo impounded by Senegalese soldiers at the Tanaaf customs post. The convoy's escort, a Guinea-Bissau citizen, was told that the goods and crew had been detained 'because they [the Senegalese authorities] had got news that Yahya Jammeh is sending arms to Mané'.[102] Regardless of the accuracy of this intelligence, business at 'Garage Bissau' was suspended for the duration of the conflict.

On 26 January the Gambian National Assembly met to approve the deployment of a contingent to ECOMOG. Two senior opposition politicians, Hamat Bah and Sidia Jatta, resisted the proposal. Jatta insisted that Gambian troops should not be expected to fight and should withdraw as soon as new elections could be held in Bissau. Moreover, he doubted that the intervention force could fulfil a constructive role, whilst suggesting that ECOMOG might undermine the cease-fire in place. Bah raised a highly controversial issue – the reaction of a contingent on its return from a peacekeeping intervention. Concern over the consequences of participation in peacekeeping intervention was felt in all troop-contributing countries. However, it was acute in Gambia. Referring to the coup that brought Jammeh to power in July 1994, Bah pointed out that 'the very people we sent to Liberia [as part of ECOMOG] are the ones who came back and flushed out a democratically elected government'.[103]

Niger

The assassination of President Ibrahim Baré Mainassara lent a deep irony to the involvement of the Nigerien contingent in the operation. The unpopular, authoritarian Mainassara was shot by his own Presidential Guard on 9 April 1999 in, what was described by the BBC's correspondent, as 'a copybook coup d'état'.[104] The coup was condemned by Lansana Kouyate on behalf of ECOWAS leaving the regional organisation in the bizarre position of denouncing events in a country presently contributing to an intervention to manage conflict in a country undergoing similar political collapse. It is uncertain whether the absence of Niger's senior field officers from Niamey facilitated the action of junior officers led by Major Daouda Mallam Wanké. Niger's participation in the intervention was most likely an attempt to curry favour with Paris. Mainassara was desperate for support from France following the refusal of Nigeria to renew an agreement signed with his predecessor Sani Abacha that involved Nigeria paying the salaries of the Nigerien Presidential Guard.[105] Mainassara was in Paris just a month before his assassination. During an official banquet at the Quai d'Orsay, Bernard Kouchner emphasised France's intention to develop a 'multi-faceted aid programme', as well as French satisfaction at Niger's decision to participate in ECOMOG.[106]

Benin

Since his return to power in 1996 Benin's President Mathieu Kérékou has sought to convince the international community that his government had abandoned the Marxist ideology that characterised his previous administration. In 1996, the Gaullist Minister of Cooperation, Jacques Godfrain, commended Benin's shift to market economics and financial rigour.[107] Furthermore, a battalion of Beninois troops had just finished training under the US peacekeeping project, the African Crisis Response

Initiative (ACRI). Despite these two spurs to participation, Benin gave the impression that it was the least engaged of the troop-contributing states. Cotonou acted unilaterally to declare the withdrawal of its contingent following Mané's final assault. Although there were calls in some quarters for ECOMOG to stay to help with the proposed elections, officials in Cotonou announced that 'the situation and objective reasons for maintaining the Beninois contingent in Guinea-Bissau have radically changed and...rendered pointless the ECOMOG buffer force and security mission'.[108]

France

The line taken by Paris during the Guinea-Bissau crisis and the ECOMOG intervention was reckless given the scant rewards for success and the significant international embarrassment of defeat. Belying the more detached official line taken by the *Quai d'Orsay*, involvement in Guinea-Bissau demonstrated a continued willingness to intervene in the *pré-carré*, albeit in a less overt fashion.

France's relations with Guinea-Bissau in the 1990s were crude and redolent of a nineteenth century colonial power struggle. Since Vieira's first overtures to join the Franc Zone in 1987, Paris pursued a policy of usurping Portugal's influence and incorporating Guinea-Bissau in its own extensive sphere of interest in West Africa.[109] In geopolitical terms Paris saw closer ties with Guinea-Bissau as strengthening the hand of French-speaking states in the continuing francophone/anglophone rivalry within ECOWAS. Moreover, by undermining Portugal's role in Bissau, France underlined that whilst its African policy was undergoing reappraisal this did not dilute an essential engagement with the continent. Finally increased influence in Guinea-Bissau allowed for a possible solution to the Casamance conflict together with the concomitant security benefits for Senegal. Senegal and France enjoy close diplomatic and military relations. As an important proxy in the sub-region what is good for Senegal is good for France.

The onset of violence brought the opportunity to demonstrate French resolve. Whilst France's instinct was to support the Senegalese intervention, public pronouncements maintained the non-interventionist position.[110] France's propensity for 'creative ambiguity' in African policy statements endures.[111] In fact throughout the duration of the conflict there were reports of French troops supporting Forex. When the conflict reignited in late January, prime minister Fadul accused France of using the ship carrying the ECOMOG troops, the *Siroco*, in concert with Senegalese warships, to bombard *Junta* positions. Tellingly, this period marked the most serious reversals for rebel forces. Further, as many as 300, white, francophone soldiers were reported openly supporting Forex troops.[112] French naval officials responded that the *Siroco* had no guns capable of reaching *Junta* positions from its anchorage thirty miles off the Bissau coast.[113]

A priest who has lived in Suzana on the Casamance border since 1968, Father Guiseppe Fumagalli known as Padre Ze, reported sightings of French soldiers involved in the fighting in a series of polemical letters:

> What are the French doing with guns in their hands? What can explain this? Can we speak here of good intentions and altruism? It would suffice for France to tell Senegal to stop, so that this process can get back on track – they [the Senegalese] have always been attentive students. Instead, they [France] do the contrary and give them [Senegal] ground support.[114]

These accusations, reported in the Portuguese newspaper *Público*, caused international embarrassment to France, especially as they coincided with a visit by President Chirac to Lisbon. Chirac redoubled the emphasis that French forces were not involved.[115] Future reports moderated this absolute denial. Writing on 22 February Hugo Sada noted that, whilst French policy had been non-interventionist, exceptions should be made when the security of French citizens was at risk.[116] Yet, France's effort to minimise and hide their support for the Vieira cause was compromised. Following the meeting between Chirac and his Portuguese counterpart President Jorge Sampaio reported sightings of French troops involved in fighting diminished.

French and Senegalese efforts in late January to alter the course of the war proved inadequate. Henceforward, French policy depended on the influence that they could exert on the ECOMOG force. In this respect, given the mainly francophone composition of the force, French policy in wider aspects of the conflict was sure to have an impact on the way in which ECOMOG was perceived by Bissauans. The *Junta* leadership remained highly sceptical, whilst the peacekeeping troops themselves were met with studied indifference by much of the population with whom they came into contact.

The operation was a first opportunity to test the RECAMP theory of prepositioned materiel for use by regional troops outside exercise conditions. It was also a chance to see if RECAMP could be used as an instrument to further French interests in the region. French meddling in the composition and deployment of ECOMOG both reinforced the existing animosity between the anglophone and francophone members of ECOWAS and undermined, possibly fatally, future RECAMP-funded ECOMOG interventions.

By manipulating its regional proxies in Dakar and Lomé, France managed to position itself behind two of the three groupings in the conflict. They supported the Vieira government through the connection with Senegal, whilst also underwriting the ECOWAS initiative and ensuring a majority francophone composition. It is symptomatic of France's decaying African policy that the other grouping in the conflict, the *Junta* and its MFDC allies, was victorious.

To what extent do French activities during the conflict in Guinea-Bissau and the ECOMOG intervention clarify France's reappraisal of its African policy? Sada seeks to accentuate the positive. He notes that France is in a transitional period between a direct interventionist presence, and support for all-African peacekeeping interventions. He further commends French support for ECOMOG in Guinea-Bissau as an expression of this new policy.[117]

Such an analysis does not look beyond the 'spin' emanating from the *Quai d'Orsay*. French involvement in the conflict might have moved away from the former policy of direct intervention. Certainly Paris made every effort to avoid accusations of supporting the loyalist position with arms. Yet, the supposed diplomacy and support for the ECOMOG intervention hid a failed attempt to retain influence in the region by other means. Paris must decide. In future crises, France must either rely on diplomacy, with its limitations, or revert to a more strenuous interventionist policy.

The defeat for French policy rankled. Paris maintained a hostile posture toward Bissau, suspending aid and cooperation until after elections were held. During a visit to Lomé President Chirac praised Togo's efforts as part of ECOMOG whilst condemning the 'brutal' manner in which the Abuja accords had been broken by Mané through the 'unacceptable and inadmissible' tactic of a coup d'état.[118]

Portugal

Portugal's relations with the Vieira regime had been strained throughout the 1990s. Lisbon was aware of the attempt by Paris to poach Guinea-Bissau. The impracticality of a proposed 'Escudo Zone' led to Vieira opting to join the Franc Zone. When fighting erupted in June 1998 Portugal saw an opportunity to reassert its influence. There were early reports of covert aid to the Mané's forces, although these were assumed to refer to the supply of satellite communications equipment ostensibly for use in the mediation process. Throughout the conflict all parties recognised that Portugal held a preference for the *Junta*.

The CPLP's function was to offer Lisbon a plausible entrée into the mediation process.[119] By the time of the Abuja accords events on the ground convinced Lisbon that Vieira's cause was lost prompting the CPLP to assume a secondary role in the construction of the intervention force.

If Portugal felt it unnecessary to pursue an interest in an intervention in circumstances that it felt were essentially decided, it remained vigilant against any efforts to reorient the direction of the conflict. The response to French involvement in the renewed fighting at the end of January was swift and robust. Lisbon conducted a naval exercise off the Bissauan coast that was held to be the main factor dissuading French and Senegalese ships from bombarding *Junta* positions. On 10 February Vieira made a limited protest against Portugal's efforts to undermine his external support by suspending a long-standing technical-military cooperation programme.[120] The move implied that Guinea-Bissau no longer needed military cooperation with Lisbon, preferring support from Paris. Following a Portuguese communiqué expressing 'displeasure', a spokesman for Vieira stated that the move was intended to 'suspend' rather than end cooperation.[121]

Conclusion

United Nations Secretary-General Koffi Annan has warned of the prevalence of 'military adventurism' in Africa and voiced concern over 'countries sending forces across borders to fight in other countries conflicts'.[122] Between 1998 and 1999 African armies intervened in other African nations 19 times.[123]

Military 'intervention' can be initiated for numerous reasons and is subject to subdivision.[124] Beyond the contending factions of the Guinea-Bissau armed forces, civil war provoked overlapping intervention by armed forces from seven militaries and a secessionist movement from a neighbouring state. Senegal and Guinea intervened on spurious legal grounds. Senegal, in particular, saw intervention as a chance to outflank the long-running rebellion in Casamance. France was unable to intervene in its formerly ubiquitous far-reaching and decisive manner. Nonetheless, Paris lent covert military support to the bilateral intervention. The failure of *Opération Gabou* saw France attempt to influence, through finance and logistics, the ECOMOG peacekeeping intervention. The francophone contributing states, especially Togo, took the opportunity to enhance their relations with France and as part of the French-speaking block within ECOWAS. France's efforts were to no avail. Mané's *Junta Militar* troops, supported by MFDC rebels, fought the Senegalese and Guineans to a standstill, and then swept past Vieira's remaining loyal forces.

For Senegal and Guinea intervention was costly not only in lives and material, but also proved a serious setback to their respective regional policies. Despite hopes that a change of government in Dakar might enhance relations between Senegal and Guinea-Bissau, tensions between the new government of President Wade and Mané's armed forces remain high.

Tacit support for *Opération Gabou* and French involvement in the ECOMOG intervention signalled a further reversal for France's African policy. Victory went to the only alliance involved in the conflict, the *Junta* and MFDC, that did not receive French backing. Hopes that the RECAMP initiative might allow Paris to exert influence in the region by proxy were premature. France's discomfort was Portugal's gain. However, given Guinea-Bissau's continued membership of the Franc Zone, the rapprochement with Lisbon should not be overstated. However, the important mediation role played by the CPLP suggests a more assertive role for lusophone states in regional conflict management.

The outcome for ECOMOG and the troop-contributing states was mixed. Togo and Gambia, in particular, used the peacekeeping intervention to further limited foreign policy aims. Togo, despite being unable to sway events on the ground, resuscitated its reputation with France and enhanced its prestige in ECOWAS. Gambia consolidated its position as a leading facilitator in regional conflict mediation. Whether the coup in Niger was influenced by the absence of senior commanders in Guinea-Bissau must remain conjecture. Given its size and composition it was predictable that ECOMOG was unable to prevent Vieira's overthrow. However, the narrow aim of the operation, the extrication of the beleaguered Senegalese and Guinean forces, justified ECOWAS' decision to intervene.

Notes

1 *Economist*, 15 May 1999, p. 48.

2 Quoted in Davidson, Basil (1981), *No Fist is Big Enough to Hide the Sky: The Liberation of Guinea-Bissau and Cape Verde*, Zed Press: London and New Jersey, p.165; see also Cabral, Amilcar (1980), *Unity and Struggle*, Heinemann: London; Forrest, Joshua B. (1992), *Guinea-Bissau: Power, Conflict and Renewal in a West African State*, Westview Press: Boulder; Galli, Rosemary E., and Jones, Jocelyn (1987), *Guinea-Bissau: Politics, Economics and Society,* Frances Pinter: London; Lopes, Carlos (1987), *Guinea-Bissau: From Liberation Struggle to Independent Statehood,* Zed Books: London and New Jersey; Rudebeck, Lars (1974), *Guinea-Bissau: A Study of Political Mobilization,* Scandinavian Institute of African Studies, Uppsala.

3 Quoted in Rudebeck, Lars (1997), ‘”To seek happiness”: Development in a West African village in the era of Democratisation’, *Review of African Political Economy*, 71, p. 84.

4 Clapham, Christopher (1996), *Africa and the International System: The Politics of State Survival*,Cambridge University Press: Cambridge, p. 60.

5 Faye, Ousseynou (1994), ‘La crise casamançaise et les relations du Sénégal avec la Gambie et la Guinée-Bissau (1980-1992)’, in Momar-Coumba (ed.), *Le Sénégal et ses voisins*, Sociétés-Espaces-Temps: Dakar-Etoile, p. 202.

6 Marut, Jean-Claude (1996), ‘Après avoir perdu l'est, la Guinée-Bissau perd-elle aussi le nord’, *Lusotopie*, p. 84.

7 Ibid., p. 84.

8 Handem Piette, Luisa (1998), ‘Guinea-Bissau: Recent History’, in *Africa South of the Sahara 1999*, Europa: London, p. 555.

9 Radio France Internationale, Paris, 12 February 1995; Antenna-1 Radio, Lisbon, 28 February 1995.

10 Marut, op.cit., p. 86.

11 US Department of State Bureau of Democracy, Human Rights, and Labour, ‘Guinea-Bissau Country Report on Human Rights Practices for 1999’, 25 February 2000.

12 *Afrique Express*, 13 May 1999, p. 3.

13 IRIN-WA, Weekly Roundup, 52, 12 June 1998; Rudebeck, Lars (1998), ‘Guinea-Bissau: Military Fighting Breaks Out’, *Review of African political Economy*, 77, pp. 484-486.

14 Interview with Dr Sadat Jobe (Minister for External Affairs, Gambia) and Ansumana Ceesay (Director of Political Affairs) Banjul, 27-28 January 2000.

15 IRIN-WA, Update, 230, 16 June 1998.

16 *Le Soleil en ligne,* <http://www.primature.sn/lesoleil/archi4/report.htm>, 25 May 1999.

17 Ibid.

18 *Jeune Afrique*, 'Les Sénégalais pris au piège', 1956, 7-13 March 1998.

19 IRIN-WA, Weekly Roundup, 56, 10 July 1998.

20 EIU (1998), *Country Report: Guinea-Bissau*, 3rd Quarter, p. 32.

21 IRIN-WA, Weekly Roundup, 57, 17 July 1998.

22 UNHCR Press Release, 'Ogata warns of refugee crisis in Guinea-Bissau', <http://www.unhcr.ch/news/pr/pr980622/htm>, 22 June 1998.

23 *Africa Research Bulletin*, 1-30 June 1998, p. 13133.

24 UNHCR, 'Refugees and Others of Concern to UNHCR – 1998 Statistical Overview', <http://www.unhcr.ch/statist/98oview/intro.htm>, 13 January 2000.

25 Amnesty International, 'Guinea-Bissau: Human rights in war and peace', AI Index AFR 30/07/99.

26 US Department of State Bureau of Democracy, Human Rights, and Labour (1999), 'Guinea-Bissau Country Report on Human Rights Practices for 1998', 26 February.

27 Panafrican News Agency, 'OAU Calls for Restoration of Legality in Guinea-Bissau', 15 July 1998.

28 OAU Conflict Management Division, 'OAU and the Conflict in Guinea-Bissau', <http://www.oau-oua.org/document/mechanism/english/mech10.htm>, 6 January 2000.

29 Interview with Essan Khan (Deputy Permanent Secretary in the Ministry of Defence), Banjul, 24 January 2000.

30 First joint meeting of ECOWAS ministers of foreign affairs and defence on Guinea-Bissau, Abidjan, 3 July 1998; Key articles of the Final Communiqué:

8 The Ministers strongly condemned the mutiny in Guinea-Bissau. They warned the rebels in Guinea-Bissau against committing any atrocities against the innocent civilian population and foreign nationals.

9 The meeting called for an immediate cessation of hostilities throughout the country.

10 The Ministers reaffirmed their support for the democratically elected Government of President João Bernardo Vieira.

11 The meeting agreed that the central objective of ECOWAS in Guinea-Bissau is to restore peace to Guinea-Bissau and reassert the authority of the democratically elected Government of President Vieira throughout the country.

12 The Ministers agreed to work towards realising this objective by a combination of the following three measures: i) dialogue and negotiation; ii) imposition and sanctions and enforcement of embargo; iii) and the use of force.

13 The Ministers recommended the extension of the mandate and scope of activities of ECOMOG to cover Guinea-Bissau. In this regard, all Member States should immediately contribute additional troops to ECOMOG.

They also called on the Member States for the provision of adequate logistic support for ECOMOG.

31 *Africa Research Bulletin*, 1-31 July 1998, p. 13189.

32 IRIN-WA, Weekly Roundup, 55, 3 July 1998.

33 The Committee of Seven comprised Burkina Faso, Côte d'Ivoire, Gambia, Ghana, Guinea, Nigeria and Senegal with representatives from the secretariats of the OAU and ECOWAS.

34 Hall, Margaret (1999), 'The conflict in Guinea-Bissau: the diplomatic intervention of the community of Portuguese-speaking countries', West African Seminar Series, University College London, 5 February.

35 The members of the Contact Group were the foreign ministers of Cape Verde, Mozambique, Portugal and São Tomé and Príncipe, together with senior officials from Brazil and Angola.

36 Interview with William Joof (Permanent Secretary to the Office of the President, Gambia), Banjul, 24 January 2000.

37 EIU (1998), *Country Report: Guinea-Bissau*, 4th Quarter, p. 28.

38 Panafrican News Agency, 'Ecowas Briefs Security Council on Guinea-Bissau Situation', 15 July 1998.

39 IRIN-WA, Weekly Roundup, 56, 10 July 1998.

40 IRIN-WA, Update, 259, 27 July 1998.

41 *Marchés Tropicaux*, 31 July 1998, p. 1633.

42 Ibid., p. 1633.

43 EIU (1998), *Country Report: Guinea-Bissau*, 4th Quarter, p. 29.

44 IRIN-WA, Weekly Roundup, 69, 9 October 1998.

45 Treaty of ECOWAS, Chapter X, Article 58, Paragraph 2, Sub-paragraphs e and f, Cotonou, 24 July 1993.

46 Interview with William Joof (Permanent Secretary to the Office of the President, Gambia), Banjul, 24 January 2000.

47 AGREEMENT BETWEEN THE GOVERNMENT OF GUINEA BISSAU AND THE SELF- PROCLAIMED MILITARY JUNTA

The parties to the conflict in Guinea Bissau meeting in Abuja on 21 October and 1st November 1998 in the context of the efforts of the 21st Summit of the Authority of the Heads of State and Government of the Economic Community of West African States (ECOWAS),

HEREBY AGREE AS FOLLOWS

1 Reaffirm the cease-fire agreement signed in Praia on 26 August,
2 Total withdrawal from Guinea Bissau of all foreign troops. This withdrawal shall be done simultaneously with the deployment of an ECOMOG interposition force which will take over from the withdrawn forces.
3 The interposition force will guarantee security along the Guinea Bissau/Senegal border, keep the warring parties apart and guarantee free

access to humanitarian organisations and agencies to reach the affected civilian populations. In this regard, the Oswaldo Vieira international airport and the sea-port shall be opened immediately.

4 Immediately put in place a Government of National Unity which will include, amongst others, representatives of the Self-Proclaimed Junta, in line with the agreement already reached between the parties.

5 General and Presidential elections shall be held not later than the end of March 1999. These elections will be observed by ECOWAS, the Community of Portuguese-Speaking Countries (CPLP) and the international community.

48 Ofodile, Anthony Chukwuka (1994), 'The Legality of ECOWAS Intervention in Liberia', *Columbia Journal of Transnational Law*, 32/2, p. 418.

49 UN Security Council Resolution 1216 (1998), S/RES/1216 (1998); UN Press Release, 'Security Council Calls for Urgent Establishment of Government of National Unity in Guinea-Bissau', SC/6614, 21 December 1998.

50 Jackson, Richard (1999), 'African Solutions to African Problems', Paper Presented to the AFSAAP Conference, 26-28 November 1999, Perth, Australia.

51 Ibid.

52 Ibid.

53 Ibid.

54 *Africa Research Bulletin*, 1-30 November 1998, p. 13331.

55 UN Security Council Resolution 1216 (1998), S/RES/1216 (1998).

56 Jackson, op.cit.

57 *L'Humanité*, 28 July 1998; Interview with William Joof (Permanent Secretary to the Office of the President, Gambia), Banjul, 24 January 2000.

58 *Africa Research Bulletin*, 1-30 November 1998, p. 13331.

59 *The Spectator* (Banjul), 31 December-14 January 1999, p. 18.

60 *Afrique Express*, 177, 12 November 1998, pp. 3-4.

61 IRIN-WA, Weekly Roundup, 2, 15 January 1999.

62 BBC Online Network, 'Guinea Bissau deaths', <http://news.bbc.co.uk /hi/english /world/africa>, 6 February 1999.

63 EIU (1999), *Country Report: Guinea-Bissau*, 2nd Quarter, p. 32.

64 IRIN-WA, Weekly Roundup, 3, 22 January 1999.

65 Interviews with senior Gambian officials, Banjul, 24-28 January 2000; Letter from HE President Yahya Jammeh to HE President Gnassingbé Eyadéma, 29 December 1998.

66 BBC Online Network, 'Nigeria not to send troops to Guinea-Bissau', <http://news.bbc.co.uk/hi/english/world/africa>, 7 February 1999.

67 IRIN-WA, Weekly Roundup, 76, 27 November 1998.

68 IRIN-WA, Update, 389, 27 January 1999.

69 Interviews with senior Gambian officials, Banjul, 24-28 January 2000; Letter from ECOWAS Executive Secretary Lansana Kouyate to President Yahya Jammeh, 20 January 1999.

70 Niger and Togo offered 500 men, Benin offered 300 men and Gambia offered 150 men.

71 Interviews with senior Gambian officials, Banjul, 24-28 January 2000; the force comprised 173 troops from Togo, 146 troops from Niger, 145 troops from Benin and 136 troops from Gambia.

72 Interviews with senior Gambian officials, Banjul, 24-28 January 2000; Support included 40 vans, 10 4x4 vehicles, helicopter support, uniforms, relief materials, camp beds, signals equipment, materials for the repair of the health infrastructure, fuel and spare parts.

73 Interviews with senior Gambian officials, Banjul, 24-28 January 2000; 'Convention d'Aide Budgetaire' between HE N'jogou Saer Bah (Gambian Ambassador to France) on behalf of HE Dr Sadat Jobe (Gambian Minister for External Affairs) and M. Charles Josselin (French Minister for Cooperation and the Francophonie), article 2, 18 March 1999.

74 Communiqué du Ministère de la Défense, 'Soutien de la France à la Force Interafricaine de maintien de la paix', Paris, 28 January 1999; Sada, Hugo, 'Guinée-Bissau: La France apporte une aide logistique à l'ECOMOG', *défense nationale*, April 1999, p.180.

75 Interviews with senior Gambian officials, Banjul, 24-28 January 2000.

76 US Department of State Bureau of Democracy, Human Rights, and Labour, 'Togo Country report on Human Rights Practices for 1998', 26 February 1999; EIU (1999), *Country Report: Togo*, 1st Quarter, p. 8.

77 EIU (1999), *Country Report: Togo*, 1st Quarter, p. 11.

78 *Agência Lusa*, 'Guinea-Bissau; Senegalese troop withdrawal not immediate, President Diouf reportedly says', 9 February 1999.

79 *Agência Lusa*, 'Guinea-Bissau: Swedish diplomat rebuked for statements to French radio', 9 February 1999.

80 *Agência Lusa*, 'Guinea-Bissau: Accord reached on foreign troop withdrawal, deployment of peacekeepers', 10 February 1999.

81 *Agência Lusa*, 'Guinea-Bissau: Fighting breaks out in Bissau, residents flee to port district', 6 May 1999; *Agence France Presse*, 'Guinea-Bissau President ousted, reportedly has asylum in Portugal', 7 May 1999; BBC Online Network, 'Guinea-Bissau palace ablaze', <http://news.bbc.co.uk/hi/english/world/africa>, 7 May 1999.

82 BBC Online Network, 'Second day of Bissau fighting' <http://news.bbc.co.uk/hi/ english/world/africa> 7 May 1999.

83 EIU (1999), *Country Report: Guinea-Bissau*, 3rd Quarter, p. 31.

84 BBC Online Network, 'Guinea-Bissau palace ablaze', <http://news.bbc.co.uk/hi/ english/world/africa>, 7 May 1999.

85 Interviews with senior Gambian officials, Banjul, 24-28 January 2000.
86 *Agence France Presse*, 'Paris confirme que ses fonctionnaires ont quitté le centre culturel', 7 May 1999.
87 Mekencamp, Monique (1999), 'Guinea-Bissau: Democracy Restored by a Military Coup', in Monique Mekencamp, Paul van Tongeren and Hans van de Veen (eds), *Searching for Peace in Africa: an Overview of Conflict Prevention and Management Activitie,* European Platform for Conflict Management and Transformation, Utrecht, p. 303.
88 Andrén, Ulla (2000), 'The Forgotten Conflict in Guinea-Bissau', *News from the Nordic Africa Institute*, 1, January, pp. 5-6.
89 Herbst, Jeffrey (2000), 'Western and African Peacekeepers: Motives and Opportunities', in John W. Harbeson and Donald Rothchild, *Africa in World Politics: The African State System in Flux*, Westview Press: Boulder, p. 313.
90 Ibid., p. 313.
91 EIU (1998), *Country Report: Senegal,* 3rd Quarter, p. 15.
92 *Africa Confidential*, 41/7, 31 March 2000, p. 3.
93 Marut, Jean-Claude (1998), 'Ligne dure face à la Casamance', *Monde Diplomatique*, October, p. 4.
94 Beck, Linda (1999), 'Sovereignty in Africa: From Colonial Inheritance to Ethnic Entitlement?', Conference paper delivered at the American Political Science Association Annual Meeting, Atlanta, September 2-5 1999.
95 *Le Soleil en ligne,* <http://www.primature.sn/lesoleil/archi4/report.htm>, 12 May 1999.
96 EIU (1998), *Country Report: Guinea,* 1st Quarter, p. 14.
97 EIU (1998), *Country Report: Guinea,* 3rd Quarter, p. 10.
98 EIU (1998), *Country Report: Guinea,* 1st Quarter, p. 13.
99 Eyadéma, Gnassingbé (1999), 'La force d'interposition africaine', *défense nationale*, 2, February, pp. 5-9.
100 EIU (1998), *Country Report: The Gambia,* 3rd Quarter, p. 27.
101 *Daily Observer* [Banjul], 9 February 1999.
102 *Daily Observer* [Banjul], 15 July 1998.
103 *Gambia Daily News* [Banjul], 28 January 1999; *Daily Observer* [Banjul], 28 January 1999.
104 BBC Online Network, 'Niger: A copybook coup d'état', <http://news.bbc.co.uk/hi/ english/world/africa>, 9 April 1999.
105 *Independent* [Accra], 22 June 1999.
106 'Toast du Sécretaire d'Etat à la Santé et à l'Action Sociale, M.Bernard Kouchner, au dîner offert au Palais des Affaires Etrangeres en l'honneur du Président de la République du Niger, M.Ibrahim Mainassara Baré, Paris, 25 February 1999.

107 'Discours du Ministre Délégué à la Coopération, M. Jacques Godfrain, à l'occasion du dîner offert en l'honneur du Président du Bénin, M. Mathieu Kérékou', Paris, 8 August 1996.
108 *Agence France Presse*, 'ECOWAS Credibility Dented in Guinea-Bissau', 10 May 1999.
109 Koudawo, Fafali (1997), 'Guinée-Bissau: la carte francophone', *L'Afrique politique*, pp. 213-228.
110 Ministère des Affaires Etrangères, Point de Presse Déclarations du Porte-Parole, 'Guinée-Bissao', Paris, 22 June 1998.
111 Martin, Guy (1995), 'Francophone Africa in the Context of Franco-American Relations', in John W. Harbeson and Donald Rothchild (eds) *Africa in World Politics: Post-Cold War Challenges*, Westview Press: Boulder, p. 182.
112 EIU (1999), *Country Report: Guinea-Bissau*, 2nd Quarter, p. 33.
113 CNN.com, 'Guinea-Bissau strife strands civilians, peacekeepers', 2 February 1999, <http://clinton.cnn.com/WORLD/africa/9902/02/guinea-bissau>.
114 Letter from Father Guiseppe Fumagalli, Suzana, 1 February 1999, <http://www.geocities.com/TheTropics/Cabana/8248/padrezee.html>.
115 'Visite au Portugal Point de Presse Conjoint du Président de la République, M. Jacques Chirac, et du Président de la République Portugaise, M. Jorge Sampaio - Propos du Président', Lisbon, 4 February 1999.
116 Sada, op.cit., p. 180.
117 Ibid., p. 180.
118 'Visite en Afrique allocution du Président de la République, M. Jacques Chirac, devant la communauté française', Lomé, 22 July 1999.
119 Wegemund, Regina (1999), 'Die CPLP und der Burgerkrieg in Guinea-Bissau', *Internationales Afrikaforum*, 35/2, pp.165-176.
120 *Agência Lusa*, 'Guinea-Bissau: Lisbon 'displeased' with president Vieira ending military cooperation programmes', 11 February 1999.
121 *Agência Lusa*, 'Guinea-Bissau: Vieira adviser says military cooperation with Portugal will be resumed', 12 February 1999.
122 BBC Online Network <http://news.bbc.co.uk/hi/english/world/africa> posted 12 February 1999.
123 Thom, William (2000), 'Africa's Security issues Through 2010', *Military Review*, July-August, p. 7.
124 Connaughton, Richard (1992), *Military Intervention in the 1990s: A New Logic of War*, Routledge: London and New York, p. 1.

13 Interventionist Companies: Privatising the Military Option

Gerry Cleaver

Introduction

During the 1990s there has been much debate in both political and academic circles about the role of so-called private security companies and mercenaries in Africa's conflict zones. In some of the literature the terms private security company and mercenary are treated as being synonymous and therefore I intend to devote some space to an attempt to reach more individual definitions of both phenomena. I believe that it is also important to put the current situation in its historical context especially with regard to Africa's post-independence history. This is a subject that stirs up a great deal of emotion wherever it is debated. It is possible to find passionate arguments for and against the use of private security companies and mercenaries in much of the recent literature on the subject, though it must be said that there is far more of the latter than the former. It is not my intention in this chapter to adopt any particular moral position but to analyse the facts as I see them.[1]

This chapter will also highlight the particular circumstances pertaining in sub-Saharan Africa that facilitate the privatisation of security. Examples of recent operations by private security companies and mercenaries and their effectiveness will be analysed in the context of the claims made by the advocates of security privatisation and the allegations made by their opponents. Finally I will look at the reaction of individual states and supranational organisations to this emerging phenomenon and their attempts at 'controlling' it.

Definitions

Given that much of the contemporary debate concerning private security companies centres on the legality of their operations and whether or not they should be viewed as mercenaries, I believe it is necessary to examine the definitions of 'mercenary' currently in use by the international community. There have been a number of attempts at defining mercenaries in international law. These include the 1977 Convention for the Elimination of Mercenarism in Africa established by the Organisation of African Unity, Article 47 of the 1977 Additional Protocol I of the Geneva Conventions and the 1989 International Convention against the Recruitment, Use, Financing and Training of Mercenaries.[2] Article 47 of the Additional Protocol to the Geneva Conventions describes a mercenary, inter alia, as someone participating in a particular conflict who has been specifically recruited for that purpose and who is motivated purely by personal gain. They also have to have been promised rewards, by a party to the conflict, in excess of those available to their equivalents in the forces of that party. In addition to qualify as a mercenary they must not be a national or a resident of the country involved in the conflict or a member of the armed forces of another state on official duty in the state in which the conflict takes place. All of these criteria need to apply before an individual can be classified as a mercenary.[3]

Article 47 is generally deemed to apply only to interstate conflicts and to 'wars of national liberation' and therefore it might be argued that civil wars remain outside its provisions. These conflicts are precisely the ones in which the business of private security companies has flourished in recent years in Africa. Article 47 also suffers from a lack of whole-hearted support from the major western powers, many of whom are also dragging their feet on ratification of the 1989 International Convention. This latter Convention and its OAU counterpart are more wide-ranging when it comes to the types of conflict covered by their definitions of what constitutes mercenary activity. To those states which have signed up to these international agreements, mercenaries are criminals, outside the protection of international law and not entitled to be treated as prisoners of war if captured.

Reference to these international conventions does not greatly help clarify matters when consideration is given to the status of private security companies. For the purposes of this chapter, I will join with other writers on this subject in excluding from the term private security company, those organisations that merely provide security guards for buildings or individuals or who are engaged in neighbourhood security schemes to counteract crimes such as burglary, mugging, car-jacking etc.[4] The type of private security company upon which this article will concentrate is that which provides military expertise of a kind more traditionally associated with the armed forces of a nation state. The activities of these companies are often multifarious and they may well be engaged in the provision of personal security and the protection of static installations. However what sets them apart is their ability to provide military expertise whether it be technical, logistical, organisational or actual combat.

Defining these companies and their employees as mercenaries, as laid down within international law, becomes problematical. It seems that many categories of advisor employed by these companies cannot be considered mercenaries, as they do not actually participate in combat. If as they claim they do, these private security companies restrict their employment to legitimate governments, then it is difficult to categorise them as mercenaries, especially if the definition used in international conventions refers to someone engaged in overthrowing the constitutional order. Things become even more complex when these companies operate alongside international forces engaged in a humanitarian intervention. The confusion as to the status of these private security companies is reflected in the reports of the United Nations Special Rapporteur of the Commission on Human Rights, Enrique Ballesteros. While deprecating the development of such companies he admits that within the terms of the international law currently established it would not be possible definitively to categorise them as mercenaries. Ballesteros makes the point that this is an issue that requires clarification at the international level as the current legislation is open to a variety of interpretations.[5] However he feels more certain when asserting that the continued employment of such companies by governments has serious implications for state sovereignty, especially in Africa.[6]

Historical Background

The use of mercenaries is by no means a modern phenomenon and is nearly as old as organised warfare itself. Historical examples are legion and quoted at length in the literature. It was the rise of the nation state and the concomitant creation of national armies that led to the demonisation of mercenaries. It became almost dishonourable to be seen as fighting merely for money rather than for one's country and employing 'foreigners' in your army was deemed to be, at the very least, an underhand tactic. There is a sizeable element of hypocrisy in all of this as all the European colonial powers employed troops recruited from their colonies both during the acquisition of empire and in the two World Wars.

There were a variety of reasons for the employment of colonial troops but chief among them was that they were generally much cheaper than their European counterparts, often available in greater numbers and better suited to tropical environments. As a bonus they often turned out to be excellent soldiers. Were these troops mercenaries? Or did their status as imperial subjects mean that they could be counted as members of the 'national' forces of the colonial power? A soldier in the King's African Rifles in World War One may have been fighting for Britain but his imperial masters most certainly would not have considered him to be British. This might be considered a moot historical point but in the contemporary debate much is made of the foreign origins of mercenaries as being a defining characteristic. What happens if the putative mercenary adopts, or is given, the nationality of the country in which he is fighting? The nationality issue is further complicated if he is an employee of a private company with multinational connections.

The employment of mercenaries by major European powers continues to this day. Both the French Foreign Legion and Britain's Gurkhas are recruited from people who are not citizens of the employing state.[7] Although incorporated into the armies of these two countries and officered by their nationals, these units hark back to an earlier tradition of hiring foreigners to do your fighting for you. Participation in 'Blue Helmet' operations has given these units de facto recognition by the United Nations. Since the origins of both these units date back to the first half of the nineteenth century then perhaps tradition and longevity have bestowed an element of legitimacy upon them.

Prior to the advent of the private security companies in the last decade, mercenary activity in post colonial Africa was typified by the operations of groups led by such notorious individuals as Mike Hoare, Bob Denard, Rolf Steiner and Costas Georgiou better known as 'Callan'.[8] These names and others like them can be found associated with all the continent's hot-spots, the Congo, Comoros, Seychelles, Zimbabwe, Benin and Angola, to name but a few. They were used to prop up regimes and to overthrow them. They were employed in civil wars and struggles for liberation and earned a reputation for brutality that led to their being nicknamed *'les affreux'* - the terrible ones.

These mercenary activities were by and large funded by means of direct payments to either the individuals concerned or to a 'front' company that acted as a recruiting agency. Although this funding may have come directly or indirectly from the resources of the state, the direct exploitation of a state's natural resources by the mercenaries themselves or their associates was not part of the bargain. To be sure mineral exploitation companies may well have benefited from the activities of these mercenaries and even encouraged them. But the connection was always kept covert and certainly not formalised through identifiable corporate linkages. In this one respect at least, the activities of today's private security companies differ markedly from those of the earlier 'soldiers of fortune'.

Although the activities of these individuals achieved a certain amount of notoriety they were by no means the only examples of foreign military interference in the affairs of independent African states. African and non-African states intervened both covertly and overtly in the affairs of the newly independent states of sub-Saharan Africa. A great many of these interventions, whilst reprehensible for many reasons, could not justifiably be termed mercenary. However, one might question the role played by the Cubans in Angola and Ethiopia for example or South Africa's use of units such as the famous 32 Battalion in Angola in support of UNITA.[9] African states also 'loaned' their troops in support of their political allies.[10] Morocco lent troops to President Mobutu of Zaire in the 1970s when his regime was under threat from Katangan rebels. In his turn Mobutu provided some of the better units of his otherwise disreputable army, in support of the Habyarimana regime in Rwanda in the early 1990s. These two examples, out of the many that have been documented, may provide evidence to counterbalance the impression that might be obtained from some of the literature, that up until the advent of private security companies, African states had relied solely on their own resources for the provision of security.

Typologies

Attempts to produce a typology of contemporary private military activity are made more difficult by the involvement of individuals and companies in a variety of military-related activities at the same time. However notwithstanding these problems of classification, it is possible to identify a number of general categories of private military activity in Africa. The first type is the 'classical' mercenary. Individuals recruited for their military expertise to fight in a specific conflict. A recent example of this are the Serbs allegedly recruited by former officers of the French military to fight for Mobutu in 1997.[11] This vain attempt to shore up a collapsing regime ended up with the Serbs turning on their erstwhile allies in the Zairean army whilst fleeing from the advancing rebels. Nowadays many of these mercenaries are employed for their technical knowledge rather than just for their prowess in combat. They are contracted to operate and maintain the more sophisticated weaponry now to be found on all the world's battlefields, such as aircraft, helicopters and artillery. It has been noted that the provision of this type of expertise can be directly linked with contracts to supply such equipment.[12] Increasingly much of this work now falls into the second general category of privatised security activity, namely the private security company.

The activities of these companies can be further subdivided. Firstly there is actual participation in combat, leading and supporting the forces of the employer state. The best known exponent in this field is Executive Outcomes. Next are the types of activity associated with the enhancement of the capabilities of the employer state. These include the provision of training, especially at the higher command level, military intelligence and analysis and weapons supply. A major player in this area is the US company, Military Professional Resources Incorporated (MPRI).[13]

Thirdly, as mentioned earlier, private companies are also involved in supplying security for installations and personnel. In addition private companies are increasingly employed to provide logistical support and maintenance facilities, not only for the militaries of individual states but also for the United Nations. Many western militaries are moving toward the privatisation of the 'non-teeth' or 'tail end' aspects of military operations including logistics and base support.[14] This is increasingly the case when forces are deployed abroad in humanitarian operations. This is part of a more general process of divesting the state of activities that are believed to be more properly the province of private companies. The companies involved in the provision of this type of support to the military may not, themselves, have military origins or structure and are usually divorced from the actual fighting. It may be safely assumed that they would nevertheless be employed to provide some sort of military advantage to the host army, if only to release their own logistics troops for front line duty. In this case they might well find themselves included in any broader definition of mercenary activity adopted by the international community.

Much of the literature concentrates on the activities of companies such as Executive Outcomes and MPRI who are involved in the first two categories of private security company activity. Although private security companies have operated in many parts of the world, it is in Africa that they have found their most profitable market.

The Operating Environment

Private security companies have, in the last decade, prospered in an international environment of increasing instability and insecurity. Whilst this is a global phenomenon, it is arguable that its most extreme and pernicious manifestation is to be found in sub-Saharan Africa. The factors leading to the creation of this environment are both international and African in origin.

Africa has suffered from very serious international marginalisation following on from the end of the Cold War. During that conflict Africa became a battleground for the superpowers who conducted their rivalry via proxies such as Cuba and South Africa. The consequences of this rivalry still haunt Africa today, particularly in Angola. Nevertheless during this period Africa was, to a significant degree, a centre of attention for the superpowers and many African leaders were able to exploit this to the political and pecuniary advantage of themselves and their countries. However in the immediate aftermath of the collapse of the Eastern Bloc in 1989 Africa, as one writer has described it, 'lost its political worth' and the states of sub-Saharan Africa became 'so much irrelevant international clutter'.[15] This political marginalisation has been accompanied by growing economic isolation, with the continent accounting for little more than two per cent of international trade.

The end of the Cold War saw rising expectations, especially in the West, of a peace dividend as a result of the reduction in military forces. It has led to a reduced military capacity among the Western states and an increasing reluctance to become involved in areas not deemed to be vital to national interests. Africa usually falls into this category. The reduction of military forces released a great deal of experienced manpower onto the private market and facilitated the growth of private companies through the availability of this resource as well as the increasing use of private companies by Western militaries to provide logistical services. The change of regime in South Africa had a similar effect, releasing onto the market a large number of combat-experienced personnel, no longer required by the new, smaller South African National Defence Force (SANDF). This post Cold War military retrenchment also released a great deal of hardware for private use and international export. In the economically depressed states of Eastern Europe and the former USSR, the arms industries were often the most advanced and competitive segments of the economy. It is therefore understandable that these states should seek to maximise their foreign currency earnings through increased arms exports to the world's trouble spots.[16]

The early years of this decade also saw a dramatic decline in international participation in peacekeeping on the African continent. The debacles in Somalia and Rwanda have effectively crippled the reputation of the United Nations in Africa.[17] The humiliation suffered by US forces in Somalia led to a radical rethink of the US commitment to United Nations peacekeeping operations. This culminated in the issuing of Presidential Decision Directive 25 in May 1994. This document laid down a number of criteria which would have to be satisfied before the US would participate in future United Nations peacekeeping operations. Effectively the future use of US combat forces in such operations was ruled out.[18] Because of its veto and ability to block budgets the US exercises enormous influence over the United Nations' ability to conduct peacekeeping operations. Without active US participation the other Western powers would be most reluctant to become involved in any United Nations peacekeeping operations in Africa. These developments combined with mistakes within the United Nations itself led to the disaster of UNAMIR I in Rwanda.[19] In reality peacekeeping in Africa has been devolved down to African states themselves and they are woefully ill-equipped for this task.[20] The US, Britain and France are prepared to provided some assistance to African peacekeeping operations but at one step removed from the actual participation of their forces.[21] The French have now started to restructure their armed forces and withdraw some of their troops from Africa where they have had a long-term military presence in the postcolonial era.[22] Western disengagement and limited African capacities have created a security vacuum, into which the private security companies have moved.

Within Africa itself a number of factors have contributed to this poor security environment. The post colonial African state has been typified by a lack of popular legitimacy for the institutions of the state and its political processes. Widespread systemic corruption on the continent has undermined the legitimacy of politicians and the state itself as well as contributing directly to the poor performance of local security forces. Chronic economic failure, the debilitating impact of Structural Adjustment Policies and fierce competition for ever scarcer resources have facilitated the creation of an environment where recourse to violence is often seen as the only way out of a desperate situation. The overthrow of long-serving dictators and the effective collapse of some states has added to the overall air of insecurity and the military retrenchment in South Africa following the demise of apartheid has created a pool of experienced manpower available for private employment. These political and economic circumstances together with Africa's underdeveloped natural resources created an opportunity for those able to exploit it.

Executive Outcomes: The Archetype Private Security Company

Executive Outcomes is probably the most widely known private security company amongst the general public. Part of this notoriety derives from the reports of their apparent 'success' in bringing a form of peace to parts of Angola and Sierra Leone. However Executive Outcomes has become the primary target of those who are critical of the roles of private security companies in general. This is largely due to its origins. Executive Outcomes started in 1989 as an incorporated company registered in South Africa and Britain. Its founders were both former members of South Africa's apartheid era special forces, Eeben Barlow and Lafras Luitingh. In 1997 both men left Executive Outcomes and the company was then headed by Nick van den Bergh, a former officer in the South African parachute regiment. It appears that his past was a little less controversial than those of his predecessors and thus better for the corporate image.[23]

Most of Executive Outcomes' front line operatives have been recruited from former members of South Africa's special forces units that operated in the apartheid era. These units, such 32 Battalion, Koevoet, Paratroops and Reconnaissance Commandos were all heavily involved in South African military operations in Namibia, Angola and Mozambique.[24] The Namibian settlement in 1990 and the end of apartheid in 1994 led to the disbandment of these units and the creation of a reserve of potential recruits for organisations such as Executive Outcomes. The officers employed are almost exclusively white while many of the soldiers are of Angolan or Namibian origin. Executive Outcomes does not maintain a standing army as such but recruits to meet its contractual needs. The common experiences of its recruiting base make welding them into an effective force less problematical than with a more eclectic group.

However it is these origins at the cutting edge of apartheid South Africa's military that have caused such problems for Executive Outcomes' image makers. Many commentators, especially African ones, cannot help but ascribe evil motives to anything done by what have been described as 'apartheid's attack dogs'. This tends to bring a mixture of emotions to any debate on private security companies in Africa. There is revulsion at the involvement of these representatives of a pariah system in the affairs of independent sub-Saharan African states. This is compounded by embarrassment that these states can not sort out their own security problems without recourse to such people.

The corporate connections of Executive Outcomes are difficult to pin down.[25] Formerly part of a now defunct holding company, Strategic Resources Corporation, Executive Outcomes is closely connected to a number of other private security companies such as Lifeguard Security and Saracen Security. Executive Outcomes also has a business relationship with the Branch-Heritage Group which is based in the same London office building as agents acting for Executive Outcomes. A former British SAS veteran, Anthony Buckingham, heads the Branch Heritage Group. The group includes a number of mineral extraction companies such as Branch Energy, Branch Minerals, Diamond Works and Heritage Oil and Gas. It also includes the private security company, Sandline International. The mineral companies operate in places such as Angola and Sierra Leone and have employed Executive Outcomes or its affiliates for the purposes of providing security. They have all benefited from the consequences of Executive Outcomes interventions in these two countries. Officially there is no corporate link between Executive Outcomes and the Branch Heritage Group, although they share interests in Ibis Air often referred to as Executive Outcomes' air force. But the two organisations seem to operate to each other's benefit. The mineral companies provide the introduction for Executive Outcomes who then provide the security environment that allows for the profitable extraction of the minerals that might otherwise be impossible to access. This close association puts the mineral companies at an advantage when negotiating contracts as they can link their operations with the provision of security. When one looks at the oil and diamond reserves of Angola and the diamonds of Sierra Leone the sums of money at stake are vast and from the mineral companies' point of view well worth the risk. The cost of employing private security companies is small in comparison to the potential rewards, and it is all to the good if you can get the host government to pay the bill.

The origins of Executive Outcomes activities in Angola are not entirely clear. It appears that they were initially retained by a number of oil companies in 1992 to protect their installations in the Soyo region of Angola where Heritage Oil and Gas had interests.[26] This area was overrun by UNITA and Executive Outcomes was contracted in March 1993 by the Angolan government to assist in the recapture of this strategically vital region. Backed by Angolan troops Executive Outcomes operatives, numbering less than 100, recaptured the facilities. Although they were subsequently lost again after Executive Outcomes departure this action so impressed the Angolan government that it offered Executive Outcomes a $40 million dollar one-year contract to train its forces. The contract was continuously renewed until January 1996. Over 500 Executive Outcomes personnel were employed, many in combat roles. They are credited with turning around the fortunes of the Angolan government and its military and in forcing UNITA to the negotiating table. Executive Outcomes was principally concerned with recapturing diamond and oil fields as these are crucial to financing war in Africa. Because many had fought with UNITA in the past they had excellent knowledge of their tactics and limitations. Executive Outcomes eventually left Angola after pressure on the Angolans from the US.[27]

Executive Outcomes was called into Sierra Leone by the besieged government of Valentine Strasser in March 1995. Much of the country including the valuable diamond and rutile mines was in the hands of the Revolutionary United Front, headed by Foday Sankoh. The civil war in Sierra Leone was a spill-over from the Liberian conflict and was conducted with almost inconceivable barbarity mostly against unarmed civilians. The government forces had effectively ceased to exist as an organised force and the soldiers and rebels became so indistinguishable as to lead to the coining of a new term, 'sobels'.[28] All this needs to be borne in mind when placing the actions of firstly Executive Outcomes and later on Sandline, into context. The RUF were no liberation movement struggling against foreign oppression. They are no better than murderous gangsters that use mutilation as a deliberate weapon against defenceless civilians, and the international community, at both the global and regional level had singularly failed to find a resolution to this particular conflict.

Between December 1995 and October 1996 Executive Outcomes launched a series of offensives that secured the Freetown area, reoccupied the diamond and rutile mines and eliminated the RUF bases. They established sufficient security for elections to be held in March 1996 that led to a civilian regime and forced the RUF to sign up to a peace accord in November 1996. The cost to Sierra Leone of the involvement of Executive Outcomes was some $35 million. This was to be paid in cash by monthly instalments. There is no evidence that Executive Outcomes itself obtained diamond concessions though Branch Energy did.[29] This was a heavy burden on an economy such as Sierra Leone's, nevertheless the security provided was essential for its future well being and in reality, it was not available elsewhere. It is interesting to note that both UNITA and the RUF made the departure of Executive Outcomes a condition of their agreeing to a peace deal. Both of them subsequently reneged on these deals. A criticism levelled at private security companies in general and Executive Outcomes in particular is that they have failed to deliver lasting solutions to the problems of Angola and Sierra Leone. In their defence it must be stated that they never claimed that that was what they were trying to do. They offered particular solutions to specific problems. As for long term solutions it is not just private security companies that have failed; so have the United Nations and regional organisations. Executive Outcomes has always claimed that it worked only for legitimate governments. While one might argue over the legitimacy of the MPLA regime in Angola there is an even bigger question mark over that of Valentine Strasser in Sierra Leone. In Africa the definition of legitimate can be very elastic. Criticism that focuses on this element of their activities might be easier to sustain.

Executive Outcomes has also operated in a number of other African states including Kenya and Uganda but these operations have been of a much lower profile. The reputation of Executive Outcomes personnel is such that they are sought by many parties to conflict. There are stories that the Mobutu regime in Zaire attempted to recruit ex-Executive Outcomes personnel during its dying days in 1997.[30] Former Executive Outcomes operatives are said to involved on both sides of the conflict in Angola today. The company itself officially went out of business on 1 January 1999. The statement at the time said that Executive Outcomes no longer saw itself as having a role to play in conflict resolution in Africa. Its closure may be connected with South African legislation on private security companies but reports suggest that its offices in Pretoria remain staffed and that some its personnel are now employed by Lifeguard Security. It may well be that this archetypal private security company could yet reappear under another name.[31]

Sandline: Exposing the Conundrum

The furore surrounding the so-called 'arms to Sierra Leone affair' had rather more to do with the machinations of the British political system than any deep seated concern for the fate of a small West African country.[32] Nevertheless the inquiry of the Parliamentary Foreign Affairs Committee into the relationship between the Foreign Office and Sandline International did bring the role of private security companies in Africa to the attention of the wider British public. It also exposed the conundrum facing most Western powers, in this case the British government, when faced with international crises. They feel obliged by the pressures of public opinion, to be seen to be doing something, but equally are aware that the same public will rarely countenance the dispatch of national forces to remote and dangerous corners of the world.

As the pronouncements of international organisations appear increasingly as ineffective window dressing and sanctions become something of a joke, governments might well view the possibilities provided by private security companies with favour. However the stigma still attached to such companies means that governments and their officials prefer to keep such relationships away from public scrutiny.

Sandline International is very closely associated corporately with the Branch Heritage Group, headed by Anthony Buckingham. Another company in the group, Diamondworks, has extensive diamond mining interests in Sierra Leone, which it took over from Branch Energy in 1996. Sandline is headed by a former colonel in the British army, Timothy Spicer, and operates out of offices in London, though it is registered in the Bahamas. It offers military training, logistics, supplies, planning and threat analysis. It had a close working relationship with Executive Outcomes with whom it was involved in an abortive contract in Papua New Guinea in February 1997.[33]

The involvement of Sandline International in the affairs of Sierra Leone came as a result of the overthrow in May 1997 of the democratically elected civilian government of Ahmed Tejan Kabbah. His regime was overthrown by an Armed Forces Revolutionary Council headed by Major Johnny Paul Koroma. This junta immediately allied itself with the Revolutionary United Front, to form a 'Peoples Army'.[34] The military had resented the loss of access to the diamonds and other economic resources of Sierra Leone that a civilian government had brought. In addition they resented the growing influence of the Kamajor civilian militia who had been very effective in assisting Executive Outcomes in defeating the RUF the previous year. This new alliance between the junta and the RUF merely made public something that had been suspected for a long time, namely that elements of the army had co-operated with the RUF to plunder the natural resources of Sierra Leone.

The Koroma junta was internationally isolated but proved immune to diplomatic efforts aimed at its removal. The junta embarked on a series of murders to stamp out opposition and to all intents and purposes behaved in a decidedly criminal manner. Despite this the international community seemed reluctant actually to do anything to remove them. The United Nations passed Security Council resolution 1132 (1997) imposing an arms embargo on Sierra Leone.[35] However this can be interpreted as gesture politics given the state of impotence to which the United Nations has been reduced, especially in Africa, and the ease with which the purveyors of arms evade regulation and border controls.

President Kabbah, in exile in Guinea, was put in contact with Sandline International allegedly by the British High Commissioner to Sierra Leone, Mr Penfold, who had also relocated to Guinea. Sandline International were contracted to supply weapons and equipment to forces loyal to President Kabbah and also to the Nigerian-led ECOMOG forces who were stationed in Sierra Leone and who were preparing to confront the junta militarily. The arms came from Bulgaria and were shipped via Nigeria and possibly Guinea. The deal was financed to the tune of $10 million by an Asian businessman, Rakesh Saxena. He has a major interest in Diamondworks which was promised major diamond concessions in return for this finance.[36]

Whether or not the arms supplied by Sandline International helped in the overthrow of the junta is debatable, as ECOMOG forces succeeded in this task, at least as far as Freetown was concerned, by 10 March 1998, before the bulk of the arms arrived. Nevertheless the arms, equipment and expertise provided by Sandline International did assist the government of President Kabbah in the following months to extend some control beyond the capital. However the Junta/RUF forces remained undefeated and capable of launching further murderous attacks. The Kabbah government was compelled to sign a peace agreement with the RUF in July 1999 which allowed them a significant share of power.

The uproar in Britain over Sandline International and Sierra Leone centred on the extent to which Foreign Office officials and Ministers were aware that Sandline International was in breach of a United Nations arms embargo to which the British was a signatory. There were also arguments as to whether or not the embargo was meant to apply to the forces of the legitimate government. The fact remains that a private security company was instrumental to some degree in the restoration of a democratically elected government and the removal of a murderous military junta.

Regulating Private Security Companies

In his latest report, the United Nations Special Rapporteur on mercenaries, Mr Enrique Ballesteros, makes the point that current international legislation is extremely limited in its effectiveness in dealing with the question of mercenaries.[37] The only current international legislation in force, is Article 47 of the 1977 Protocol I Addition to the 1949 Geneva Conventions. However this legislation does not attempt to ban mercenary activity as such but merely defines the legal status of mercenaries. The International Convention against the Recruitment, Use, Financing and Training of Mercenaries was adopted by the United Nations General Assembly in December 1989. In order for it to enter into force it needs to be ratified by 22 states. At the time of writing, nearly a decade later, it has only been ratified by 19 states.[38] All this international legislation is riddled with loopholes and this is especially the case with regard to private security companies which are not catered for in the above treaties. As Ballesteros points out, the interest of the international community would appear to lie in the regulation of the activities of these companies. He argues that these companies are usurping responsibilities that are the obligations of states, namely defence and security, and that in permitting and often encouraging this, for whatever reasons, states are undermining their own legitimacy.[39]

The United Nations Special Rapporteur seems to imply that there are no circumstances in which a state ought to resort to the use of private security companies for the provision of security. This rather absolutist view appears to be based on a belief that they employ mercenaries, whose use is universally detestable and that the price of these companies is usually met from the precious natural resources of states already in dire economic straits. Nevertheless in what appears to be tantamount to an admission that private security companies can be useful, Ballesteros pointedly calls for their activities to be regulated, not outlawed.[40]

In 1998 South Africa enacted the Regulation of Foreign Military Assistance Act which sought to place limits on the activities of private security companies based in that country. Essentially companies who were based in South Africa and who wished to provide military services abroad would in future need the permission of the South African government. Such permission could be refused if the proposed activity conflicted with South Africa's international obligations, would lead to human rights infringements in the host country, cause or exacerbate instability, support terrorism, worsen regional conflicts, be against South Africa's national interest or be unacceptable for any other reason.[41] This legislation was obviously aimed at organisations such as Executive Outcomes. Though they persistently stated that they saw no difficulties in complying with the Act, shortly after its introduction they closed their Pretoria offices, possibly with the intent of relocating to somewhere where the legislative environment was more conducive to their activities.

In October 1999 it was reported that the British government was considering the introduction of legislation to regulate the activities of private security companies based in the UK.[42] Britain is not a signatory to the 1989 United Nations Convention on Mercenaries and obviously believes that it is impractical to outlaw the activities of private security companies. The British Foreign office has studied the South African law and a spokesman stated that the government had 'decided to initiate a thorough and open debate on the problem (of private security companies) and the options for dealing with it both nationally and internationally'.[43] The act of engaging in mercenary activity in a foreign state at peace with Britain, is already outlawed by the Foreign Enlistment Act of 1870, which will have to be repealed to accommodate any new legislation. A Green Paper on the proposals is promised for 2000 and these moves would appear to indicate some form of official admission as to the potential usefulness of private security companies, notwithstanding the embarrassment caused by the Sandline affair. In support of this belief Donald Anderson MP, chairman of the House of Commons Foreign Affairs Select Committee, was quoted as saying with regard to private security companies 'in some cases there is a legitimate role for their work, particularly when they are involved in the protection of workers abroad'.[44]

An indirect form of regulation may come from the increasing international awareness that it is natural resources that help fund the activities of private security companies, mercenaries and rebel movements alike. This is particularly the case with diamonds. Africa produces diamonds of exceptional quality and size and many are relatively easy to mine, close to the surface.[45] This is especially so in Angola and Sierra Leone. The diamond trade is one of the most heavily regulated in the world and dominated by one company: De Beers. Their London-based Central Selling Organisation artificially keeps the price of diamonds high by maintaining a large stockpile.[46] Nevertheless rebel groups such as UNITA have very successfully used illegal diamond mining to fund their military campaigns, often to the tune of hundreds of millions of dollars per year.[47] On October 3 1999 a campaign called 'Fatal Attractions' was launched to get the diamond-buying public to question the source of their purchases and boycott illegally mined diamonds.[48] De Beers quickly followed with an embargo on all Angolan diamonds not from approved government sources.[49] The impact of these policies, as well as a recent United Nations ban on diamonds from Sierra Leone,[50] may be limited as it will be difficult to enforce.[51] However it does demonstrate a growing awareness that it is Africa's natural resources that are the ultimate attraction for freebooters of all persuasions whether they be private security companies, multinational corporations or mercenaries. If governments especially can be dissuaded from selling off the 'family silver' to pay for security then maybe the climate for private security companies will be less amenable. This seems to be unlikely in the short term and especially when one considers that the employment of Executive Outcomes by the government of Sierra Leone was given tacit approval by the IMF.[52]

Conclusions

The present circumstances in much of sub-Saharan Africa provide a fertile environment for private security companies, mercenaries and rapacious mineral companies. International companies want access to Africa's natural resources and desperate governments need to raise revenue from their exploitation. In regions of insecurity the personnel and equipment needed for these industries need protection. The local security forces are simply not up to the task and so the private sector steps in. It is the resource-rich regions that are the centres of conflict, Angola, Sierra Leone and the Democratic Republic of Congo to name but three. Africa's enormous economic, political and social problems are leading to increasing levels of conflict on the continent. The wider international community has effectively abandoned any idea of intervening militarily in Africa's conflicts, regardless of the humanitarian suffering. Different standards are applied to Africa than are applied to the former Yugoslavia. It is unpleasant, it may even be racist, but it is a fact. The United Nations is in no position to intervene either. It is financially crippled and its actions hamstrung by a reliance on American support for effective action. Its actions in Somalia and Rwanda have also fatally undermined its credibility in Africa.

African peacekeeping resources are limited and the track record of African peacekeeping operations is at best patchy.[53] The present Nigerian government seems disinclined to continue to act in the expensive role of regional policeman for West Africa and this must cast into doubt the future of ECOMOG as a regional intervention force.[54] In many cases it is the states' own security forces that are part of the problem. In Sierra Leone the army united with the RUF rebels to unseat the democratically elected government. This again was about control of valuable resources, in this case diamonds. When a government has ineffective or unreliable security forces, and the international community either can't or will not intervene, where else can it turn in a crisis other than to private security companies?

Despite the liquidation of Executive Outcomes as a corporate entity, 'mercenaries' and private security companies of all types abound in Africa today. From the old fashioned soldiers of fortune to skilled technicians operating expensive imported equipment, to the 'corporate' private security companies, their services are much in demand.[55] At present a former employee of Executive Outcomes is piloting the Sierra Leonean government's helicopter gunships (allegedly for free!).[56] The importance of his impact in countering the RUF has been tacitly recognised by the Indian government which recently dispatched three similar helicopters to reinforce their contingent of the United Nations force in Sierra Leone.[57]

The demand comes not just from desperate African governments or rebel groups. Multinational corporations use them to protect their interests and facilitate their access to Africa's natural wealth, in some cases they have developed very close and mutually beneficial working relationships. Foreign governments also see them as a useful substitute for intervention by their own forces. As has been demonstrated in the past, these private military forces can achieve remarkable results using relatively small numbers of personnel. What they are patently not suited for are the more traditional peacekeeping operations associated with the United Nations. Even if they all cooperated together they could not muster the necessary manpower. For example the current United Nations operation in Sierra Leone, UNAMSIL, consists of nearly 13,000 troops. However it is arguable that in Sierra Leone the United Nations is engaged more in peace enforcement or war fighting than peacekeeping and it is in these circumstances that private security companies may have a role to play. They could act as combat auxiliaries to the intervention force for the kind of tasks that contributing states might be reluctant to see their forces involved in. Given the realities of life on the ground in Africa, some sort of 'modus vivendi' needs to be worked out between the private sector and international organisations such as the United Nations, OAU and ECOWAS.

It is important to remember that these companies are driven by profit, they are not charitable institutions. They do not claim to be able to solve all a state's problems but are employed for a specific task and in many cases they are remarkably effective given their small numbers. In order to pay for them states have to resort to what resources they have, often mining concessions. But before private security companies are universally condemned for this impact on African economies, questions have to be asked about the involvement of African states in the affairs of their neighbours. Zimbabwe's intervention in the Democratic Republic of the Congo has far more to do with the exploitation of that country's natural resources by the Zimbabwean elite than any deeply felt affection for Laurent Kabila.[58]

Much of the criticism of private security companies is justified but a lot is predicated on there being a viable alternative to their employment available to desperate African governments. This is just not the case. In an ideal world there would be no need for the services of private security companies. Unfortunately contemporary sub-Saharan Africa is a far from ideal world.

Notes

1 There has been much recent literature n this subject. I found the most useful general overviews to be: Adams, Thomas, K. (1999), 'The New Mercenaries and the Privatization of Conflict', *Parameters,* US Army War College Quarterly, Summer. Accessible at http://carlisle-www.army.mil/usawc /parameters/99summer/adams.htm. Isenberg, David (1997) 'Soldiers of Fortune Ltd: A Profile of Today's Private Sector Corporate Mercenary Firms', a paper for the Center for Defense Information, Washington DC November 1997. Accessible at: http://www.cdi.org. Shearer, David (1998), 'Private Armies and Military Intervention', *Adelphi Paper 316,* published by Oxford University Press in February 1998 for the International Institute for Strategic Studies London.

2 Adams, Isenberg and Shearer, ibid.

3 Shearer, ibid., p. 17.

4 Adams, ibid., p. 1.

5 Enrique Ballesteros, United Nations Special Rapporteur: Report on the question of the use of mercenaries as a means of violating human rights and impeding the exercise of the right of peoples to self determination. United Nations Document E/CN.4/1998/31, 27 January 1998. Paragraphs 67-92.

6 Ballesteros, E/CN.4/1998/31, ibid.

7 Britain still recruits for the Royal Gurkha Rilfes in Nepal and many nationalities are to be found within the ranks of the Foreign Legion.

8 Shearer, ibid, p. 15. See also Tickler, Peter (1987) *The Modern Mercenary: Dog of War or Soldier of Honour?,* Patrick Stephens Ltd: Wellingborough UK and Hoare, Mike (1991) *Congo Mercenary,* Robert Hale Ltd: London.

9 32 Battalion was largely made up of Angolans led by South African officers and NCOs.

10 See May, Roy and Hughes, Arnold (1986) 'Armies on loan: Toward an explanation of transnational military intervention among Black African

states' in Baynham, S. (ed), *Military Power & Politics in Black Africa,* Croom Helm: London.

11 'Des ex-gendarmes de l'Elysee participeraient au recrutement de mercenaires pour le Zaire', *Le Monde* 81/97. 'Mercenaries bark but don't bite', *New African,* April 1997.

12 Adams, ibid, p. 3.

13 See MPRI's website at http://www.mpri.com.

14 Dogan, Rhys and Pugh, Michael (1996), 'From Military to Market Imperatives: Peacekeeping and the New Public Policy', a paper presented at the Britain International Studies Association Conference, University of Durham, 17-18 December.

15 Decalo, S. (1992) 'The Process, Prospects and Constraints of Democratisation in Africa', *African Affairs*, 91.

16 'Eastern Europe's Arsenal on the Loose: Managing Light Weapons Flows to Conflict Zones', BASIC occasional paper 26 May 1998. Accessible at http://www.bacisint.org. Venter, A. (1999) 'Arms into Africa', *New African,* January.

17 May, Roy and Cleaver, Gerry (1997), 'African peacekeeping: Still dependent?' *International Peacekeeping,* Summer, Vol. 4, No. 2.

18 May and Cleaver, ibid.

19 May and Cleaver, ibid.

20 Cleaver, Gerry and May, Roy (1997), 'Peacekeeping the African Dimension', *Review of African Political Economy,* No. 66. Cleaver, Gerry and May, Roy (1998) 'African perspectives: regional peacekeeping', in May, R., and Furley, O. (eds) *Peacekeeping in Africa,* Ashgate: Aldershot.

21 May and Cleaver (1997), ibid. Cleaver, G. (1998), 'The African Crisis Response Initiative', a paper presented at the biennial conference of the African Studies Association of the UK, University of London 14-16 September.

22 *West Africa,* 28 July 1997 – 3 August 1997, pp. 1196 and 1199. Pan African News Agency, 30 July 1997, 'Gabon, France discuss military bases'.

23 Shearer, ibid, p. 41, and Isenberg, ibid. 'Africa's new enforcers', *The Independent*, 16 September 1996. 'Corporate dogs of war who grow fat amid the anarchy of Africa', *The Observer*, 19 January 1997.

24 Unlike the other units mentioned, Koevoet was a highly effective counter insurgency unit of the South West Africa Police. See Heithman, H. and Hannon, P. (1991) *Modern African Wars 3: South West Africa,* Osprey Men at Arms series no. 242, Osprey publishing: London.

25 Shearer and Isenberg, ibid.

26 Shearer, ibid., p. 46.

27 Isenberg, ibid.

28 Zack-Williams, A. B. (1999) 'Dimensions on West African Conflicts', a paper presented to the one day ASAUK Symposium Dimensions of Vulnerabilities held at Coventry University, 16 September.

29 Francis, D. J., 'Mercenary Intervention in Sierra Leone: providing national security or international exploitation?', *Third World Quarterly,* Vol. 20, No. 2 p. 326.
30 Thorneycroft, P. (1999) 'Mobutu couldn't afford South African mercenaries', *Weekly Mail & Guardian,* 18 July, at http://www.sn.apc.organisation/wmail.
31 Adams, ibid. Pons, S. (1999) 'Executive Outcomes to close "on its own terms"', *Daily Mail & Guardian*, Johannesburg, 11 November, http://www.mg. co.za.
32 See The Report of the Select Committee on Foreign Affairs, ibid.
33 Isenberg, ibid. Enrique Ballesteros (1999), Report on the question of the use of mercenaries as a means of violating human rights and impeding the exercise of the right of peoples to self determination, United Nations Document E/CN.4/1999/11, 13 January.
34 Francis, ibid., p. 327.
35 Ballesteros, ibid, E/CN.4/1999/11, 13 January 1999, para. 27.
36 Francis, ibid., p. 328.
37 Enrique Ballesteros Report on the question of the use of mercenaries as a means of violating human rights and impeding the exercise of the right of peoples to self determination, United Nations Document A/54/326 7/9/99, para. 52.
38 Ibid., para. 73.
39 Ibid., para. 66.
40 Ibid., para. 62.
41 Regulation of Foreign Military Assistance Bill, South African Ministry of Defence (B54-97), para. 6.
42 'Cook to lift ban on mercenaries', *The Sunday Times,* 3 October 1999.
43 Ibid.
44 Ibid. See also 'Double edged Sword: The case for a pragmatic assessment of mercenary forces', *The Times*, 5 May 1998.
45 'Rough Diamonds', *The Guardian Education Section,* 7 September 1999.
46 Ibid.
47 Ibid.
48 'Diamonds traded for guns lose their sparkle', *The Sunday Telegraph,* 3 October 1999.
49 'De Beers ban on gem sales hits UNITA', *The Daily Telegraph*, 8 October 1999.
50 'Back diamond ban, Cook urges traders', *The Guardian*, 7 July 2000.
51 'Liberia selling arms for diamonds', BBC 6 July 2000 accessed at http://news.bbc.co.uk.
52 Isenberg, ibid.
53 Cleaver, Gerry and May, Roy (1998) 'African perspectives: regional peacekeeping', in May, Roy, and Furley, Oliver (eds) *Peacekeeping in Africa* Ashgate: Aldershot.

54 'Nigerian troops announce Sierra Leone pullout', BBC World Service 21 October 1999, http://news,bbc.co.uk.

55 Venter, A. J. (1999) 'Security in the Badlands', *Combat and Survival,* Vol. 11, Issue 9, December.

56 'Airborne adventurer keeps Freetown free', *The Sunday Telegraph*, 18 June 2000.

57 *Air Forces Monthly*, August 2000, p. 14, 'Indian Air Force Mi 35s in Sierra Leone'.

58 'Zimbabwe losses add up in Congo', BBC World Service 25 November 1999, http://news.bbc.co.uk.